NGOs IN LIVELIHOOD IMPROVEMENT
Nepalese Experience

NGOs IN LIVELIHOOD IMPROVEMENT
Nepalese Experience

TEK NATH DHAKAL

ADROIT PUBLISHERS

Published by
ADROIT PUBLISHERS
4675/21, Ganpati Bhawan, Ansari Road,
Daryaganj, New Delhi-110 002
Phones : 011-23266030

Distributors
AKHIL BOOK DISTRIBUTORS
e-mail: akhilbooks@yahoo.com
akhilbooks@hotmail.com

ISBN : 81-87392-69-X

Laser Typeset by
Arpit Printographers
E-mail : arpitprinto@yahoo.com

Printed in India on behalf of
M/s Adroit Publishers by Arpit Printographers
Phones : 09350809192, 011-22825424

Contents

1

Introduction

BACKGROUND

The World Bank Vice President Moeen Qureshi said about the World Bank–NGO relation, "more effective...efforts to eliminate mass poverty" (quoted in Salmen and Eaves, 1991:94). About the same time, Cernea concluded, as "the essence of the NGO approach is not to induce development financially, but to mobilise people into organised structures of voluntary group action for self-reliance and self-development" (1988:7). Why should people be mobilized? Because development should be initiated and carried out *by people* and should be *for people* to take the benefit of the development. For this, people should be mobilized and organized to achieve self-reliance and self-development and ultimately to eliminate mass poverty particularly from the developing countries. People's organisations, which are also called non-governmental organisations (NGOs), could play an important role in mobilizing people in the development process. Therefore, third sector organisation (TSO) or the NGO sector has been an area of interest about their roles among the different stakeholders such as academicians, practitioners, planners, policy implementers, taxpayers and also the beneficiaries at large. In other words, the turn of the twentieth century has become a period of critical assessment/analysis of the NGOs as they have been developing at the cutting point of market, the state, and the civil society (Siistiänen: 2000, 7). Therefore, a rise in the non-profit organisations and their activities in the developing countries can play an important role in the process of improving livelihood of the people, economic upliftment, and political change (Drabek, 1987; Brown & Korten, 1991; Fisher, 1993; Salamon, 1994). However, there could be a significant variation between scope and the roles of the NGOs among northern countries and the international agencies like the World Bank, UNDP, etc. and the NGOs in the southern countries. The northern countries/international agencies often use these NGOs as an 'alternate institutional mechanism' for the transfer of the resources to the developing countries and also for understanding the reality of the developing countries for building relations. On the other hand, the southern countries have been using these organisations both for improving the socio-economic conditions of their people/ societies and also the means of resources transformation.

Several reasons are attributed to the emergence and proliferation of non-governmental organisations (NGOs) since the 1970s. Among them 'market failure' and 'government failure' are considered leading reasons in European, Asian, African, and Latin American countries. Researchers and policy-makers have started to examine the role of NGOs as a possible remedy for the 'crisis of the welfare state'. This growth of NGOs, at least in part, is a reflection of dissatisfaction with both state and market. On the other hand, the use of NGOs has been consistent with both the new right aid policies of governments in the USA and UK and the 'alternative' aid policies of the conscience of the donor community in the nordic countries and the Netherlands. Other OECD countries have also from time to time used NGOs as an effective channel for development of capital transfer in the form of foreign aid. The restructuring policies of the World Bank and other influential donor institutions led to a planned reduction in the role of the state in the south and increased space for NGOs especially since the 1980s (see also UNDP, 1994a: 26). Measures are therefore directed towards effective institutional mechanisms for mobilising local resources and unleashing the local force in a co-ordinated manner to speed up development process. In 1970,Western support channelled through NGOs in the developing countries was US$ 0.9 billion, while this volume recorded a steep growth to US$ 505 billion in 1987 (World Bank: 1991, 136). The total development aid from OECD countries channelled through NGOs increased from 0.7 per cent to 5 per cent in 1993–4 (Vuorela, Airaksinen and Ulvila 1996: i in Hossain, 1998). The role of states in building up the international NGO system has also been significantly increased during the early 1990s (Tvedt, 1998a: 49; also see Smillie and Helmich, 1993; Riddell et al., 1995). Apart from this, the breakdown of the Soviet Union and one-party system and non-function of state economies in the Eastern Europe the role of the NGOs and the civil society organisations could be an important actor of the alternative model of development (Tvedt 1998a: 167–8). As a result the growth of NGOs both in northern and southern countries has dramatically increased since the 1980s and also in the 1990s.

One of the major issues in southern countries like Nepal is fighting poverty and how to improve the livelihood[1] condition of the poor people and bring them into the mainstream of developmental process. This has been a great challenge. Malnutrition, illiteracy, disease, squalid surroundings, high infant mortality, and low level of life expectancy are some of the basic problems of the country. Apart from these problems, the other socio-cultural-psychological problems are child-marriage, indebtedness, malnutrition, factionalism, groupism, child labour, girl trafficking, gambling, drugs, female discrimination, and illiteracy as a result of orthodox society and demonstrative effect particularly the youngsters towards the consumption-oriented modern society. Nepal's 144th position in the Human Development Index is enough to explain the situation of the country (UNDP, 1999). How to solve all these problems has been a big challenge, for the government and also for other developmental organisations. However, Nepal has been in the process of four decades' planning efforts for her development. As a result little progress in age-specific mortality rate, high life-expectancy, increase in literacy rate, improvement in nutritional characteristics, protection of illness, priority to social security, and increase in consumption level are a few of the positive examples. Despite the government's efforts, the depressing and desperate situation of rural lives of Nepal has attracted different development experts to address the problems and undertake amicable, reasonable, and effective solutions.

So far Nepal's socio-economic condition could not become healthy as majority of her people are still facing rampant poverty, illiteracy, poor health, deteriorating natural resources, and social ill-practices (CBS, 1996). The degree of poverty confined the majority of the rural poor, due to the faulty process of income distribution among the households, to limited access to productive resources, high levels of underemployment and/or unemployment, and augmented the indebtedness of the poor which widens the gap between urban and rural areas and also between the haves and the have nots. Though the agriculture sector has been providing up to 89% of the total employment for the economically active people, most of them have only subsistence-level jobs CBS, 1999; 118).

The role of NGOs has been recognised as important to solve the multifarious problems and particularly to help improve the livelihood of the rural people. For achieving substantial and sustained poverty reduction, there is a need in the inclusion of civil society, non-governmental organisations and local democracy to enable the governance system. NGOs are considered development partners in Nepal. However, questions such as, "Are NGOs better institutional options particularly for improving the livelihood of the poor people?" have been coming from different quarters. In this context, this present study is mainly focused on the role of NGOs for improving the livelihood condition of the poor people who are living in the rural areas. For the purpose of this study, the functions of PLAN International–an international NGO working in Markhu Village Development Committee[2] (VDC) of the Central Hill of Nepal and Backward Society Education (BASE)–a national NGO working in Hekuli VDC of the inner Terai[3] of mid-western Nepal were selected.

LITERATURE REVIEW

An examination of the available literature relevant to this study reveals that it is relatively limited. However, towards the later part of the 1980s and particularly during the 1990s, both foreign and Nepalese scholars began to research on Nepal's NGO problems. While some of the authors on Nepalese socio-economic development pointed to the problems of NGO movement in a brief passage or two, others have devoted a chapter(s), and a few books are fully written about NGOs in Nepal[4]. Scholars conducted some of the studies for their doctoral dissertation and Licentiate and Master's degree dissertations. Apart from these, some independent researches and various research-oriented articles can also be found.

Research Dissertation

In 1998, Maskay brought out a comprehensive study covering theories on the perspectives of NGO development, the Nepalese experiences and trends of NGO movement, empirical assessment of perception and perspectives of NGOs, and the policy perspectives of NGOs in Nepal. It was based on both primary and secondary sources. The primary data were collected through a structured questionnaire with 110 educated elite who have directly or indirectly affiliated with the national NGOs. Another 15 key persons from among the members of the social sector think-tank with long work experience were interviewed (Maskay, 1998:110). The study revealed that there is an important role of NGOs for the development of Nepal. However, NGOs should prove themselves as people's organisations, and need to cultivate willingness and ability to institute and sustain for empowerment and self-reliance (Ibid: 124–5). Finally, he concluded that there is a need for policy liberalisation, i.e., for 'NGO empowerment'; consideration of NGOs' role in development; that there should not be a gap between the intentions or the pronouncements and profile of performance; that channelling of external assistance for 'capacity-building' of the NGOs, etc. are contributory for NGO-utopia and the NGO-reality as 'a catalyst of development' (Ibid: 167–171).

Dhakal made a case study on the role of NGOs to find out the change brought about by an international NGO's (Save the Children Federation) programmes and to identify the existing bottlenecks for implementing the NGO programme in rural Nepal (1989: 10). The study conducted field surveys in two village *Panchayats* (now Village Development Committees) of Gorkha District. The NGO activities covered health, agriculture and economic development, human resource development, water resources and physical infrastructure development and resource conservation (Ibid: 33). The NGO programme successfully delivered services, such as drinking water, and positive feelings towards health care and educational development activities. The NGO was found, to some extent, to bring attention owards the enrolment of their children to the school. However, due to the faulty process of taking all communities as a single entity, the disparities of haves and have nots, conscious and less conscious make upper and better communities/families were benefited from the project (Ibid: 128–9).

Odegaard (1997) made a study on the cultural perspective of the Tharu caste/ethnic group. One aspect of the study was how the NGOs such as Tharu Welfare Society, BASE, Tharu Culture Society, and The Rana Reform Movement are playing their role as an entrepreneur to educate and empower the community. A case study was made by using observations and interview methods. The researcher thinks that the NGO movement helps the Tharu community to build up unity, create awareness as "knowledge is power", means of "ethnic incorporation", and also a drive to acquire modern skills and means of livelihood.

Backer (1998) made a case study of an NGO–Backward Society Education (BASE)–in Nepal and discusses the dichotomies of the NGO accountability. The research was based mainly on the role of NGOs with management and accountability perspectives (Backer, 1998: 14–15). The study was made by observation of BASE's activities, and through interview with the president and other members of the NGO. The study revealed that the management capacity should be strengthened for maintaining accountability. It can also be possible by inculcating the functional and formal training. As BASE was found running as an "organized anarchy or ad-hocracy" (Ibid: 97), the downward accountability should also not be fully ignored, which could also require considerable adjustments for the co-operational climate based on trust and confidence (i.e., allowing for a learning-by-doing process). However, research on the accountability issue was not extensively explored (Ibid: 100).

K.C. studied the state of environment within which rural-based NGOs have been operating; their management systems; organisational culture; performance; and the interrelationships between environment, management system, and organisational capacity (K.C., 1998: 5–6). This study was made on the interview and a survey questionnaire with a sample of NGO executives during the years 1996 and 1997. The study concluded that NGOs were moderately capable of mobilising local resources, but had little success in discouraging social ills and evils. Moderate success of the NGOs was observed in involving income and equipment-generating activities (Ibid: 86). Of the total 80 NGOs studied, most were "either low performers or fair performers due to the weak organisational culture, low performance and very unfavourable environment". The high performers owed their success to high positive association with strong organisational culture, transparent management practices, and highly favourable environment.

Hossain (1998) made a study on the sustainability aspect of NGO-related project administration. Apart from the literature reviews, the study was conducted by using thematic interviews with the donors, NGO executives, and the concerned governmental people. The study covered different aspects, such as NGO and their projects' sustainability, NGOs and the development of southern countries like Bangladesh and Nepal, and NGOs and nordic development aid perspectives. He has highlighted some of the problems faced by the Nepalese NGOs for implementing their programmes (1998: 103–4). The researcher concluded that the NGOs in the southern countries like Bangladesh and Nepal are often led by the educated middle class and local elite, who also perceive this sector as an alternative source of employment. However, the NGOs of these countries are "at the heart of voluntary sector development activities" and play as intermediary actors between the northern NGOs and member organisations (Ibid: 236). He argued that sustainability of the project largely depends upon management capacity, financial factors, commitment, government policies, technological factors, socio-cultural factor, and environmental factors. Though the working environment for the NGOs in Bangladesh and Nepal are conducive, the NGOs largely suffered from weak management capacity, heavy dependency on foreign funding, and less participation from among the women..

Shah (1999) researched the role of International NGOs (INGOs) for mobilising resources for the development of Nepal. The study was conducted by interview and literature survey. The study covers the volume of resources and the sectoral benefits and also the negative aspects of INGO funding for the development of Nepal. The study revealed that the health and community development sectors benefited by the INGO resource mobilisation; however, the problems of transparency, critical choice of projects, and accountability are often overlooked.

In 1992, CECI made an in-depth study, which covered the nature of community-based NGO activities, institutional and policy environment of NGOs; potentials of different types of NGOs; and need to strengthen the institutional capabilities required for effective institutionalisation of NGOs in Nepal (CECI, 1992: 3). For the purpose of study, 47 NGOs were selected from among local self-help and local service organisations from six different districts. The study classified the different NGOs into local self-help organisations, local service NGOs, regional and national NGOs, and professional NGOs; assessed the legal and policy environment for working for the NGOs, their potential and limitation for scaling up; and recommended for their capacity building. The study revealed that due to the lack of NGO credibility, lack of appropriate culture, involvement in the partisan politics, NGOs have often failed to scale up their functions. Moreover, the government can facilitate the NGOs by simplifying the NGO-related rules and regulations, and by developing co-operation mechanisms. Similarly, the NGOs themselves also should develop human resource management systems, project planning and monitoring systems, try to be development facilitators rather than implementing the projects, maintain financial accountability, and develop organisational systems for their enhanced capabilities.

Articles Published in the Periodicals

Beginning with the 1990s, articles covering some aspects of the role of NGOs in Nepal started appearing in periodicals and in books.

Dahal considers that voluntary organisations (VOs) are the social space grounded by the people at the local level and rooted in the shared interest of the members (1997: 67). Such VOs play for strengthening local self-governance and the socialisation and mobilisation of people for networking and promoting the public good, which help by providing a number of institutional arrangements for the production and allocation of public goods, by developing self-organising capabilities of people, and by maintaining policy continuity and coherence so that high-level predictability is attained in the anticipation of relationship between consumers and the citizens and the rational assignment of service responsibility (Ibid: 69–70).

Singh raises some issues–urban concentration of NGOs, heavy dependence on foreign money, restriction of open membership–are some of the problems regarding NGOs, though the NGO sector could contribute to the socio-economic development of the country (1992: 70–73). The INGOs either implement directly or through their DONGOs, which have their own management, goals, and priorities. She concluded that the NGO could play crucial roles in alleviating poverty by engaging NGOs at the grass-roots level and above, to complement the government in its endeavour to deliver services towards alleviating it (Ibid: 76).

Nickson argues the role of INGO with respect to rural development, particularly to empower the poor and to alleviate poverty, which requires organisational independence and programme flexibility (1992: 47). The author concluded that due to a "very negative" approach toward development, and non co-operative one to the INGOs, the public administration is non-functional. It requires a co-operative environment to better the functioning of INGOs (Ibid: 61).

Lama et. al. tried to deal with the historical background, level of current performance, definitional, and legal framework of NGOs and the grass-roots development cultures. Instead of facilitating the NGOs, the existing Act and regulations became more control oriented, which could help in flourshing the NGOs and reach the grass-roots more efficiently (Lama et al. 1992: 95–6). However, NGOs should also work "towards the collective empowerment of the poor and the disadvantaged which leads towards the enhancement of the better live situation for them" (Ibid: 97).

Dhakal highlights the growing size of NGOs in number and, scope and the facilitation role of SWC. However, NGOs could not work to the desired extent unless they confined themselves to the urban areas, and far from reaching the real needy communities and also government agency like SWC's promotional strategy and monitoring and evaluation capacity would be developed (Dhakal, 1999: 310–312).

Acharya in her article "Non-Governmental Organisation (NGO)-Led Development Strategy in Nepal" deals with a theoretical discussion on NGOs; NGO–INGO relations; and policies related to (I)NGOs, their functions, strategies, impacts, and problems in Nepal. NGOs' flexibility in methods of communication, timing of interventions, and in the mode of operations are advantages. Scarcity of resources, lack of commitment, transparency, accountability, and corruption often make them inefficient to reach the poor and empower the people (1997: 86–93). She concludes that there should be good policies to facilitate and control the NGOs for functioning well.

Ghimire said that though NGOs are making some

contributions for awareness creation, income generation, and delivery of health services, there are also some negative aspects such as abuse of voluntary organisation for unethical activities, working as "dollar-growers", working as the workers of political parties, working for foreign mission interests (1999a: 8–11). He thinks transparent policy and regulation are important vehicles for controlling unethical and illegal works in the name of social service.

Keeping in mind the growing role of NGOs, Chand concluded that there is a need to chalk out a specific action plan and to develop a mechanism to monitor and evaluate the functions, which help to assess their potentials for furthering nation building (1999: 20).

Joshi thinks social service empowers oneself with tremendous inner strength to face all circumstances in life with poise and peace. So it should not be taken as a business (1999: 2–3).

Timilsina (1999) concluded that there is lack of understanding between the CSOs and the government about the roles and functions of CSOs. However, there is a need of CSOs' roles specially in building awareness and educating the people in the first quarter of 21st century (1999: 30).

Making a critical analysis, Panday said NGOs and self-help organisations should work as catalytic agents of change; however, they often become the cost of the society. This is because of over politicisation, NGOs themselves working as private companies for "easy money", and external invation through NGOs by giving money to 'crony' NGOs (2000b: 5). In another work Panday again comments that the "NGO sector has not been able to play the role in development and to establish checks against anti-democratic, anti-people policies, tendencies, and action" as NGOs are clearly lacking in accountability, transparency and often autonomy in their working styles (1999b: 135).

In viewing the role of NGOs, Bhattachan raised five questions related to the relationship between class contradiction and the (I)NGOs, class-consciousness and (I)NGOs, class struggle and (I)NGOs, sincerity and effectiveness to help the poor, and the relationship amongest the state, (I)NGO, market and the community (1999: 274–7). He concluded that only those (I)NGOs which are pro-poor, field-based, transparent for the programmes and budgets, and willing to contribute to poverty alleviation and "rural self-reliance" should be funded (Ibid: 277–78).

Hossain highlights some of the problems of development NGOs for implementing their programmes: uneven regional distribution, representation by local elite and rich people, and lack of clear NGO policy (Hossain, 1998: 116). He concluded that some of the challenges are legitimacy, resources problems, relations between government and the NGOs, change in roles in development, issues of accountability, and lack of professionalism by Nepalese NGOs (Ibid: 121).

Similarly, Odegaard (1998) made a study of an NGO, its role on democratisation and development of a developing country like Nepal. According to the writer, BASE as an NGO plays a good role to bringing help to illiterate people and in shaping a social policy. Though the NGO has a problem of "management", its role to mobilise the group action to the community awareness should be appreciated.

Writing on how NGOs can be important institutions, their growth, and functions in Nepal, Pokharel (2000) raised some issues such as financial transparency, discipline, internal democracy, and the performances of the NGOs. Similarly, the relationships and co-ordination between NGOs and the government, and high transaction cost of the donor money and motive of creating DONGOs are often the problem between the local NGOs and the donor NGOs in Nepal (2000: 61–3).

Chand made some historical remarks and explored strategies such as developing their capacity and facilitate for development-oriented NGOs (2000: 69). He opined that the voluntary actions of both NGOs and CBOs are important. For this, mobilisation of internal resources, good relations between the government and the NGOs, clear-cut policies about the role of NGOs, adoption of transparent and accountability of the NGO functions, etc. are some of the conditions to take into account.

Bhattachan (2000) explores indigenous voluntary action in Nepal. He discusses how voluntary organisations were formed among nationalities and their immediate past activities. Instead of project activities, the movement approach is more helpful to strengthen the nationality interests. He also opined that the (I)NGOs should help the nationalities to gear advocacy for the egalitarian society.

Sharma (1999) highlights that NGOs could not work due to the lack of clear policy about their role of development, lack of proper co-ordination system including financial weakness, and weak management. Some of the negative trends are religious conversion, making money, and over-politicisation.

Apart from the above articles a few leading dailies also highlighted some burning issues regarding the roles and functions of NGOs in Nepal. Such issues are: weak regulation for the mobilization of resources through NGOs; lack of transparency and accountability; lack of clear policy toward NGOs to work as development partners; NGOs' lack of quality works; lack of right strategies to activate the NGOs in the livelihood improvement; misuse of foreign funding rather than developmental activities (for details see *Gorkhapata* (23 Jan., 1999); *Kantipur* (8 Jan., 1998); *The Rising Nepal* (23 Dec, 1997; 14 Feb., 1998); *The Kathmandu Post* (12 Feb., 1999; 25 Feb., 1999).

STUDY PROBLEM

An estimated 1.3 billion people in the world (according to World Bank US$ 1/day criterion) are living under poverty (UNDP, 1997:5) and have problems meeting their basic needs, and lack clean water, adequate sanitation, housing, or basic health services. Many of them often struggle to make today's ends meet instead of looking for long-term work. Even children have to work for family income instead of going to school. Looking into such a grave problem, the recent trend of donors mostly concentrate on the programmes focused on poverty alleviation and social sector development, local empowerment, and gender issues in the poverty alleviation programme.

With regard to the concentration on poverty issues, the Asian Development Bank has formulated operational objectives, developed a strategic approach, identified areas of emphasis, and worked out operational instruments/approaches to reduce poverty as its major development thrust (ADB, 1999). The World Bank (1999) has stressed its major assistance in addressing deprivation, inequality, transparency, capacity building and issues related to gender disparities. The Common Country Assessment of UN System has addressed issues related to human poverty, environmental implications, economic development, and democratic experiments, concentrating mostly on decentralized government and participatory development, employment and income generation, and women and development with an aim to support poverty eradication (UNDP, 1999). The International Fund for Agricultural Development (IFAD) has emphasized the involvement of civil society and the private sector, social mobilisation, community ownership, and human resources development as the strategic instruments to trickle down the benefits to the poor (IFAD, 1999). Similarly, one of the seven major priorities in Japan's New Development Strategy is the reduction of poverty by one-half of the people living in extreme poverty by 2015 (Ministry of Foreign Affairs, 1998). The white paper of the British Government on international development also has focused its international development effort on the elimination of poverty and encouragement of economic growth, which benefits the poor (DFID, 1997). German Agency for Technical Cooperation has focused its poverty component by emphasizing wider involvement of local bodies and the user groups in a decentralized structure in community forestry, green road, and micro-credit schemes (GTZ, 1999). Likewise, the Danish government's future funding is set to focus on poverty reduction as the central objective of their multilateral efforts (OECD, 1997).

The new approach towards the poverty problem, particularly in the developing countries like Nepal, shows a new policy drive to alleviate poverty. Due to this close attachment with grass-roots people and local institutions, NGOs can play a critical role in ensuring that benefits go to marginalised groups, and in mobilising community organisation to benefit the poor section of society; they can also be the better implementers in the rural sector. They may have a comparative advantage in developing participatory and targeting approaches that effectively involve poor people, and their work is often grounded in local realities, in a way bigger programmes find it difficult. The firmer incorporation of civil society and NGOs into the picture also has distinct advantages. However, learning from NGOs has been highly selective and has not generally gone very far, though many of today's models of micro-level development are NGO-sponsored.

However, the professional and technical limitations, poor co-ordination, and problems of representativeness and accountability in the NGO sector also could not been far from the debate of success or failure to be an effective institutional channel for the aid and for the delivery of services to the needy people. Though there are some case studies of individual NGOs, similar theoretical and empirical works on the NGOs in developing countries is only beginning to emerge (Paul, 1991). Korten studied the overall development picture of NGOs (Korten, 1988; 1990; 1992). Salmen, Eaves (1991), and Beckman offer a micro-level view of NGO experiences; similarly Salamon and Anheire studied origin, legal systems, their comparative advantage of non-profit organisations both in developed and developing countries (Anheier–Salamon, 1996; 1998). Tvedt also studied the development role of NGOs and how they can be effective means of channelling resources (Tvedt, 1998). However, the role of NGOs in the case of developing countries, particularly the grass-roots level and its policy impact both at the national and international level, is less studied.

The Government of Nepal has taken the NGOs as development partners for community and rural development, urban slums improvement, empowerment of women, improvement of the environment, delivery of public health, irrigation, health education like AIDS and drug abuse, youth activities, and development of moral values (see NPC, 1992; 1998). There are around 20,000 registered NGOs, of which half are affiliated with the Social Welfare Council[5] (SWC) in the country. Apart from this, around 90 INGOs are also working in the country. However, the country still has been facing the problem of socio-economic issues related to the poor, women, and children. On the one hand, foreign aid channelling, both from bi-lateral and multilateral sources and in grants and loan, and also both through governmental and NGOs have been increasing; on the other hand, questions regarding their proper utilisation, addressing the need and requirements particularly of the poor people have been coming out (Panday, 1999: 11). Unfortunately, the majority of the people, especially in the rural areas, are forced to struggle with the poverty for their better livelihood.

The recent issues and concerns of the people and the government regarding NGOs are related with their roles for improving livelihood of the poor rural people, sustainable development of the country, project sustainability of NGO-led development projects and management capability of the NGOs. The other aspects of institutionalisation, voluntary services, transparency, cost effectiveness, and accountability are in discussion among donors, practitioners, and academicians. Some pertinent questions behind these NGOs are: What would be the appropriate areas of functions through these NGOs or voluntary organisations? Should these organisations be controlled or set free for working? What would be the relation with the government and external donor agencies?

Therefore, the search for the role of NGOs has become one of the major policy issues facing both government and NGOs in Nepal, as much of the literature also fails to address the core issues. It is difficult to come to an agreement on the roles, potentials, and limits of NGOs, and some of the emerging issues in dealing with their role on how can these sectors be more capable. Due to the limited knowledge of the NGO sector, there is no consensus on the definition of NGO, as they also lack systematic management system, proper accounting, and even human resource development, including the quantitative and qualitative dimensions of NGO activities.

There are only a few studies on the NGO sector in Nepal. A number of studies focusing on the potential role of the NGOs in development has also been undertaken by international donors who are very much interested on involving the NGOs in the development process. They have undertaken very few careful assessments of NGOs' collaboration with international donors. Some of the academic researches and other freelance research studies show that there are both positive and negative impacts of NGOs in Nepal. However, the literature regarding development aid, roles of organisations like NGOs, and appropriate policies regarding the operations of such organisations has been still lacking in Nepal, which could be a valuable insight to overcome the shortcoming and bottlenecks for achieving even greater success in future.

This study was conducted to understand how the NGO programmes could be useful to uplift the livelihood level of the needy people in a developing country like Nepal. The outcome of this study, thus, would help the local and international policy makers, and donor agencies in implementing NGO-led development actors in directing their resources in good projects, in managing the projects more efficiently, and in implementing them effectively for creating a welfare society. For the purpose of research, two aspects–roles of the NGOs and improvement of livelihood of the beneficiaries–are addressed. For addressing the role, the nature and volume of activities of the NGOs, support or contradicting of the existing developmental policies, concerned NGOs' roles and strategies were assessed. To study livelihood improvement, the level of poverty and the changes brought about by the NGOs' activities were assessed. However, it is difficult to find a universally accepted meaning or measuring rod of the term 'livelihood', because this terminology could be defined in different ways by different countries or organisations as per the existing economic level of the country, social value of the society, and also the community/individual perceptions. On the other hand, there is also a problem of the extent to which the level of livelihood should be uplifted, which has become an important agenda of debate. In this context, this study was based on how the beneficiaries are perceived for the requirement of their livelihood and to what extent with regard to the concerned NGOs functions are able to meet their needs at their local level.

PURPOSE OF THE STUDY

The main purpose of this study is to discuss whether NGOs are better institutional options for benefiting the poor people. More specifically, this study aims:

- To assess the organisational landscape of NGOs in relation to the needs of the poor;
- To review the existing policies with regard to NGOs' role in the improvement of livelihood in Nepal;
- To examine the NGOs' activities in relation to the improvement of livelihood of target communities; and
- To find out the strengths and weakness of the NGOs' role in improving the livelihood level of the target people.

METHODOLOGY

This research is descriptive cum analytical in nature and has been conducted empirically. Mostly primary data were collected for analysing the primary information; however, some secondary data were also collected as per necessity. As part of the research work, the studies conducted by Dhakal and Ulvila (1999), *Institutional Analysis of Markhu VDC with Emphasis on Non-Governmental Organisation* (An Unpublished Report on NGOs in Development Research Project Working Document 3); Hossain and Dhakal (1999), Public, Private & Non-Profits: Institutional Analysis of Hekuli VDC of Dang District in Mid-Western Nepal (Unpublished Draft Report on NGOs in Development Research Project Working Document 6); and Dhakal and Hossain, (1999): The Fate of Ghewa and Mercy of Non-governmental Organisations: The Impact & Relevance of Development Initiatives in Nepal (Unpublished Draft Report on NGOs in Development Research Project Working Document 7) were also used for the necessary information.

Selection of Study Area

For collecting primary information, two village areas–

Markhu Village Development Committee (MVDC) and Hekuli Village Development Committee (HVDC)–were selected by the researcher himself. The location of these MVDC and HVDC are shown in a map of Nepal, which is given in Chapter Five.

These places were selected keeping in mind that Markhu VDC features central hilly parts and Hekuli VDC the mid-western Terai of the country. It was assumed that NGOs working in these selected villages could give a clear picture of how these NGOs work for different rural communities interacting with various actors such as public, profit, and the non-profits for the welfare of people particularly in the livelihood issues. Nepal is a country of multi-caste/ethnic populace, and these VDCs also hold major castes such as Tamang, Newar, Brahmin/Chhetri, Magar, Chaudhary (also called Tharu), Damai/Kami, Gurungs, Sanyasi, etc. (further description about the people and communities are given in respective case studies in Chapter Five). Apart from this, different governmental field offices and financial institutions have already existed before the modern NGOs entered in these places. However, NGOs like PLAN International (one of the biggest INGOs in terms of resource investment with integrated programmes in Nepal) in the case of Markhu VDC and BASE –one of the biggest national NGOs in Hekuli VDC– have been studied in these villages. On top of that, local groups or the centuries-old traditional voluntary organisations have also been existed in the area. Similarly, both organised and/or unorganised forms of private enterprises exist as well.

Primary Information

Primary information was collected from the local beneficiaries, NGO activists, NGO executives, local-level governmental employees, non-governmental employees, and private sector executives including policy-level executives. Local beneficiaries were contacted to find out the impact of NGO activities in terms of the livelihood improvement of the NGO programmes. Similarly, local-level NGO executives were discussed on the issue related to livelihood improvement of the beneficiaries and also to find out the strength and weakness of their performance in the implementation of their programmnmes. Governmental executives such as those working at Ministry of Women, Children and Social Welfare; Social Welfare Council; Ministry of Local Development, and NGO leaders were also contacted to discuss the policies with regard to NGOs for directing their resources and efforts for improving the rural livelihood of the country.

Secondary Information

Apart from the primary information, secondary information was also collected from different sources. For this, office records of the concerned organisation, published and unpublished information, planning documents, and other research documents were collected and reviewed.

Selection of NGOs

For the purpose of study two NGOs–one from Markhu VDC and the other from Hekuli VDC, respectively–were selected on a judgemental basis. Selection was based on volume of activities, coverage, and their existence in the study areas. These selected sample NGOs are as follows:

PLAN International was selected as a sample NGO from Markhu VDC (the details of this NGO are given in Chapter Five). PLAN International was the leading NGO, with diversified activities and cooperating with other NGOs, CBOs, users' groups, women's group, local VDC, and schools. However, there were a few other NGOs, CBOs, and traditional organisations in Markhu. These NGOs such as Centre for Self-help Development (CSD), Community Support Association of Nepal (COSAN), Tamang Ghedung Sang (TGS), and local NGO–Satteswari Youth Club (SYC), Indrasarobar Youth Club (IYC)–were working as co-partners of PLAN International.

Similarly, Backward Society Education (BASE) in Hekuli was selected because this organisation was the largest national NGO for mobilising foreign resources and working with diversified activities (also see Chapter Five for details). However, Chandra Smriti Youth Club, Social Upgrade in Progress of Education Region (SUPER), Janashiksha Social

Association, and Chure Mahabharat Sewa Samaj have also been established and they had only limited activities.

Data Collection Procedure

Primary data were collected at various time intervals by different methods and tools such as reconnaissance survey, household survey, interviews, group discussion, field observation, and Participatory Rural Appraisal (PRA) exercise. During reconnaissance, a survey was conducted by visiting with concerned NGO executives, local people, and some of the project beneficiaries at the selected fields. The researcher himself was involved in obtaining the field information. However, my colleague Marko Ulvila was working with me for conducting the PRA exercise and the household survey in Markhu, and Farhad Hossain for conducting the PRA exercise in Hekuli. A structured questionnaire was administered to obtain household survey in both places (see questionnaire in Appendix I). This questionnaire was distributed to 150 households both in Markhu and Hekuli, however, the effective size of these questionnaire was 104 from both places. The questionnaire was distributed in Nepali language and translated into English for presentation. Some trained assistants were recruited for conducting PRA exercises and administering the questionnaire in both places.

Interviews were conducted with various persons. Altogethers 16 common people from the study areas, 12 NGO executives (both NGO leaders and NGO employees), and 10 government employees (both working at central level and field level) were interviewed to get information. The names of these interviewees are given in Appendix II. Reconnaissance Survey, PRA, Group discussion, Interview, Household survey and the Observation were employed during the field visit.

Analysis of Data

After collecting primary and secondary information, data were analysed mostly in a descriptive way while the quantitative data are presented in tables, figures, and percentages. Some of the analytical tools such as social

TABLE 1.1: Description of Information Collection and Fieldwork

S.N.	*Tools applied for collecting information*	*Markhu Village*	*Hekuli Village*	*Informants*
1	Reconnaissance Survey	1998 March	1999 May	NGO staff, Local people
2	PRA	1998 October	1999 July	2 male groups, 2 female groups
3	Follow-up & group discussion for feedback on initial findings	1998 November May 2000	1999 October	Beneficiary + NGO employees/ workers and govt. officials
4	Interview	2000 February, March, April	2000 March, April, May	16 local people from both Markhu and Hekuli, 12 NGO executives both activists and employees, and 10 various level government empooyees
5	Household Survey	2000 February	2000 April	104 respondents in each VDC
6	Observation	During the field stay	During the field stay	

mapping, timeline, pair-wise ranking, time trend analysis, and content analysis were used for the purpose of analysis. The case study method was employed for analysing two case studies (see Chapter 5). For the purpose of analysing the data, computer, electronic calculator, and manual methods were used.

SCOPE AND LIMITATION OF THE STUDY

There is a growing concern among the intellectual community, development partners, NGOs, project implementers, and beneficiaries on the role of NGOs in development aid transfer, socio-economic improvement of the country, and the effective service delivery to the needy community. It can be hoped that this study would contribute to understanding how the NGO programmes could be useful to uplift the livelihood status of the needy people. As the development aid literature has been lacking in Nepal, this study can contribute to an academic assessment of NGO works, which could provide valuable insights to overcome the shortcomings and bottlenecks for achieving even greater success in future. The outcome of this study, thus, would help the local and international policy makers, donor agencies, and environmentalists in implementing NGO-led development activities in directing their resources in good projects; in managing the projects more efficiently; and in implementing them effectively for creating a welfare society.

Despite the above scope, this study is also limited in the following ways:

Though this study was conducted in a scientific way the findings and conclusions of the study could not be generalized in macro or broader perspective, as the study was limited within two NGOs working in a few VDCs. The selected areas had reasonable basic infrastructure such as road links, village communication and other institutional infrastructure; however, in other remote places such service delivery agencies could have other form of impacts. The assumption was that the intervening agencies could have better performance if the project area already would have created the development infrastructures and the visible changes could be easily identified.

This study was mostly confined to assessing the role of NGOs for addressing the livelihood issues; however, other areas of functions and the programmes of the NGOs were lacking in this study though they are also equally important in the development discourse.

Analysis of this study was based on the data and the information collected during the period 1998–2000 as given in Table 1.1. Any change or development in the beneficiary's status or the NGOs' roles in uplifting livelihood does not necessarily represent the findings of this study.

Some of the terminologies such as the definition of livelihood required for a living, status of change in the livelihood level of the beneficiaries and so on have been used for analysis on the basis of local perspectives (i.e., beneficiaries' perspectives rather than other established standards). The role of public, profit, and the non-profit institutions was analysed only in the local perspectives at the field level, however, emphasis was given in the NGOs' activities only.

STRUCTURE OF THE STUDY

Altogether this book comprises six chapters. Some chapters are devoted to theoretical aspects, while the others focus on empirical studies. Most of the chapters such as the first, third, fourth and the sixth are devoted to both empirical and theoretical aspects. The second chapter covers mostly the theoretical aspects, while the fifth deals with empirical studies. The first chapter covers background, literature review, research problem, objectives and methodology, and the scope and the limitation of the study.

The second chapter mainly discusses the conceptual and theoretical debate on poverty and livelihood, people-centred development as required for livelihood improvement. The other areas covered in this chapter are meaning and the concepts of NGOs and its emergence and role in development including the NGOs' better option.

Similarly, the third chapter presents an elaborate coverage of the poverty situation of Nepal. This chapter covers a general development scenario, social setting, occupation and employment, and the income distribution situation of the country. It also reviews incidence of poverty and the efforts and challenges for addressing the problem of poverty in Nepal.

The fourth chapter mainly explains the NGOs in Nepalese perspective. The subjects covered in this chapter are the traditional welfare services in Nepal, expansion of modern NGOs in Nepal, legal system and the institutional arrangements for administering the NGOs in Nepal. This chapter also explains the national development plan and the

NGO-related development policies for working in Nepal.

The fifth chapter presents two case studies covering various functions of NGOs with regard to the improvement of livelihood of the beneficiaries in the selected VDCs. This chapter documents the existing socio-economic situation of the studied areas and analyses the concerned NGOs' functions with regard to the improvement of the beneficiaries. It also discusses the problems and prospects of NGOs as a better option.

On the basis of theoretical discussion and empirical studies, the whole text is concluded in the sixth chapter. This chapter includes changing organisational landscape for people-centred development, livelihood management through NGOs, problems NGOs encounter in performing their functions, and the contributions of this thesis for further research.

END NOTES

1. The terms poverty and livelihood are defined in the second chapter.
2. Village Development Committee (VDC) is a political and administrative grass-roots unit of local government in Nepal. There are 4913 VDCs all over the country. A VDC is divided into nine wards (parts). People residing in a VDC elect an eleven-membered Executive Committee (EC) for a period of five years. The EC comprises a chairman, vice-chairman and nine members (representing one each from a ward). The people residing in a ward elect five members including a woman representative. A government appointed civil servant works as secretary of the VDC (HMG/N 1998/2055, 3-15).
3. Topographically Nepal is divided into three zones such as Terai, Hills and the Mountain. Terai lies in the southern part of the country covering 17% of the total area. As the land is plain and fertile which is also called as the 'granary of the food stuff' of Nepal. Similarly, Hill area covers 68% of the country's total area, which falls in the middle range of the country. Finally, the Mountain area covers 15% of the total land, which is located at the northern belt of the country.
4. Books covering some issues related to the roles of NGOs, its functions in Nepal are: Chand, (1991; 1999), Maskay, (2000; 1998): Vartola, Juha et al., (2000); Rademacher & Tamang, (1995);

Bhattachan & Mishra, (1997); Gurung, (1998); Dahal & Gurugharana, (1996); Dahal & Horst, (1996); Community Development Service Association (1999).

5. The Social Welfare Council (SWC) is a Governmental NGO bureau which facilitates, coordinates, monitors, evaluates the (I)NGOs working in the country. An NGO registered in the concerned governmental department must be affiliated with SWC to get grant (s) or aid from the INGO(s) and/or the donor agency (ies).

2

Theoretical Framework for Studying Livelihood Issues and NGO Roles

How life can be happy is a debatable issue and could have only a subjective answer. Food, shelter, clothing, education, and good health are considered basic requirements for living. However, other elements such as social well-being, self-respect, social inclusion, mental peace, etc. are also important for living. Deprivation these elements stakes a condition of vulnerability and the manifestations of poverty. Narrowly or broadly, the concept of development is moving around the management of these aspects, which requires human inputs for the development. In this context, the definition of poverty (and how it can best be addressed for a better livelihood), and how intervening agencies such as non-governmental organisations could be more effective, are often the central questions at conceptual and practical levels in the development discourse. This chapter focuses on poverty and livelihoods with emphasis on its meaning and concepts and a need for people-centred development for improving livelihood. It also discusses concept, emergence, and the roles of NGOs as a better option in the development discourse of livelihood management.

UNDERSTANDING POVERTY AND LIVELIHOOD

Conceptualising Poverty

It is curious that some people are compelled to live in

poverty. Is this because of the individual inability or mistakes, or because of the influence of the existing environments? These are some of the pertinent question, which initiate understanding the poverty and livelihoods issues. Whatever the reasons may be, living in poverty is painful to the individual person(s) and also a challenging issue confronting civilised societies, particularly the respective governments and the development organisations. Therefore, how poverty can best be addressed for a better livelihood often becomes the central question for analysis, as the amount of basic requirements for a human living is a debatable issue. However, the term *poverty* or *vulnerability* has been discussed and conceptualized by different persons/organisations differently. Robert Chambers has identified some elements that constitute the 'cluster of disadvantages' which contribute to poverty– what the author terms the 'deprivation trap'. These clusters include poor household, physically weak household, isolated household, vulnerable household, powerless household. The author also believes that all these disadvantages are interlinked and cannot be isolated but rather constitute 'deprivation' or the 'poverty trap' with an interlocking set of factors such as poverty itself, physical weakness, vulnerability, isolation, and powerlessness (Chambers, 1983).

Poverty became a subject of research inquiry at the beginning of the last century. Rowntree (1901) conceptualised the poverty issue from a biological perspective. The author distinguished poverty as primary poverty and secondary poverty, which could be compensated by enlarging income. Primary poverty is an income level below which households fail to buy essentials of food, clothing, shelter, warmth, etc. while the secondary poverty, is a household's failure to purchase minimum subsistence/needs because of inappropriate, inefficient use of income otherwise adequate to meet the needs. About the same time, Booth (1903) made a study about poverty and tried to distinguish the concept of poor and very poor. However, income equivalent of poverty can be changed after changing the standards of nutrition. Both Rowntree and Booth tried to conceptualise the poverty problem from the consumption or the survival perspective.

According to this school, the poor are defined on the basis of their inability to maintain their consumption. The measurement was based on income level necessary to purchase the required volume of minimum nutritional intake for sustaining the life and calorie counts, which often became the key measure of poverty. Absolute poverty and relative poverty are the basis of measures. Absolute poverty is taken as a notion failing for supply of minimum subsistence appropriate to certain circumstances. On the other hand, relative poverty is measured in terms of the inequalities in income distribution.

Though this approach makes it easier to calculate the level of poverty, it cannot present the actual reasons for and level of poverty. Therefore, this approach was criticised by many other writers. Due to the variations in the physical features, climatic conditions, work habits, and consumption habits, the requirement of consumption basket might be different. It also depends on costs and the availability of the consumption items at the time of purchase (see Rein 1971, Townsend, 1974 Sukhatme 1977, Srinivasan 1977, 1979). Such factors affect the nutrient content and the amount of income or expenditures to buy such food items. Again, the quantity of measure has also been taken in different ways. Madalgi (1968), and Dandekar and Rath (1971) used a nutritional norm of 2,250 calories, and Parnab Bardhan (1974) used 2,100 calories per day per adult unit in one context and the National Planning Commission in Nepal, for example, used a norm of 2256 calorie required per day per adult unit (NPC 1977 in Koirala et al. 1992:5; also see Ojha, 1971; Minhas 1974; Joshi, 1979; Jain, 1981). On the other hand, Lipton (1983) used the percentage of household expenditure spent on food as the basis of poverty line demarcation. According to Lipton, households spending more than 70% of the total expenditure on food alone are considered poor. But how much food can be purchased from that 70% of income is also another issue. Miller and Rein (1970) drew up a rather different list of items governing poverty, such as political, legal, and educational components of social well-being. They believe, for example, that despite material affluence, the deprivation of human rights is a kind of poverty in a political sense.

As consumption alone is insufficient to explain poverty, the definition expanded to incorporate other basic needs. This approach helps to identify a list of both food and non-food items required for basic needs. The poor according to this concept are those deprived from fulfilling basic needs. (See ILO, 1976; Streeten, et. al, 1981). To comfortably identify 'poor' from 'non poor,' items of the basic needs are taken together. This approach incorporates a satisfactory level of food, healthcare, housing, education, and other aspects. Households are defined as poor if their food, clothing, medical, education and other needs are not met. The basic needs concept is more elaborative to describe the poor or poverty. However, it is again difficult to specify the amount of items, types of items, and the characteristics of the items (for example nutrient value, etc.) of the basic needs. Similarly, how much income is needed to fulfil a set of basic needs has also become an issue. This approach also does not explain how the items could be accessible or not accessible to the people.

Sen proposed another shift in argument that broadened the understanding of poverty. He argued that poverty must be studied both from the "causation of poverty and effects of poverty" which affects the well-being of the poor rather than counting poor using a ratio of poverty (Sen, 1981: 10). The author discusses the biological, inequality, and relative deprivation approaches of studying poverty. Due to the vagueness of requirement, differences on individual habits, cultures, and other factors biological approach is not enough to explain the poverty problem.

The inequality approach explores the social (political and economic) factors that cover economic inequality and poverty as well. The role of inequality in the prevalence of poverty can help in analyzing poverty. The redistribution of wealth or the ownership of the means of production even without an expansion of the country's productive capabilities can significantly reduce the incidence of poverty (Ibid: 14–15).

The relative deprivation approach underscores that the

definition of poverty confines both objectively and culturally. However, different arguments such as 'feelings of deprivation' and 'condition of deprivation' could be advanced. The basic necessities of life are socially determined. What is a necessity for a citizen in one society or in a country could be a luxury or insufficient for another citizen in other contexts because the values, custom, styles of living, and habits of a particular social condition could be the determinant factors. So, one may 'feel' deprived of something compared to another society. Even in the same society, this feeling may occur. Thus, 'feeling' is rather a subjective terminology that divides people in specific social groupings and strata (Ibid. 15–17).

In this context, Sen discussed the notion of 'entitlements', which is premised on the "ability of people to command food through the legal means available in the society, including the use of production possibilities, trade opportunities" required for life and livelihood. (Sen, 1981: 45). Sen's entitlement approach discussed the capability or the ability to command food, and starvation is a failure to be entitled to a bundle of food (Ibid. 45). The work usefully directs the attention not just to the incomes people have (or have not) realized, but also to the bundles of assets or endowments held by the poor; the nature of the rights associated with those assets and, the nature and the vulnerability of particular claiming systems. Here, the measure of poverty takes into account the number of poor, the depth or severity of poverty, and the distribution of income among the poor. This approach describes the relationship of the resources that poor people have and the commodities that are essential to meet their basic requirements. Therefore, livelihood can be measured on the basis of the set of commodity bundles. It can be claimed on the basis of a given set of tangible and intangible endowments, either through direct use of the endowments, or by using them to access other goods through market and other forms of claiming systems such as moral or legal ones.

The UNDP conceptualised that "human dimensions" to the concept of standard of living, which consist of income, educational (attainment for gaining knowledge), and life expectancy (health, nutrition, and sanitation) are required for living without poverty (UNDP, 1991). For basic human development, opportunity and choices are considered important. Here, choice has been defined as long, healthy, creative life, and to enjoy a decent standard of living including freedom, self-respect, and respect to others (UNDP, 1997: 15). This approach also confirms that poverty is more than consumption, as it has many dimensions in human life. The UNDP viewed poverty from three perspectives: income, basic needs, and capability. The income perspective tries to define poverty on the basis of a certain amount required for survival, i.e., a defined cut-off level of income should be needed for buying required food. Similarly, the basic needs concept considers the lack of income for managing other human needs such as basic health and education including essential services apart from the food requirements. The capability perspective explains the absence of basic capabilities to function — a person lacking the opportunity to achieve some minimally acceptable levels of these functions. UNDP in its 1997 report introduced a human poverty index (HPI) as a concept by integrating the multiple dimensions of human poverty. The indicators for measuring the deprivation of human life relate to survival, knowledge, and a decent standard of living.

Haq broadens the definition of human poverty. Critical for human progress is important for the poverty of opportunity. According to Haq, the term Poverty of Opportunity Index (POPI) could broaden the scope of poverty definition. Poverty of income concerns the result; poverty of opportunity is concerned with the cause (The Mahabub ul Haque 1999: 12) which is required for human development. On the other hand, the World Bank considers poverty as a state of deprivation due to economic, social and psychological factors (World Bank, 1980).

From the above discussion it can be said that poverty is a state of vulnerability, disadvantages, ill-being, or other various forms of deprivations that a person or household has to suffer. Such deprivation can include physical, social, psychological, mental, and legal dimensions. The issue of poverty is due to both cause and effect, and also to the poor people's powerlessness and inefficiency. The diversity of poverty can be found due to the gender situation and bias of the society. The women often become vulnerable and destitute, and ultimately fall into the poverty trap. Similarly, other forms of poverty are due to environmental catastrophe. Floods, landside, and drought including lack of vegitation spread the vulnerable secton of the society. Another form of poverty is due to migration patterns particularly the job and unskilled migrants who shift from rural to urbans. Traditionally, the standard of living is measured either by income, consumption, or a combination of some other indicators such as human dimensions of the individual or a family. Low level of income alone is not enough to explain or define poverty. Other factors such as basic needs, capabilities, opportunities, empowerment, etc. are also important indicators to understand and define poverty.

Concepts and Meaning of Livelihood

As an academic discourse the concept of livelihood to address poverty issues has developed in the recent past. Initially this was conceptualized by the World Commission on Environment and Development. It aimed to maintain or enhance natural resource productivity, secure ownership of and access to assets and income-earning activities, as well as to ensure adequate stocks and flows of food and cash to meet basic needs (United Nations, 1992). Similarly the Copenhagen Social Summit highlights in its *Commitment Three* "governments accept responsibility for promoting full employment, as well as the attainment of sustainable livelihoods for all through productive employment and work" (United Nations, 1995: 2). It also emphasizes the interrelatedness of its main thematic elements such as poverty, unemployment and social exclusion. This shows that productive employment and work are vital elements for livelihoods; however, poverty, unemployment and social exclusions are the basic threats to be taken into account. The Institute of Development Studies (IDS) and the International

Institute for Sustainable Development (IISD) also advocate a sustainable livelihood approach with their emphasis on how households and members within households diversify their activities in order to increase income, reduce vulnerability, and improve the quality of their lives.

The concept of livelihood may evolve in different ways in response to different circumstances and aspirations. The meaning, for example, in the Nepalese context can be taken as an easy living by meeting needs for food, clothes, shelter, heath, education, and environment, which could provide substantial degree of local needs and self-reliance. The Webster's New World Dictionary defines livelihood as "a means of living or of supporting life". The literature in religion also explains livelihood. The Americal Evangelical Society—a religious organisation—defines livelihood as "the means by which life is sustained" (http://www.elca.org/dcs/economiclife.html on 02.11.00). However, livelihood is more than income or a consumption package. Sustainability comes if there is a long-term perspective of means for sustenance. A sustainable livelihood approach draws an improved understanding of poverty and analysis relating to gender, governance, and farming systems, bringing together more holistically (Farrington et al., 1999). Chambers and Conway define livelihood more comprehensively as "the capabilities, assets (stores, resources, claims and access) and activities required for a means of living" (Chambers and Conway, 1992: 7). This definition tries to establish a relationship among different variables such as capabilities of the person/household, various forms of assets, and the type of activities required for living. Different forms of assets could be different alternatives for a livelihood. The notion of capabilities can be taken in terms of physical and mental and social capabilities for doing work.

Frank Ellis, one of the leading scholars on this issue, says "livelihood comprises the assets (natural, physical, human, financial and social capital), the activities, and the access to these (mediated by institutions and social relations) that together determine the living gained by the individual or household." (Ellis, 2000: 10). In this definition of livelihood,

Ellis also identified three important variables comprising assets, activities and access. These elements are mediated by institutional and social relation processes for the ultimate outcome of the livelihood strategies. A livelihood programme should help the poor to gain better access to opportunities and may turn out to be substantially more cost effective for poverty reduction than attempting, artificially, to support particular sectors or sub-sectors of rural economic activity (Ellis, 1998; also see Gyawali, 1998: 73; Mishra, 1998).

For better understanding the livelihood process and analysing it, Ellis has developed a framework for the analysis of rural livelihoods (see Figure 2.1). Similar frameworks have also developed by Scoones (1998). The framework identifies entry points and critical processes, and assists with prioritising catalysts for change that can improve people's livelihoods. This is a version of the 'assets-mediating process-activities' framework, which can be utilised for poverty alleviation, sustainability, and building livelihood strategies.

FIGURE 2.1 A framework for micro-policy analysis of rural livelihoods

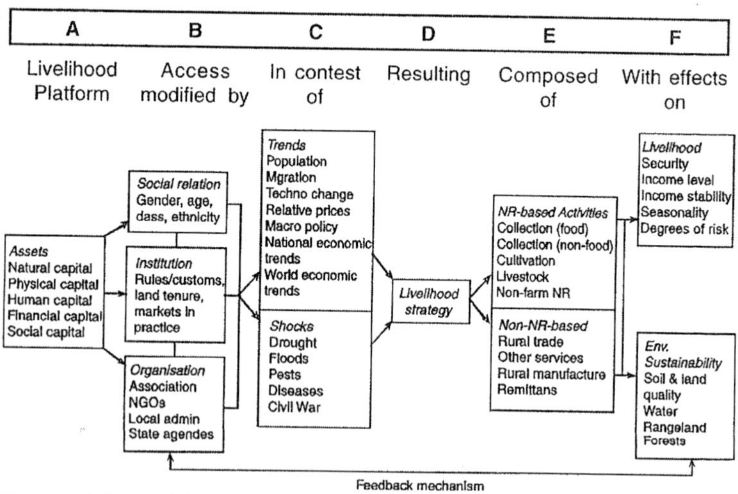

Source: Adopted from Ellis, 2000: 30.

The framework starts with assets owned, controlled, claimed, or accessed by the household. Assets can be an important element in the livelihood framework, which enables the individual/family to undertake directly or indirectly for production, or use as a means of survival, engage in labour markets, participate in reciprocal exchanges with other households. Therefore, to get rid of vulnerability or the poverty trap, various forms of assets such as human capital, physical capital, financial capital, social capital and natural capital are considered necessary (Ibid. 31). Some others such as Swift (1989) divide assets among the investments, stores, and claims; Maxwell and Smith (1992) between productive capital, non-productive capital, human capital, income, and claims. Similarly, Reardon and Vosti (1995) consider assets as natural and human resource assets and on-farm and off-farm physical and financial resources, while Mosher (1998) takes labour, human capital, productive assets, households relations, and social capital. Among these various types of assets natural capital comprises land, water, and other forms of biological resources that can be used for generating means of living, while physical capital comprises roads, buildings, irrigation canals, pumps, etc. used for generating income. Similarly, human capital is an important factor in poor people's homes, as they can use their own labour. The usefulness and effectiveness of human capital depend heavily on the education, training, and healthy condition of the people (see also Carney, 1998). Financial capital is the stock of money to which the poor household has to access it. The saving and credit and also the saleability of other assets comprise financial capital, which is important for generating means of living. Among these assets social capital has been recently considered as an important asset required for generating means of livelihood (Ibid. 32–7).

Social capital can be defined as a "reciprocity within communities and between households based on trust deriving from social ties" (Moser, 1998 cited in Ellis, 2000: 36). Social capital does not cost money but is built up by individuals, groups, communities, societies, and other forms of human associations that are effective for managing and carrying out various forms of survival activities (see also Putnam, 1993). In short, assets is one of the key variables required for solving poverty or attaining a better livelihood.

Assets alone are not enough as activity is required for generating income. The outputs depend on how it is mediated or processed. Ellis, in this framework, draws important factors that influence access to assets and their use in pursuit of viable livelihoods. Accordingly, social relations, institutions, and organisations in one category; and trends and shocks in the other category are classified. Social relations within their immediate gender, class, age, or ethnic groups are also important. Apart from this, existing rules and regulations regarding asset ownership, transfer (including marketing system as an institution and existing organisations such as local associations, NGOs, local or state agencies) are some of the important factors for influencing livelihood strategies. Both governmental and non-governmental organisations can play effective roles through their policies and activities of the livelihood outcomes. For this, people should be taken as the centre point of the development policy, strategies, and programmes. Ellis argues that a sustainable livelihood approach puts the people at the centre of development because people are the input as a capital in the form of people's organisations or networks and also the objective for enjoying the benefit. Chambers argues for the need for local participation for solving poverty issues because the people in the community can define criteria of well-being and the key elements of deprivation as they appear in the local context. On the basis of participatory studies in Asia and sub-Saharan Africa, local people defined poverty and ill-being in the following ways:

- "being disabled (for example, blind, crippled, mentally impaired, chronically sick),
- lacking land, livestock, farm equipment, a grinding mill,
- being unable to decently bury their dead,
- being unable to send their children to school,
- having more mouths to feed, fewer hands to help,
- lacking able-bodied family members who can feed their families in a crisis,

- having bad housing,
- suffering the effects of destructive behaviours (for example, alcoholism),
- being "poor in people", lacking social support,
- having to put children in employment,
- being single parents,
- having to accept demeaning or low status work,
- having food security for only a few months each year, and
- being dependent on common property resources. (Chambers 1997 in UNDP, 1997: 17).

The asset, mediating process, and activities should have a good relationship in the livelihood framework, however, often influenced by trends and shocks to the household and local circumstances. Due to the change in population, migration pattern, technology, market prices, including national and international policies and shocks such as natural calamities, drought, floods, pests, diseases, civil war, etc. the livelihood strategy and activities could be affected, necessitating redesigning the policies and implementation strategies.

On the basis of the asset situation, the social factors—including risk factors strategies—should be developed. Ellis remarks, "livelihood strategies are dynamic; they respond to changing pressures and opportunities and they adapt accordingly... and are composed of activities that generate the means of household survival" (Ellis, 2000: 40). Such activities could be both agricultural and non-agricultural, including natural based and non-natural based. On the basis of resource availability, existing legal situation, market situation, and interest, the individual/household activities could be diversified. Income could be earned from both farm and off-farm activities. A single activity could not be enough due to seasonality and other unfavourable environments. For this, different households should adopt different strategies according to their particular assets and access status. The positive impacts of such diversification include seasonality, risk reduction, employment creation, credit and asset improvement, environmental benefits, and gender benefits;

however, some negative effects could be on income distribution, farm output and adverse gender effects (UNDP, 199b; Ellis, 1998; Farrington et.al., 1999; Scoones, 1998).

On the basis of asset, mediating process, and activity-strategies, the outcome of the livelihood could be expected. Such outcome could be related to income level, income stability, reduction in adverse seasonal effects, and reduction in the overall risk profile of the income portfolio while preserving environmental sustainability. Despite the framework expected for planning and implementing a livelihood programme, various extraneous factors may affect assets and the activities. As Illis argues, substitution capabilities should be introduced, and household asset management could be a key feature for fighting the crisis (Ellis, 2000: 42–45).

Various factors such as social system (e.g., gender, racism or caste, religion), economic factors (unequal distribution of wealth), political system (none or limited participation in the decision making process), and other factors such as lack of knowledge, lack of good health, etc. are the reasons for poverty or vulnerability. There is no limit of potential requirements that can be determined because a rich person can feel poor and a poor person can also feel rich. How much is enough is also a question of debate (Alan, 1992). Therefore the concept of poverty is subject to time and place, which has to be perpetually rethought and redefined. However, both man-made and nature-made shocks and trends also make rural living more difficult. As a subject of study, the concept of livelihood or sustainable livelihood can be taken as a development strategy that can be a useful tool to help poor people by developing various assets capacity and mediating with useful activities for a better outcome. Since the basic notion of livelihood gives its prime concern to people (i.e, needy people both at the decision making and implementation of the livelihood activities), their roles for generating a means of living could be expected to a much better extent. However, how livelihood programmes can be best managed and how such programmes can be useful toos in varying contexts and situations has not been developed.

PEOPLE-CENTRED DEVELOPMENT: A NEED FOR LIVELIHOOD IMPROVEMENT

There is much talk and discussion about the development of the society/nation especially after the Second World War. Since then different models of economic development have been in practice, particularly to change the face of developing countries. Therefore, the development practitioners and the academicians started to debate the active participation of the people at the developmental process, when the 1950s' 'trickle-down' approach of development which favoured the economic growth model failed to address the poverty and powerlessness of the masses. It has to embody a process, which leads to a rise in the capacity of rural people to control their environment, accompanied by wider distribution of benefits resulting from such control. The developmental efforts can be meaningful only if poverty is alleviated by a sustained increase in productivity and incomes of the rural people, particularly in the case of developing countries. Though the role of state was highlighted during the 1960s for playing a catalytic and innovative role by employing *development administration*[1], the public sector performance could not meet the needs and aspirations of the people, particularly in the developing countries. Consequently, change in the conception of people-centred development, i.e., given more emphasis on people, has been noticed particularly since the 1970s. The conventional development indicator to measure GNP, therefore, has been gradually replaced by Basic Needs Approach (see ILO, 1976), which emphasizes the lives of majority of people living in miserable condition.

Schumacher (1977) pointed out that development does not start with goods, it starts with people and their education, organisation, and discipline. Without these, all resources remain latent and the resource potentiality could not be tapped for the benefit of the people. The author also argued that it requires an informed, disciplined, and organised people for development. Unless the living of the people is properly considered and managed accordingly, the developmental process becomes a useless effort because economic growth alone can not represent real development (Ramana, 1977).

Therefore, development processes must carry the aspirations and the 'defined needs' of the people for allocating, mobilizing, and managing resources which can strengthen the communities (Korten, 1988: 9). The community-based model of resource management could entertain and facilitate local participation, which can also control decision-making for representing the local responses and encouraging the mobilization of local initiative and resources (Ibid. 11–12). Development is not like a substance which can be borrowed from outside, i.e., real development cannot be purchased with foreign aid or assistance, rather it depends on people's ability and interest for using the local resources efficiently (Korten, 1995: 5). People must be involved in carrying out developmental activities that require authentic participation if they want to take benefit from the developmental process (Oakley, 1991).

For encouraging and involving people in development, social development is taken as a necessary condition. In the absence of social development, the scale of poverty, income disparities, unemployment, different forms of social stress including the loss of moral values in the society could create more problems. The Copenhagen Declaration and Program of Action of United Nations (1995) is a pronouncement for putting the needs, rights, and aspirations of the people at the core of decision making of the development programme. The summit expressed its full commitment to "strengthening community organisations and non-governmental organisations in the area of education, health, poverty, social integration, human rights, improvement of the quality of life, and relief and rehabilitation, and enabling them to participate constructively in policy making and implementation" (Ibid, 78). Therefore, a "bottom-up" approach should be adopted through income-generating and social welfare activities to empower the downtrodden as they are not united or able to advocate for their rights. People's participation in decision-making, implementation, benefits sharing, and the evaluation process is the necessary condition in this bottom-up approach.

Dahal views the important role of people as, "human factor

alone can contribute to a cohesive and adaptive society for it has proved so far to be a powerful engine for accumulating social capital as well as raising people's confidence in partnership for collective action" (Dahal, 1996:8).

People should be taken as the centre point in the process of development. Cernea argues about the people's importance in the development as "*people* are .. and should be.. the *starting* point, the *centre* and the *end goal* of each development intervention" (Cernea, 1985: ix, emphasis added). When people's participation is taken as a *means* participation seems as a process for mobilizing local manpower and resources including extracting external funding. On the other hand, when people's participation is taken as an *end goal*, it can be expressed as empowering the people in terms of their acquiring the skills, knowledge, and experience to take greater responsibility for their development. In the case of poverty due to exclusion it can be solved by involving them in the development activities. Similar views are presented in Acharya's (1997) work on a people-centred development approach which emphasizes the need of an active role of people in reshaping their lives. They should make the decisions, which can change for betterment. Therefore, people's participation and empowerment of the people to control their own destinies should be the primary objective of development. This approach puts the people at the centre and leads to:

- "basic needs satisfaction of the majority of the population—this means access to food, shelter, clothing, primary education and healthcare,
- equal opportunity for all groups of people, including women and ethnic minorities to develop their maximum potential—this may be defined as human development, and
- sustainable development, which does not put excessive pressure on environmental resources." (Acharya, 1997: 70–71).

For development, people must be active and the central focus from decision making to implementation. For this, people's organisation could be effective institutions to carry out people's sentiments and aspirations. People's organisation such as Non-Governmental Development Organisation (NGDO) could assist people-centred development if the knowledge, experiences, and values of the poor or marginalised (particularly women and powerless minorities including local resources) are well considered. Instead of imposing external expertise, resources, and technological know-how, there should be better understanding of the local potentialities which could be more effective in producing sustainable impacts in terms of reducing poverty and increasing social justice (Fowler, 2000: 17).

NGO—CONCEPTS AND DEFINITION

The present era demands optimum participation from different communities and formal and informal groups, agencies or organisations to constitute the society in the direction of becoming prosperous and reducing the level of agony that scattered the life of the people. One of the reasons that the governmental efforts could not be very productive was the faulty delivery mechanism up to the grass-roots level. The other reasons behind the failure of government are many, such as: highly constrained with rigid and often outmoded rules and regulations, vested political interests, apathy and lack of initiatives on the part of government employees, rampant corruption, and procedural red-tapism. Therefore, the dissatisfaction and criticism of public sector performance for the state development, i.e., reaching the grass-roots more directly and efficiently a new institutional mechanism both for resource transfer and grassroots actors has been realised, particularly since the 1970s. This new institutional force, which is often considered by NGOs for tackling the multifarious problems for providing basic needs facilities, creation of awareness, delivery of health facilities and providing a better livelihood, led to the search of alternative institutional mechanisms in the developing countries. These entities, therefore, are being looked upon as 'a major collective actor' in development activities and on the public agenda in general.

This situation demands appropriate alternative institutional measures for mobilising local resources and unleashing the forces of development in a co-ordinated manner to speed up socio-economic enhancement. Anheier (1990) presented this actor with social, economic, political, and cultural arguments for its 'comparative advantage' particularly for the development of the developing countries. Similarly, Brown (1988:21) considers that NGOs can also be taken as potentially critical catalysts for unlocking the energies and resources of the poor and voiceless, and for building pluralistic and democratic societies.

However, the term NGO covers everything from a small grass-roots traditional organisation to the international big organisation, from rural to urban, with varying and diversified objectives and capacities which often make it difficult to demarcate the boundary of its area of functions and responsibilities. Therefore the defining term, *non-governmental organisation* (NGO) has become a complex task. There are plenty of terminologies often found interchangeable and also overlapping one another. Some of the frequently used ones in the talkshops and also in different writings are: Non-Governmental Institutions (NGI), Non-Profit Organisation (NPO), Non-Governmental Development Organisation (NGDO), Private Voluntary Organisation (PVOs), Third Sector Organisation (TSO), Voluntary Organisation (VO), Public Service Contractor (PSC), People's Organisation (PO), Governmental Non-Governmental Organisation (GoNGO), Charitable Organisation (CO); Grassroots Organisation (GO); Civil Society Organisation (CSO); Independent Organisation (IO); Associational Organisation (AO); Private Organisation (PO), Community-based Organisation (CBO); Quasi-Non-governmental Organisation (QUANGO) (IDS, 1985,1; Anheier and Seibel, 1992: 1; Etzioni, A., 1973); Korten, 1990: 2; Tvedt, 1998:12). Other catchwords such as "new solidarity", "sociabilite", "private initiative", "self-reliance", "alternative to both market and state", and "reduction of big government" are also often used for this sector (Anheier and Seibel 1990: 8). Apart from this, some negative terminology is also found:

Briefcase NGO (BRINGO), Come and Go NGO (ComeN'GO), Commercial NGO (CONGO), Criminal NGO (CRINGO), Fake NGO (FANGO), Mafia NGO (MANGO), Non-Governmental Individual (NGI), Party NGO (PANGO), Phantom NGO (PHANGO), Politician's NGO (PONGO), etc. (Fowler, 1997: 32).

In this context, due to NGOs' diversified role, structure, and mode of interaction with clientele, it makes it difficult to draw a clear perception regarding their roles. Depending upon the functional characteristics and their roles, NGOs can be defined both from broad and narrow perspectives. The conventional approach implied towards the definitions of NGOs, based upon 'functional criteria', specifically confined the entire activities of NGOs within the realm of 'social and welfare' services. The terms "social service", "social work", "welfare service", and such related phrases as "social administration" and "social welfare administration" (and most of the policies and programmes involving these terms) are essentially formulations and practices of the 20th century (*Encyclopaedia Britannica*, 1980). In this way NGOs are swinging around philanthropic, altruistic, and charity-based activities. But recent considerations towards the roles of NGOs are taken as the critical contributors to basic economic growth and to the broader civic infrastructure and regarded as alternative development institutions (see North, 1990; Putnam, 1993; Fukuyama, 1995; OECD, 1995; World Bank, 1995). The third sector also has taken as a remedy for the "crisis of the welfare state" (Anheier and Seibel, 1990:1) and can be defined as "third sector organisations are different in relative, not in absolute terms: they may be less means-rational and less formal, and they may put more emphasis on solidarity and direct exchanges than do organisations in other sectors" (Anheier and Seibel, 1990:12). This gives a clear notion that NGOs or the third sector organisations rely on solidarity or the people's strengths and understanding rather than means rational like other public or for-profit sectors. In the Western welfare states, NGOs are organisations created for some public purpose, which can be separated both from government and the private sector (see Gidron, Kramer, & Salamon, 1992; Pardon; 1987). But others such as Bebbington et al. (1993), and OECD include "commercial private sector" and also business ventures as NGOs.

Anheier and Salamon try to discuss the conceptual issue of non-profit organisations and the NGO concept, and attempt to define them in a more comprehensive way. They defined NGOs from four perspectives: *legal, economic/financial, functional,* and *structural-operational* (Salamon & Anheier, 1992). According to legal definition, the creation of an NGO should be based on legal provision. This definition seeks a more formal definition of NGOs; however, the scope of flexibility working jurisdiction could differ from country to country, which makes it difficult to put the NGOs in the same legal basket. Secondly, what about the century-old traditional organisations which existed on trust and understanding of the people? The economic/financial definition tries to limit the NGO funding from government to not more than fifty per cent. Again, problems could occur as many of the NGOs in developing countries are funded either by bilateral money or official grant funds (Salamon & Anheier, 1992: 133). The functional approach emphasizes functions, purposes, and working methods of the NGO. Despite the scientific temperament of this approach, the functional roles and principles could differ from organisation to organisation (also see UNDP 1993, 84).

Finally, the structural/operational definition tries to sketch the boundary of non-profit sector from the market and the state. It does not recognise only the purposes of the organisations or their sources of income, but also their basic structure and operation. According to this notion the non-profit sector is defined on the basis of some basic characteristics. Thus, a non-profit organisation should be:

- *organised* (i.e., as a legal entity),
- *private* (i.e., institutionally separate from government),
- *non-profit* (i.e., not returning any profits generated to their owners or directors),
- *self-governing* (i.e., not overruled by the government), and

- *voluntary* (i.e., at least should have some voluntary part) (Anheier & Salamon, 1992; 1998: 20–21).

Indeed this definition gives a "what" of NGO, however, lacking "why" and "how" it should work.

Pokharel also tries to define NGO. According to him an NGO is that entity which should have at least four features such as: development oriented, non-political, democratic in character, and non-profit making (Pokharel, 2000: 55).

Tvedt said "the term 'NGO' should be used as a common denominator, a collective term, for all organisations within the aid channel that are institutionally separate from the state apparatus and are non-profit-distributing... At the same time it is important to avoid the 'catch-all' quality and the political flavour which past usage the channel, whether on political, institutional or value-based grounds" (Tvedt, 1998: 16). He tries to discuss the concept of NGOs for analysing organisational hybrids. He thinks many types of NGOs such as DONGO, QUANGO, GONGOs are hybrids, combining many characteristics with a strong relationship with both public and for-profit organisations could be only the sub-class of NGOs (Ibid. 17–8). Tvedt tried to focus on the specific and independent role of NGOs.

Korten thinks the civil society organisations are composed of the informed individual, which "also leads naturally to an authentic market economy in which the goal is to provide productive and satisfying livelihoods for all, most enterprises are local, and every person has an ownership stake in the productive assets on which their livelihood depends. Such of society would embody the principles of radical self-organisation common to all healthy living systems and provide maximum opportunity for each individual to develop and express their full creative potential toward the continued unfolding of the possibilities of the living whole" (Korten, 2000: 9).

Korten highlights the role of civil societies organisations towards meeting livelihoods and the welfare of people in society. A developed civil society can contribute in the interest of people as citizens, voters, and workers. An autonomous civil society can only be realised when power and authority is decentralised to the development actors in various forms. NGOs as development actors are in the best position to help create, strengthen and sustain autonomous organisations that can relate to and debate with each other, advocate and lobby for policy changes, assess the options presented by political parties and forces, experiment with alternative relations of production, conscientize their vision of an alternative political order, and create participatory structures that will no longer allow the elite and self-appointed parties and personalities to speak in the name of the people (Korten op.cit). Chand (1991) thinks a broad and multidimensional approach is required to define and interpret the term NGO, because NGO today has been forging ahead as a development-oriented institution embedded with the capability to function as 'supplementary' and 'complementary' entities in addressing the diversified needs of the community. Chand suggests working as development-oriented organisations. The World Bank's operational directive on NGOs defines NGO as "a wide variety of groups and institutions that are entirely or largely independent of government and characterised primarily by humanitarian or co-operative, rather than commercial objectives". This term is also used to refer "principally to those private organisations that pursue activities to relieve suffering, promote the interests of the poor, protect the environment, or undertake community development" (in Korten, 1991: 21). The OECD views NGOs as organisations "established and governed by a group of private citizens for a stated philanthropic purpose and supported by voluntary individual contributions" (OECD: 1988, 14). However, neither the World Bank nor the OECD definition speaks about NGO-government relations but suggests project approaches to do specific functions. The UN Conference on the Least Developed countries (UNCLDC) also refers in the same line as NGOs whether northern, southern, or international should be committed for solidarity, justice, and pay particular attention to the plight of the poor.

The National Planning Commission in Nepal presented

the definition of NGO in a more elaborate form. Accordingly, to be a development NGO it should have the following common attributes:

- naturally conceived voluntary by nature,
- not committed to profit making for distributing dividends among its own members,
- politically neutral,
- liberal in conducting programmes,
- oriented towards the upliftment of the poor, needy, and helpless,
- active in arousing social awareness,
- carry out works of public importance,
- involve maximum people's participation,
- follow democratic practice in selecting the board of directors from among volunteers,
- conduct other economic programmes that meet public requirements, and
- make their policies, programmes, and budget open and transparent (NPC, 1992: 719).

Though the content in the list covers both functional and normative aspects, it lacks what should be the relation between NGO and the state/market. However, how it should be governed, how to manage resources for carrying out their functions, which are the priority areas of function, and what should be the relation with other sector has not been missing. The diversity in NGO functions and relation with government and private organisations also complicate the role of NGO 'what is' and 'what to be done' through voluntary associations has become a matter of debate.

EMERGENCE OF NGOs

At present different organisations are found existing with certain purpose(s). Studies regarding organisations and their roles started from the late 19th century. Frank Oppenheimer (1896) made a study on 'law of transformation', and Michel's 'iron law of political parties' predicts a general convergence and assimilation of organisational types. Later Max Weber's

(1983) bureaucracy may evolve as the ubiquitous organisational type of modern society. Since then many authors have given their concerns on roles, functions, types of organisational fields, environment, etc. (Hannan & Freeman 1977; 1983). The 20th century has become the century of organisations. Reichard (1988) thinks modern organisations normally have four variables for the basis of organisations. They are: means rationality, formality, solidarity, and type of exchange. Third sector organisations tend to be characterised by lower degrees of means rationality and formality and higher degree of solidarity and direct exchange (Seibel & Anheier, 1990: 12). However, it would be curious to know the reasons and the theoretical understanding behind the existence of NGOs, and their roles in undertaking development responsibility of the society. There are different schools of thought to explain the emergence of NGOs and their roles. Many of them are borrowed from economic theories that NGOs are considered as an institutional response due to the failure of state and market.

According to *public goods theory* or the 'performance failure theory', NGOs exist to satisfy the residual unsatisfied demand for public goods in society. Weispord (1977) argues that people construct or form their alternative organisations (i.e., people's organisation or NGOs) when the government or the market can not fulfil the demand of public goods for all the people or serve all the interests at least at the minimum level. This situation arises if the social values or the interests are more diverse and heterogeneous. In such cases people should have instinct and awareness about the role of the organisation. Brown and Korten also sported similar views and said, "a widely recognised failure of large-scale government bureaucracies is their inflexibility and conservatism". This political form of state failure creates a situation in which NGOs emerge as innovative responses to novel problems, because of their activities for experimentation and flexibility" (Brown & Korten, 1991: 48). However, Douglas (1987) thinks NGOs arise as a response to a situation where people are sovereign but diverse—with competing and sometimes contradictory wishes.

This theory stipulates that where there are many competing and contradictory wills, a great number of NGOs will eventually grow to meet and institutionalise this social diversity.

On the other hand, in a situation of the government failure/ market failure, the unsatisfied demand for public goods left by such failure calls for the emergence of non-profit organisations, which are social entrepreneurs. Such organisations could fulfil unsatisfied needs such as education or health services. James (1987) argues that the more heterogeneous a society, the more conducive it becomes for creating a larger number of NGOs.

Another influential and related theory is the *contract failure theory*. When people find it difficult to perceive the sense of contract, they have to find reliable agents to fulfil their needs. Therefore 'non-profit organisations' could be more reliable or 'trusted agents' work as contract agents between the people and the commercial firms. As commercial firms could take more/undue benefits from the consumer's ignorance, in such a situation the voluntary organisation could be helpful to the people. Brown and Korton argue that organisations might come into existence to be remedies in case of 'market failure' situations because markets tend to be 'especially vulnerable to failure in developing countries', (Brown & Korton, 1991: 48). In such cases NGOs could emerge because people trust them more than the profit organisation (Krashinsky, 1986; also see Williamson, 1985).

Esman and Uphoff argued that NGOs play the role of local intermediaries to fulfil the 'organisational gap'. According to this model, a local intermediary mobilises the people to participate in government-initiated programmes. NGOs could be a potentially effective medium, which could be utilised in delivering services to the rural areas of developing countries. In this way, NGOs are taken as an alternative institutional framework through which the rural poor and socially disadvantaged groups are served better than the traditional bureaucratic mechanisms (Esman & Uphoff, 1984).

The relationship between the state and the NGO could have

both 'conflicting' and 'interdependence' and 'partnership'. In the case of sharing expertise, experiences, and resources, there could be a situation of complementing one another. There could be a situation of 'voluntary failure' for meeting the public needs which include 'philanthropic insufficiency' for generating voluntary resources to scale up their functions and 'philanthropic paternalism' an absence of self-reliance (Salamon & Anheier, 1998: 224–225). In such situations the 'theory of interdependence' or the 'partnership theory' applies to emerge NGOs as the partners (Salamon, 1987). In such situations non-profit organisation could not be alternatives to the state in the provision of public goods, but rather the state and the non-profit sector could grow in parallel, and even in co-operation with each other for expansion of public goods and work hand to hand.

The other theoretical consideration is the *social origin* approach to understanding the development of the non-profit sector (Salamon & Anheier, 1996). According to this approach, the non-profit organisation is deeply embedded in the social, economic, and political dynamics of different societies, and the emergence of non-profit organisations is rooted in the broader structure of class and social groupings in a society. There could be four models of non-profit organisation activities such as:

- a *statist model* characterised by limited state activity and a weak non-profit sector;
- a *liberal model* characterised by limited state activity but a strong non-profit sector;
- a *social democratic model* characterised by expanded state involvement in social welfare activity and limited non-profit involvement; and
- a *corporatist* or *partnership model* in which both the state and the non-profit sectors are actively involved in societal problem solving, often in co-operation with each other (Salamon & Anheier, 1998: 226–230). This theory explains the socio-economic and political environments that often determine the scope, role, and expansion of the non-profit or the NGO sector.

EXAMINING NGOs AS AN ALTERNATIVE INSTITUTION

Why do NGOs exist, what decides the distribution of functions between the state and the NGOs or between different sectors in society, and whether they represent a better option can be the central philosophical questions for studying the NGO phenomenon.

Brown argues that despite some similarities with other public or profit-making organisations, NGDOs have four specific characteristics, which produce special strengths and weakness. Such positive characteristics are *missions* that focus on social change, *shared values* and ideologies, instituted loosely and informally which allow *flexibility* for innovation and local adaptation, and can work with *diverse stakeholders* (Brown, 1988: 24). Brown also describes five problems such as 'leadership dilemmas', 'organisational cohesion', 'diverse external demands', and the tendency to interpret issues in terms of 'values and ideologies' that often are faced by this sector (Brown, 1988: 25–27). The diversity in NGO functions and relations with government and private organisations also complecate the role of NGO 'what is' and 'what to be done' as voluntary associations has become a matter of debate.

Due to the limited political accountability, inefficient allocation of resources, and urban syndrome development practices, public-sector organisations often become ineffective particularly in developing countries. Over-politicisation of bureaucracy, lack of proper skills, and massive corruption reinforce dysfunction in administration, which led to the emergence of NGOs (Lehman, 1990; Farrington & Lewis, 1993). As a result NGOs have excessively proliferated during the last three decades, particularly in the 1980s and in Nepal in the 1990s. Due to the comparative advantages such as capacity to reach rural poor and outreach to remote areas, promotion of local participation, cost effectiveness, adaptability and innovativeness, NGOs have been a major collective actor both in the developed and developing societies.

The role of NGOs in accelerating the pace of development and strengthening democracy is crucial in developing countries like Nepal. In the changed political context, NGOs are expected to function as a catalyst, as mobilizers, facilitators, analysts, and advocates of the people (Tuladhar, 1991). As people get more opportunities in democracy for the attainment of self-governance, self-reliance, and sustainable development, their organized efforts could play a crucial role in furthering democracy also. Such roles become crucial because of their interdependence of local organisations and institutions, their functional specialization, their accountability to the people, etc. This could demand people's own initiatives to solve their problems. In this way people could create their organisations as people's organisations or NGOs

The other role of NGO is related with the resource transfer from government to NGOs and also from donor countries/ agencies to developing countries. A change in the funding strategy of the major donor agencies like World Bank for reducing the state role and increasing the space of NGOs in the 1980s and also establishment of a 'New Policy Agenda' for development helped create and increasing the number of NGOs for poverty alleviation and also in social welfare activities (World Bank, 1991; Robinson, 1993; Tvedt, 1998:62, Vuorela, Airaksinen & Ulvila 1996: i.; Edwards & Hulme, 1996 in Ahmad, 2000: 18–19). Many governments in developing countries also encourage NGOs work as development partners and as agents of resource transfer from the donor agencies.

A change in the political system in the Eastern European countries and disintegration of Soviet Union has also added the new role of NGO and civil societies to the alternative model of development. During the turn of the 20th century, there was an ongoing debate on the redefinition of the relationship between society and state, where NGOs are playing a mobilising and catalysing role. In this context Tvetd argues that the role of NGOs should not be confined only 'gap-fillers' but "to substitute the state in key aspects of societal development" and also should have a "crucial role in creating a more just and democratic development" (Tvedt, 1998: 62–63). As NGOs have grass-roots attachment, flexible programming, cost effectiveness in implementing their activities, and manageable size, they can implement social development programmes such as poverty alleviation, women empowerment, and community development easily (Dkakal, 1989; Meyer, 1992). In this context the role of NGO could be important for furthering human rights, social mobilisation, good governance, and promoting pluralism.

Aminuzzaman also presents three major roles that NGOs can play which are also somewhat bit similar to Tvedt's arguments. According to him the NGOs' role should be in the area of 'creating democratic pluralist civil society', 'poverty alleviators and sustainable developers', and 'efficiency enhancers' (1998: 85–6). He argues that as the NGOs work with communities to foster development activities and rising democratic consciousness, they can help democracy. As a democratic development role, NGOs can strengthen civil society, encourage political participation on a micro-level, balance state power, advocate on development discourse, address the needs of society, motivate for citizenry power, promote pluralism, and establish mechanisms for government to become accountable (see McNulty, 2000; Farrington & Lewis 1993; Lehmann 1990). As the poverty alleviators and sustainable developer NGOs can help the poor and disadvantages by making direct contacts with the target groups at the grass-roots (Korten 1987). The citizens or the clients have to contact public office(s) if they want some sort of services while in case of NGOs their staff should reach the doorsteps to deliver their services. It enhances the efficiency for the effective service delivery mechanism at the doorsteps more directly. As they are collaborators of the government they can also influence the policy both by policy advocacy and also by good relation (see Farrington and Lewis, 1993).

About the role of the NGOs, Brown and Korten argue that the comparative advantage of NGOs lies in their ability to innovate, to adapt to local conditions, and to reach and to work with the poor. These positive features are the function of their basic values, special skills, small size, limited resources, flexibility, and freedom from political constraints. However, the weaknesses could be their value commitments, small size, independence, and administrative flexibility (Brown & Korten,

1991). They argue for the role of NGO in the political lenses and the donor perspectives. According to the political perspective, NGOs can play as 'gap fillers' in a situation of 'government failure'. But NGOs' role could be most important in 'social diversity' and also for 'experimentation and flexibility' (Ibid. 47). In the situation of social diversity, they argue that NGOs can engage in 'policy advocacy and political action' to accommodate the 'competing and sometimes contradictory wills' (Brown & Korten, 1991; also see McNulty, 2000). Apart from this, they can work as social experimentation, which could result in greater values, which the government could not undertake due to the political risk. From the donor's perspective, concern about the NGOs' role for economic efficiency and incentives. The authors conclude that the political and institutional role of NGOs is more important than the economic roles (Brown & Korten, op.cit. 48–49).

Korten notes, "many voice must be heard in shaping the directions of a nation's development, and NGOs have every right-indeed; the obligation, to give voice to their values and experience. It is also significant that NGOs are often the most active society's institutions in helping the poor to achieve a voice of their own" (Korten, 1987: 156).

NGOs can also be looked at from sectoral perspectives. Brown and Korten (1991:49) classify NGOs as a separate organisational sector other than government and private organisations. These organisations represent a distinct class of organisations that depend on energy and resources given freely by their members and supporters because they believe in organisational missions, not merely because of political imperatives or economic incentives. Among these three sectors, mobilisation of resources and their operating system mostly depend on coercion and legitimate authority in hierarchical systems in the public sector organisation. The business sector relies on negotiated exchange in market systems whereas the voluntary sector believes in shared values in consensus-based systems (Brown & Korten 1991: 49; see Table 2.1 below).

As the voluntary sector actualises social vision, it gets more support from the people to implement activities for their

TABLE 2.1: Organisational characteristics of different sectors

Category	*Commercial sector*	*Government sector*	*Voluntary sector*
Primary concern	Produce goods and services	Preserve social order	Actualise social visions
Implicit organisation	Market	Hierarchies	Clan/ consensus
Co-ordination mechanisms	Negotiated exchange	Authority and coercion	Shared values
Enforcement mechanisms	Contracts and reciprocity norms	Supervision and rules	Moral obliga-tions; profe-ssional ethics
Prototype	Corporation	Army	Church

Source: Brown and Korten, 1991: 49.

welfare. The immediate progress, as well as the long-term influence of NGOs as a social movement, depends first and foremost on the build-up of their organisational capacity. This will require strengthening the many fragile and weak NGOs that risk disappearing without a trace, and reinforcing their internal organisation, improving their accountability mechanisms both to their own membership and to the public at large.

Korten also presented generation strategies of the NGOs, their roles, problems of definition, and development orientation according to the different phases. This generation strategies concept gives a knowledge of how the role and functions of NGOs change over a period of time (see Table 3).

The first-generation strategies involve NGOs in the direct and immediate delivery of goods and services such food, health care, or shelter and relief materials to the victims of wars and natural calamities, starving children, and other needy people in the society. The role of NGOs in this generation is active and supply oriented as they work as 'doer'. Due to their quick service delivery they can provide immediate services in the crisis periods.

TABLE 2.2: The Generations of NGO Movements

	First Generation Relief and Welfare	*Second Generation Community Development*	*Third Generation Sustainable System Development*	*Fourth Generation People's Movement*
Problem definition	Shortage	Local inertia	Institutional and policy constraints	Inadequate mobilizing vision
Time frame	Immediate	Project life	Ten to twenty years	Indefinite future
Scope	Individual or family	Neighbourhood or village	Region or nation	National or global
Chief actor	NGO	NGO plus community	All relevant public and private institutions	Loosely defined networks of people & organisations
NGO Role	Doer	Mobiliser	Catalyst	Activist/ Educator
Management Orientation	Logistics management	Project management	Strategic management	Coalescing and energizing self-managing networks
Development Education	Starving children	Community self-help	Constraining policies and institutions	Spacious earth

Source: David C. Korten (1990): Getting to the 21st Century Voluntary Action: Global Agenda.

In second-generation strategies, NGOs work in co-operative ways with the local community to manage community self-help projects. Here, the role of NGO is a s a mobiliser of the local community for the management of human and material resources for the community welfare. This strategy assumes that self-reliance is neessary for grass-roots development. As self-help is the main trust of development, the local community can define their prblems more correctly and utilise their resources to get benefis.

The third-generation strategies have a broader orientation, as they look beyond individual communities and seek changes in specific policies and institutions at local, national, and global levels. These strategies focus on institutional and policy constraints that create problems for sustainable development. Here, the role of NGO becomes a catalyst and gives its concerns on strategic management. Both public and private institutions are collaborated with as and when necessary for developing appropriate policies and institutions to facilitate sustainable local development and control over local resources.

The fourth-generation strategies focus on people's movement towards the inadequacy mobilisation of vision. In this generation the scope of functions of the NGOs becomes more pervasive and broad, covering everything from national to global horizons. NGOs' role becomes as activist and educators and loosely defined networks of people and organisations are the principal actors and rely on self-management network. However, development NGOs in many parts of the world have not become revolutionary, but market oriented.

In this way the generation concept provides a notion that NGOs can play creative and active roles for short-term, medium-term, and long-term periods up to the indefinite time as doer, mobilizer, catalyst, and activist for the welfare of the people and the society at the local, national, and global level.

Despite the above roles and capacities behind NGOs, they suffer from limitations which make it difficult for them to implement their missions and visions. Due to short-term orientation and subject to the relation with the government, they often face difficulties for playing effective roles (Aminuzzaman, 2000: 86). Recent evaluation of NGOs has also brought out some deficiencies such as limited replicability, limited self-sustainability, limited technical capacity, and lack of broad programming context in the manner of their working. Furthermore, NGOs are also often lost in self-admiration. Although they do have strengths for which they are acclaimed, nevertheless, in the face of pervasive poverty 'small scale' can also mean 'insignificant'; 'politically independent' can also mean 'powerless' or 'disconnected'; 'low cost' can mean 'underfinanced' or 'poor quality'. One view is that NGO projects are often poor. The cost–benefit ratios are poor, the projects are not sustainable without subsidies, and the projects are not highly replicable. None of the donor-aided forestry projects in Africa came close to paying their costs. NGOs do not promote development of a self-reliant kind. NGOs clearly cannot replace government agencies altogether; their role is mainly to complement government-administered development efforts (Mahathur, 1992).

The roles of NGOs are also severely criticised by leftist writers. According to them, the NGO movement creates problems for the revolution because NGOs are promoting capitalism, supporting government, strengthening governance systems, and destroying morals and ethics of political activists by providing special benefits and bribing them. Similarly, most of the NGOs in the developing countries are run by foreign funding, which makes them more dependent. In a way, by using this means, neo-colonialism has been emerging for controlling developing countries. The interest of transferring resources through NGOs has also viewed as market expansion, and political control over developing countries (Adams, 1998; in Ulvila, 2000; also see Chintan, 2000). Questions regarding NGOs in developing countries have also raised concerns about the transparency and accountability of the NGOs and the efficient use of resources. Because of external funding, the local indigenous resource mobilisation systems, voluntary systems, and local co-operation systems have also been broken, and one of the prime reasons of killing the indigenous organisations in the development countries has been the external funding of the NGOs.

Some of the rightists think that as the NGOs have been provided tax exemptions, subsidies, and other forms of political concessions, there is a problem in the growth of market economy which hinders the faster development of the country.

NGOs could be a better institutional option and can be viewed both from macro and micro perspectives. In a macro role, NGOs can influence the broader policy agendas about development models, resource transfers, and furthering the democratic process. According to the micro perspective, their role should be viewed on operational roles of the grass-roots level programmes and activities, and the delivery of services for the poor and under-privileges. The operational roles can be analysed on its effectiveness and efficiency in mobilising local resources and generating awareness, including innovative the local technologies, which can support the livelihood improvement of a poor society.

END NOTE

1. The credit for the conceptualisation of this term in the present form goes to the Comparative Group (CAG) of American Society for Public Administration (ASPA). The CAG was organised in 1960-61 by a small group of political scientists and students of public administration who had been frustrated and disappointed with the US's efforts at technical assistance for public administration in developing countries. Some of the valuable literatures regarding this development administration concept are contributed by various thinkers and presented here. Besides the articles in periodicals, occasional papers, and case studies, some of the notable literatures in the field of development administration are: Ferrel Heady & Sybil L. Stokes (1962), Irving Swerdlow (1963), Fred W. Riggs (1964), Edward Weidner (1964), J.D. Montgomery & W.L. Siffin (1966), Ferrel Heady (1966), Ralph Braibanti (1969), James P. Heaphey (1970), Fred W. Riggs (1970), Dwight Waldo (1970), Ramesh Kumar Arora (1972), Irving Swerdlow (1975), Faisal S.A. Al-Salem (1977), S.K. Sharma (1978), George F. Gant (1979). Poudyal, Madhav P., (1984).

3

Livelihood in Nepal : How the Problems are Addressed

The process of modernisation of Nepal began only after the early 1950s when democracy was installed and opened herself to the world scenario. Almost five decades of planned economic development have been completed since then. However, the living condition of the people, particularly in the rural areas, has not improved. The poverty problem has stood as one of the major challenges before the people and the intervening organisations. This chapter presents the general development scenario of the country, social setting, occupation and employment situation, distribution of income, and poverty scenario. It also reviews the efforts made to address the poverty problems for bringing about a better livelihood particularly of the poor section of the society.

GENERAL DEVELOPMENT SCENARIO

Nepal is a small, landlocked Himalayan kingdom sandwiched between two Asian giants—China from the north and India from east, west, and south. One of the major characteristics of Nepal is smallness but with diversity in terms of land, people, cultures, traditions, economy, vegetation, wildlife, etc. Nepal's greatest advantage also lies in her diverse ecological zones which generate and maintain different species of vascular plants, mammals, birds, and butterflies as well as the perennial source of rivers. Since the formation of Nepal as a nation state in 1769, the country had been self-sufficient with respect to her own self-defined basic needs. She has a long history of cultural richness with her own traditions and values. Social co-operation, feeling of brotherhood and sisterhood, and unity within the diversity of various creeds and dialects have been the basic features and the national identity of the society. Due to this unity and social understanding within ethic and linguistic heterogeneity, Nepal has been surviving as an independent country.

Modern forms of development practice and people's power over the decision-making process only began after the establishment of democracy in 1951. At that time, there were just 376 km of road, 82 km of railway, 1140 kilowatts of power generation, 14,700 hectares of irrigation facility, 7950 student enrolled, and less than 200 hospital beds when the First Plan (1956-1961) was promulgated in the country (Gurung, 1989). Since then, nine periodic developmental plans have been completed, and currently the Tenth Plan (2002-07) is under way. As a result some of the productive infrastructures such as roads, means of communication, electricity, irrigation, including academic institutions and health centres have been created especially in the urban centres and in the plains.

The present socio-economic development indicators show that 47 per cent of adult people are literate, 60 per cent of children under 15 years of age are enrolled in school, life expectancy is 55 years of age, the number of hospital beds at present is 5023, and also the number of doctors and other health-related personnel have significantly increased. Almost 65 per cent of people have access to safe, clean drinking water.

Similarly, the productive infrastructure constructed by the year 1999/2000 are total length of road 13.849 km, electricity generation 342 megawatt. At least 62 districts are linked by road networks, 44 airfields are in operation, and 4.013 post offices are scattered all over the country. Almost 1528 VDCs are reached by telephone service, television service reaches 32 per cent of the country, and 47 per cent of people get benefit.

The share of agriculture sector in GDP is 39.2 per cent and non-agriculture is 60.8 per cent. The trade diversification has widened; per capita income has increased to US$ 243. The per

Box 3.1 : FACTS ABOUT NEPAL

Location: 26'22" 30'27" North latitude & 80'4" - 88'12" East longitude
Area: 147181 sq. km (Mountain Area 15%, Hill Area 68%, Terai 17%).
Total arable land: 18%.
Total forest covered: 37% (5.000 species of vascular plants, 850 species of birds, 6.000 species of butterflies, 175 species of reptiles).
Number of River & Rivulets: 6.000 (2.3 per cent of World Hydro Resource)
Administrative division: 5 Development Regions, 14 Zones, 75 Districts, 58 municipalities, VDC 3913.
Total population: 22 million (7.8% in Mountain, 45.5%, in Hills, and 46.7% in Terai)
Population in: 13 % in urban and 87% in village.
Population growth rate: 2.1%.
Life expectancy: 55 years.
No. of Hospitals 83, 13 Health Centres, 705 health posts, 275 Ayurbedic hospitals, 3,158 Sub-Health Posts and 160 Primary health Centres.
No. of Hospital Beds: 5023 (Health manpower: 923 doctors, nurses 4655, Kabiraj 211, Baidya 210, Health Assistants 5,295, Health workers 3,190, Local health workers 4015, TBA and Female Health workers 60.627).
Literacy rate: 47%.
Total number of academic institutions: 26.226 primary, 7232 lower secondary and 3939 secondary, 516 Higher Secondary, 5 Universities (with 219 colleges). Student Enrollment (in '000): Primary 3.964, Lower Secondary 927, Secondary 413, Higher Secondary 65.338, and university 1,535.
GDP contribution: Agriculture: 38%, Non-agriculture 62% .
Per capita income: US$: 243, Per capita GDP (1996/97) NPR. 13346.
Source: Nepal Year Book 1999, Ministry of Information & Communication *2000, Ministry of Finance, 2000.*

capita GDP of the people NPR 13.346 respectively (see Box 4.1; also see Ministry of Finance, 2000).

Despite nearly five decades of planned economic developmental efforts, the country could not achieve the desired results. More than half of the people are still illiterate, contraceptive users cover only 30.1 per cent, the mortality of children under age five is 118/1000 live births, and the infant morality rate is 74.7/1000, which is much higher than in other South Asian countries.

Even government documents show that the number of people under poverty is 42 per cent of the total populace; however, independent analysts estimate that the number of people living under poverty could be more than half of the total population. Though more than 80 per cent of people rely on agricultural occupation, only 21 per cent of the total arable land is irrigated so far. Therefore, agricultural production mostly relies on the weather. Instability of political system/ government, inefficient administrative mechanism, limited size of development resources (especially for creating development infrastructures), faulty processes for resource allocation, etc. contributed to the slow pace of development in the country. The per capita GDP growth rate after the 1970s does not give a positive indication of economic growth. Table 3.1 shows that agricultural growth is rather stagnant though it is the major source of living of the people.

TABLE 3.1 Per capita GDP Growth rate (percentage)

Indicator/period	*1971–80*	*1981–90*	*1991–96*
Real GDP growth rate	2.1	4.9	5.2
Agriculture/GDP	0.5	4.6	2.2
Non-agriculture GDP	7.0	5.2	7.8
Population	2.6	2.3	2.3
Per capita income	–0.5	2.6	2.9
Agriculture	–2.1	2.3	–0.1

Source: MoF, 1997 in Nepal South Asia Centre, 1998.

Due to the faulty process of distribution of income (see details in Section 3.4 of this chapter), people particularly in the rural part could not get reasonable benefits, which put them below the poverty line. The volume of foreign loans has been increasing[1], and reached as much as NPR 21.964 millions, however, the speed of development has not been as much as expected and the people at the grass-roots still have to suffer. Dahal writes, "although the Nepali economy passed through a series of crises in all the periods...the ultra-poor, the poor and the lower middle income groups have never before suffered the economic humiliation they are facing today that has accelerated the process of national disintegration resulting in the annihilation of some tribal communities, increasing human trafficking, asylum in refugee camps in other countries, and increasing socio-cultural, and ethnic resentments" (Dahal, Madan K., 1996: 2–3). The UNDP places Nepal in the 144th position in the list of Human Development Index indicating it as one of the poorest nations in the world (UNDP, 1999: 136).

SOCIAL SETTING

Population and Ethnicity

The present population size in Nepal is 23.1. million, about 21 per cent higher than in 1991 (CBS, 2001. Though population programmes got important space in national development plans, unwanted growth of population is considered one of the major problems in Nepal. The 1996/97 data show that the fertility rate is 4.58 and annual growth rate is 2.3 per cent, which is higher than in other SAARC nations (NPC, 1998: 223).

The Nepalese people originate from the different races such as Caucasian, Mongolian, Dravidian, and Proto-Australoid. At present, too, the society is segmented into caste, sub-caste, and ethnic and sub-ethnic groups. So the 1990 constitution of the Kingdom of Nepal considers the country as "multiethnic, multilingual". (HMG/N, Law Books Management Committee, 1963)). The 1991 census records more than 60 such groups and 20 major languages (CBS, 1991), while the National Ethnic Groups Development Committee has also identified 61 such groups. Similarly the National Language Policy Advisory Committee lists 52 living languages while other researchers have proposed their own lists of languages and dialects (Rastriya-bhasa Niti Sujhav Ayog, 1993: 5–6 in Gurung, Harka, 1998: 59; also see Summer Institute of Linguistics (SIL).

The caste system is fundamentally rooted in the Hindu religion, which can also be found on a hierarchical basis. According to the Muluki Ain 1910 B.S, such castes were there such as sacred thread-wearing castes, liquor-drinking castes, untouchables but purification not required, and untouchables but purification required. Brahmin, Kshetri, Vaishya, and Sudra are mostly found in the Terai, and Brahmin, Kshetri, and Dalits reside in Hills. Apart from this, other sub-ethnic or inter-ethnic categories also have somehow hierarchical practices (Nepal South Asia Centre, 1998: 8). Despite the enactment of Muluki Ain 2020 (HMG/N, Ministry of Law & Justice 1963) and also the guaranteed constitutional provision, of the right of the people against discriminate on the basis of caste, creed, sex, or religion, social practice (see also HMG/N, Law Book

Management Committee, 1991) still means that discrimination among the castes and the communities exists. As a result, some of the castes such as Kami, Damai, Pode, Khadki, Chamar, etc. are regarded as *Dalit* (oppressed groups), and reminiscences of untouchabilty can still be seen. They are both socially and economically deprived.

Religion

The 1991 census figures the size of religious groups as 86.5 per cent Hinduism, 7.8 per cent Buddhism, 3.5 per cent Islam, 1.7 per cent Kiranti, 0.2 per cent Christianity, and the rest 0.2 per cent (CBS, 1991: Vol.1, Part VII, Table 20). However, tribal traditions for the worshipping the same god/goddess, as well as tantrism transcend religious denominations in Nepal, particularly between Hinduism and Buddhism (Gurung, 1998: 36). Despite such multiplicity in religious practices in Nepal, religious tolerance and understanding with one another is one of the richest characteristics of Nepalese society. However, many academicians and activists who demand secularism believe that the Census figures rather attempted to rationalize the Hindu state and also think that the characteristic of religious tolerance has been exaggerated.

Gender

According to the Population Census 1991 females comprise 50.13 per cent (9.2 million) of the total population. However, one of the major social problems in Nepal is gender discrimination. Though the role of women in development has been emphasised in the national development plan since 1980, the status of Nepalese women has still not progressed much. In this context, the Ninth Plan (1997–2002) policy document states, "Nepalese women are still found suppressed, exploited, neglected and forced to live insecure life because of illiteracy, ill health, poverty, orthodox traditions and discriminatory legal system" (NPC, 1998: 719). Development of capacity and accessibility of opportunities are both lacking with women. Early marriage (44% of women are married by 19 years of age), early childbirth, high fertility rate, high rate of maternal mortality (539 out of 100.000) are some of the problems of women (Ministry of Health 1997 in Nepal South Asia Centre 1998: 7). Apart from these, illiteracy (women's literacy is only 28 per cent), lack of inclusion in decision-making processes such as in bureaucracy and political positions from the women is also quite low. On the other hand, women's work load in agriculture is as high as 1.4 times that of the men (Acharya & Bennett, 1981). Participation in the development mainstream has become possible from the early 1990s; however, it has not materialised due to the illiteracy, poverty, and social practices of people particularly at the grass-roots. Women often become the more deprived group of intra-household and social and legal discrimination between the sexes. Sons are considered assets, and daughters are liabilities. The education, health, and nutrition of women and girls are much lower than those are for men and boys, particularly in rural areas. The plight of poor women is a serious issue because the health and education of mothers influence the well being and future of their children and other family members.

Social Discrimination and Exclusion

The issue of the ethnic dimensions of unequal relations in Nepalese society in terms of the population engaged in commerce, government service, or the governing system was also raised during the 1980s. Such issues have also contributed to creating social and economic discriminations (see Seddon, 1995). Similarly, Bista (1990) in the early 1990s also emphasized social factors as impediments to economic development. The issue is not only related with development, the dignity of life, and the level of material comfort, the country has to cope with new social problems as well. A move into the larger volume of ethnic tension, communal competition, and other forms of social stress are all economic and social grievances over a long period of time. The violence associated with the Maoist insurgency over the last five years is assuming an alarming scale. Many political and economic analysts and also other social thinkers believe that this movement is basically a social and economic issue and is produced and sustained by failed development, though the facade of this problem is rather political (Panday, 1999: 11–12).

OCCUPATION AND EMPLOYMENT

The terms activity, work, occupation, and employment all are related to one another and concerned with human living. Work can be both remunerative and non-remunerative. But from an employment point of view, activities can be counted as work only when they are remunerative. People should be busy doing something to earn for their survival and economic progress. According to Nepal Labour Force Survey (NLFS), activities are defined as 'work' if:

works doing outside home for a wage job or any business operated by the person, and home-based activities such as agriculture, milling and other food processing, handicrafts, construction and major repairs, fetching water, collection of firewood including others such as bonded labourer (CBS, NLFS, 1999: 11).

This was the first survey carried out by CBS where work activities have been defined in line with the current ILO standards, which is based on the United Nations System of Nations Accounts (1993). 'Occupation' refers to the type of work done during the reference period by the persons employed (or kind of work done previously if unemployed), irrespective of the industry or the status in employment of the person. This new definition includes fetching water and collecting firewood as work, which expand the size of the employed population. Occupation also gives an account of description of a person's job. Job can be taken as a set of tasks and duties, which are carried out by or can be assigned to, one person.

The population of Nepal aged 15 and over is estimated to be 11.2 million, of which about 9.6 million (83 per cent) are found currently active[2] at any time. Apart from this, out of the total 7.9 million children aged 5–14 years of age, 2 million are also economically active (Ibid., 25). Of this two million, 1.5 million are in the 10–14 age group (61% of this age group), and rest from among 5–9 age group (21% of this age group) (Ibid. 65). Among this participation, girl children's rate is higher than male children's, and much higher in rural than in urban areas. As 87 per cent of total population reside in rural areas, at least 81 per cent of them have agriculture as a primary occupation. Almost 78 per cent of all workers in Nepal work for themselves, i.e., self-employed (Nepal South Asia Centre, 1998: 101). The informal sector can be defined only in respect of the non-agricultural sectors to those activities in both the urban and rural sector. About 1.7 million Nepalese people are engaged in informal sector jobs of which 73 per cent of all employment in main jobs outside the agricultural sector (Ibid., 61). The population Census 1991 indicates that 92 per cent of the workforce in the Mountains, 84 per cent in the Hills, and 74 per cent in the Terai were engaged in agriculture. As self-employment is the dominant component of the total employment structure, improvement in income of this component depends more on the development of skills, introduction of new technology, and managerial innovations rather than on the wage structure per se. Employment is both a means to generate income for livelihood and an effective measure for reducing poverty

Box 3.2 : THE UNEMPLOYED: NUMBERS AND RATES FOR THOSEAGED 15 AND OVER

	Number of unemployed			*Unemployment rate*		
	Total	*Male*	*Female*	*Both*	*Male*	*Female*
Nepal	178.000	98.000	80.000	1.8%	2.0%	1.7%
Urban	77.000	35.000	42.000	7.4%	5.9%	9.4%
Rural	101.000	63.000	37.000	1.2%	1.5%	0.9%

Source: NLFS 1998/99: 45

Only people working 40 hours a week can be considered fully employed. With this assumption, 2.6 million people (27 per cent of the currently employed population) who work less than 40 hours a week (Ibid., 51) are not fully employed. Lack of employment opportunity for the existing labour force on the one hand and addition of such forces in the market each year on the other shows disharmony between the employment opportunity and supply of labour. Therefore, the problem of unemployment and semi-employment has remained a major challenge and a prime factor of existing poverty. Of the total 178,000 unemployed persons (1.8% of the total economically active population), rurals account for 101,000 and urbans for 77,000. Those aged 15 and above from male groups are 98,000 (2%) and female are 80,000 (1.7%) (Ibid., 45). Every year 300 thousand labour forces (3 per cent of working age people) enter the labour market for employment.

Of the total employed rural people, 71.1 % of them have only subsistence-level jobs in agriculture; however, the corresponding share of urbans were just 35% (CBS, 1999: 118). Underemployment also tends to be higher among poor by as much as 50% in the rural areas (Panday, 1999 and also see World Bank, 1991: 43 'Micro-level studies in the Tarai'). Poor people suffer from larger family size, lower labour participation rates, and higher unemployment. The poor also have a higher dependency ratio than the non-poor. Due to their living in inhospitable areas, they spend more time managing fuel, fodder, and water. Often, instead of looking for long-term work, they have to look for what they can have to make today's ends meet. High level of underemployment and/or unemployment augmented the indebtedness of the poor and ultimately widens the gap between urban and rural areas and also between haves and the have-nots. Both economic and social problems are intermingled; one could be the cause of the other, and the issue is both related with development and the dignity and level of material comfort along with social problems.

Despite such underemployment or unemployment situations, children of 5–14 age group are also employed, which creates another problem. Instead of going to school and learning some other skills, they have to work for the family income.

Only 18% of the total land is arable for agriculture, the mainstay of the people. A few decades back, the contribution of the agricultural sector to the GDP was around 60%, which is down to 38% at present. The Terai is considered as the food bowl of the country because of its fertility and high potential in agricultural production compared to hilly and mountain ranges. However, primitive modes of agricultural production, high dependency on weather, and inadequate agricultural support systems including the distribution pattern of land holdings have been the major hurdles for benefiting the farming community. In other words, farming has been giving only a subsistence level of income—particularly to those of the marginalised section.

As the farming occupation has become less remunerative, the young particularly in the rural areas have to find other means of work. As the industrial sector has not developed much, it could not provide jobs as per the requirement. The tourism sector is also taken as a seasonal occupation, which provides some three hundred thousand jobs directly and eight hundred thousand indirectly. Therefore, alarge part of the labour force works mostly in India and in Gulf countries such as Saudi Arab, United Arab Emirates, Qatar, Kuwait, and in the ASEAN countries. However, the retention of income of the Nepalese workers is found to be very low due to the lack of skills. Only 45 per cent of the population aged 15 and over are literate of which 62% are males and 28% females. About 400,000 people (220,000 males and 180,000 females) have had vocational training. However, the quality of training needs to be improved. There is a limited scope for jobs even for the educated mass as the general education system has become non-functional and less creative.

DISTRIBUTION OF INCOME

Household income is an important determinant of the living condition of a person or family members. But due to the faulty process of income distribution among the households and limited access to productive resources, a wider gap can be found between poor and rich. A survey conducted by National Planning Commission in 1976/77 showed that 50% of the families in rural areas received less than 13% of the rural income, and the top 9% received 55% of the national income (Khadka, 1992: 303; see also CBS, 1997). The current estimate of average per capita income of a Nepali is US$ 243, which is one of the lowest in the world; more than half of the population survives on less than one dollar a day. However, the per capita income in the rural areas is US$ 131, against US$ 298 for urban areas and US$ 446 for Kathmandu—the capital city of Nepal. The per capita income for eastern Terai is US$ 146, western Terai US$ 107, and mountain US$ 110. (Nepal South Asia Centre, 1998: 114). The CBS 1997 shows that the household income in 1996 is 62% from farm income, 22 % from non-farm enterprises, and 16% from other sources such as financial assets (Ibid., 115). Similarly, the rate of income growth is lower than that of the Asian and South Asian countries.

Poverty can be the consequence of various factors such as illiteracy and superstition among the people, lack of sufficient productive infrastructure, primitive modes of agricultural production, lack of technical know-how, lack of marketing opportunities, etc. However, low level of per capita income growth, (e.g., 2.9% during 1991–96) and the higher population growth (2.3% estimated during 1991–96) can be the major causes for poverty in Nepal (Nepal South Asia Centre, 1998: 114).

Similarly, if we classify household income we find plenty of variations. The size of household income on the basis of rural and urban area is as seen in Table 3.2.

TABLE 3.2: Size of distribution of income by rural and urban areas (gini coefficient)

Survey	*Rural*	*Urban*	*National*
NPC 1977 (household)	0.60	0.5	-
NRB 1985 (household)	0.55	0.85	0.57
NRB 1985 (per capita income)	0.23	0.26	0.24
CBS 1996 (per capita income)	0.31	0.43	0.34
CBS 1996 (household)	0.51	0.55	0.57

Source: NPC, 1977; NRB, 1988; CBS 1996; in Nepal South Asia Centre, 1998: 115.

The concentration of income at the small number of rich is much higher than many of the poorer sections. The size of income presented Table 3.2 is based on the NPC (1977) survey on consumption and expenditure, Multipurpo... ...usehold budgeting survey (MPHBS) conducted by Nepal Rastra Bank

(NRB) in 1985 and also the Nepal Living Standard Survey (NLSS) conducted by CBS in 1996.

Distribution of income is influenced by the distribution of landholding to each of the family. As almost 82% of the total land is occupied by Hills and Mountains, only 18% of the total land area is economically feasible for agricultural production. Therefore, the best use of land often becomes a national slogan. However, the users of the land (i.e., marginal tenants) have very small size of land compared to the richer groups. Based on the two studies conducted by NRB in 1985 and again by CBS in 1996, the distribution of land is quite discriminatory between the small and higher income groups than the bigger lower income groups. The details are given in Table 3.4.

TABLE 3.3: Distribution of per capita household income by income category (percentage share of income)

Income group	*MPHBS 1985 (in %)*	*NLSS 1996 (in %)*
Bottom 40%	23	11
Middle 50%	54	37
Top 10%	23	52
Total	100	100

Source: NRB 1988; CBS, 1996.

There is a strong relationship between the size of landholding[3] and household income because the household income size is heavily dependent on landholding size of the family. In 1985, the house-holding and household income of large farm households was nearly 3 times higher than that of the marginal farmers (NRB 1988). Though the land resource is one of the major productive resources, the uneven distribution practices and uneconomic fragmentation could not be productive, fair, or just, particularly for the poor.

The Agriculture Survey conducted in 1981 also revealed that households having less than 0.5 hectare land were 50.5 per cent and occupy only 6.6% of the total cultivated land. On the other hand, households whose land holding is more than 3 hectares were just 8.9% who occupy 47.3% of the total cultivated land. The faulty process of income distribution among the households, limited access to productive resources, high levels of underemployment and/or unemployment augmented the indebtedness of the poor and ultimately widens the gap between urban and rural areas and also between the haves and the have nots. The per capita landholding is 0.14 ha. and land ownership is highly fragmented. About 69% of landholdings are less than 1 ha in size, and about 89% less than 2 ha. The average size of landholding is only 0.24 ha, with an average of more than four land parcels per holding (CBS 1993). The owners themselves cultivate almost 97% of the total landholding. The size of distribution of agricultural land ownership by household by region is given in Table 3.4.

TABLE 3.4: Size distribution of agricultural land-ownership by household/ region (in percentage)

Region/holding	*00.5 ha*	*0.5–2.0 ha*	*<2.0 ha*	*Total*
Mountains	41.6	44.3	14.1	100
Hills	45.8	47.6	6.6	100
Terai	33.2	47.1	19.7	100
Nepal	40.1	47.0	12.8	100

Source: CBS, 1997 in Nepal South Asia Centre, 1998: 118.

The estimated percentage of poor people in rural areas is 95% (Guru-gharana, 1996: 26). Out of these rural poor, four-fifth are either agricultural self-employed or agricultural labourers (with or without tenancy). The average operational landholding of a poor farmer in Terai is about 0.14 ha. per capita (one-third of average for non-poor), and in the hills about 0.05 ha. per capita (about one-half of average for non-poor). Moreover, quality (productivity) of land of the poor is usually much lower than that of the non-poor.

The only important asset that the poor possess is unskilled labour, which they are forced to sell at extremely low wages. Opportunities for non-farm employment are few, and the demand for agricultural labour is highly seasonal. The rate of rural underemployment is reported to be over 40%. In addition, the rural poor are also guided by the inherited and increasing indebtedness at a much higher rate of interest than the institutional rate (36% to 100%). The hard core or ultra poor spend 75% of their income on food alone (Ibid., 27).

In this context, the World Bank writes (World Bank 1990:23–24).

"The most fundamental factor contributing to poverty in Nepal has been the rapid increase in population. The two most critical consequences of this population explosion are unsustainable labour force growth and saturation of the agricultural land base... Availability of agricultural land has declined from 0.6 Ha. per person in 1954 to 0.24 Ha per person in 1990. As a consequence of this pressure cultivation has been expanded up hill slopes and on to poorer land on plateau and ridges. Marginal productivity is thus falling, and the land base itself is deteriorating—as soils are depleted, and erosion accelerates with encroachment onto more fragile slopelands".

Thus, Nepal's agriculture suffers from a chronic nutrient deficit. Increasing production costs stemming from environmental degradation take several forms, which cause air pollution, massive soil erosion in the Himalayan belt, water pollution, and other ecological degradation (Dahal & Dahal, 1993:ii–iii). Primarily, the poor in Nepal have been and will be paying for this if the poverty situation does not improve. The other reason for poverty is lack of knowledge and skill for proper utilisation of available resources. Therefore, the uneven distribution of income compounds the poverty problem, which also affects the global environment and ecology.

POVERTY SCENARIO IN NEPAL

Poverty Dimension in Nepal

Traditionally, one *mana cereal* (around 300 gram/per meal/per head of rice, wheat, or maize, etc.) with a vegetable or pulse, some clothes, a simple house (per family) and some extra food to entertain the guests is considered sufficient for a living, particularly in rural Nepal. Those who could not manage these items were considered poor. The former prime minister late B.P. Koirala had a vision that, living without poverty, a family should have "a house, one bigha (0.7 ha) land, a cow and a pair of oxen and the schooling opportunity including a place for primary care" (*The Kantipur*, 2 Sep., 2000). For this, government should focus on those who have lacked access to these assets. Compared to the size of population, the per capita size of land was bigger and there were also plenty of forests and other natural resources for the sustenance of the people. Apart from this, people also had not much familiarised with the modern industrial production. Therefcre, demand for living in a way was quite simple and the number of poor people was not that much bigger in size.

Time and again compared to the growth of population, developmental efforts could not keep up. Therefore concerns on poverty issues were given emphasis after the 1970s. The National Planning Commission defined poverty for the first time, through a survey on employment, income, distribution, and consumption patterns in 1976. For this, the required size of minimum subsistence level of income/consumption was taken into consideration. The cut-off level was based on the expenditure required for a day to buy 605 gram of cereal and 60 gram of pulses required to fulfil an average calorie need of 2256 (NPC 1977 in Koirala et.al, 1992: 5). To meet that quantity of food-stuff, NPR 2 per capita per day (at 1976/77 prices) was taken for the lowest actual daily consumption expenditure of the basic necessities (other than food items, clothing and footwear, education and health, and fuel and light). According to this survey, the poor were estimated to be 36% of the total population. As this definition explains only the survival aspect, NPC again revised the items of requirements for living. Accordingly poverty is defined in terms of basic needs (NPC, 2044 (1987). The basic needs contain a bundle of items which cover:

- food (2250 calories) for a person/per day,
- cloth (11metre) per person per annum,
- minimum basic health (sharply decreasing infant/child mortality and 65 years of living),
- housing (30 sq. metre floor space with kitchen, toilet, drinking water, sewage facilities),
- primary schooling (6–10 year-old children all for primary education and extensive adult literacy classes, and

- minimum security for all citizens (NPC, 2044, 1987: 4).

A similar effort was also made by Small Farmer Development Programme (SFDP), a special programme introduced by Agriculture Development Bank of Nepal (ADBN) in 1975. This programme initially developed a criterion based solely on the family landholding of 4 *bighas* (2.6 ha) of land in Terai and 20 *Ropanies* (1 ha) for Hills and Mountain. It was modified later to consider income as opposed to land. Families with NPR 720 per capita or less annual income at 1978 prices were considered small farmers. Later again ADBN envisaged two tiers of criteria for defining a small farmer. It considered size of land holding as well as income. Families with less than 0.5 ha of cultivated land and a per capita annual income of less than NPR 2500 (at 1987/88 prices) were considered as small farmers (Small Farmer Development Centre, 1996: 3). Thus, any person of this category could be the target beneficiary of SFDP.

Recently the government has created a special programme *Garib Sanga Bishweshwar Karyakram* (Bishweshwar Among the Poor) targeting the poverty problems. This programme tried to define poverty in a more holistic form of developing, which is based on the indicators (shown in Table 3.5).

TABLE 3.5: Poverty on the basis of defined indicators

Basis	*Indicators*
Property ownership status of a person/ family	Landless, or less than 0.4 ha land Houseless or a thatched roof vulnerable house Could have few chickens, goats, pigs Could have maximum NPR 2,100/per annum family income
Food and nutrition status	Can manage 3 months for a year from own land Hardly can have daily food Prevalence of malnutrition among the children/women of the family

Employment status	None of the family members in any national/international permanent job Could have unskilled wage labour Could be agriculture labour or the share cropper, or Kamaiya
Social status of the person or family	House-chief-less, widow, disabled, illiterate, lack of drinking water facility within a 15 minute walking distance, deprived from basic health service, family with many children, family without latrine
Socially deprived families	Indigenous communities such as Darai, Satar, Raute, Dhimal, Chepang, Musahar, Dom, Chamar, Rajbanshi, Kamaiya Tharu, Hyu, Chepe, Dahuwar, Kumal, Thami, etc.
Downtrodden and oppressed families	Artisan, Sarki, Kami, Badi, Damai, Lohar, Tamhara, Chyame, Pode, Majhi, etc.
Women/Children in difficult situation	Badi, deuki, Kamaiya, child labour, trafficked women, street children, etc.

Source: Bishweswar Among the Poor Programme Implementation Committee Secretariat, 1999:15–17.

This definition is comprehensive in nature as the poor people/family is defined in terms of the size of land holding, consumption, level of income, social status, and person in difficult situations. As discussed earlier, poverty can be defined not only from income or consumption but also particularly from powerlessness in making decisions on the entitlements. This definition also could not cover other poor groups such as people living under hazardous environment, women suffering due to gender discrimination, migrant people (particularly from rural to urban).

Apart from the governmental efforts some NGOs, the people's organisations also made their efforts for defining poverty. The Centre for Self-help Development (CSD) also defined in line with the SFDP definition. According to CSD, poor are those persons who may or may not have the land but whose per capita annual income could be up to NPR 2500. On the basis of this ceiling, they define poor and deliver their services (CSD Progress Report, 1996). Similarly, PLAN International conducted a well-being survey and defines the poor. According to the PLAN PRA report, each household is classified into six groups on the basis of size of landholding, source of income from the employment, condition of the house, literacy rate of the children in the house, and size of family. On this basis the poor or the target families are those whose well-being status is less than the normal standard (PLAN International PRA Report, 1995).

In fact poor people themselves can give the best definition of poverty. With this assumption, a group of 337 poor people were asked, Who are the poor? On the basis of a brainstorming session conducted with the participants, poor persons were identified on the basis of following indicators (see Table 3.6).

TABLE 3.6: Poverty in the words of poor people

Bases	*Indicators*
Lack of property	Those who don't have enough livestock, those who have no fertile land, those who don't have patrimonial property, persons with small landholding, landless, indebted persons, beggars and persons without house, those who don't have access to resources
Less remunerative employment	Dependent on daily wage, kamaiya, and bondage labour, those who go abroad for getting job, persons exploited and pressured by the rich
Bad health	Sick, lean and feeble, untidy
Political powerlessness	Those who have no access to decision-making process, who could not get any place in political field
Lack of education and skill	Who cannot manage own resources, who are not clever, who do not know the rational use of land, who make local spirit/alcohol for unnecessary expenditures, who could not work in productive time, failures in their work, unemployed due to lack of skills, who could not work in time due to working in landlords' work, who could not get opportunities to read and write, incapable for using available resources, who cannot express feelings

Social mal-practice	Those who suffered due to caste and sex, who have many children, believers in superstition, disabled, polygamy (sauta bhayaka), who are not helped by any person, unsocial, who lose self-confidence and frustration, imitators of foreign fashion, who have more expenditure than the source of income, alcoholic, gamblers, person with bad habits, who incur more expenditure on festivals, women, are lazy, dependent, polygamous, child-marriage, or marriage without understanding, children without legal status or abandoned by the father, born by kidnapped, prostitutes
Other reasons	Suffered by natural calamities, old, less beautiful or handsome, widows, person without children

Source: This list was expressed by 337 village participants of a "poverty seminar" held in Ashar 16-18, 2055 in Dhulikhel organised by three NGOs—Atmanirbhar Vikas Manch, WATCH, and Sikaule (p. 78).

Thus, poverty should not only be taken in terms of the size of income but should also consider illiteracy, bad health, social malpractices, and other forms of vulnerabilities which make living uncomfortable and difficult.

INCIDENCE OF POVERTY IN NEPAL

In Nepal, the incidence of poverty depends mostly on the economic process, uneven distribution of productive resources, high level of unemployment and/or underemployment. Most of the people in the country are still facing rampant poverty, illiteracy, poor health including the deteriorating situation of natural resources, and social ill practices. Despite continued efforts of various institutions such as government, civil society organisations, and international agencies, poverty persists in Nepal and increased from 36% to 49% between 1977 and 1992. As indicated by the Nepal Living Standard Survey (CBS, 1996), around 9 million Nepalese (45% of the population) are defined as poor; however, there are significant variations across the ecological regions. One can see the difference in the degree of poverty from simple poor to ultra poor.

Nepal Rastra Bank (NRB) also conducted a Multipurpose

House Budget Survey (MHBS) in 1984/5 and determined that 41.5% are below the poverty line. A 1989 reprocessing of the 1984 data (Nepal Rastra Bank, 1988) has calculated the proportion of population below the poverty line under three sets of assumptions (see Table 3.7).

TABLE 3.7: Incidence of poverty under different poverty lines by rural/urban residence 1989

Poverty Criteria	*Rural area %*	*Urban area %*	*Total Nepal %*
NPC/Nepal	42	15	40
US$ 150 (WB)	74	42	71
Lipton	68	51	66

Source: World Bank/UNDP 1990:8 in Nepal South Asia Centre: 1998, 127.

The first set was developed by NPC on the basis of level of income required to supply the minimum calorific requirements (2256 kcal). The amount required to supply this calorie requirement was Nepalese Rupees (NPR) 210 per person per month in the Hills and NPR 197 in the Terai (at 1988/89 prices). Those who could not manage this amount for their livelihood were estimated at about 40% of population who were absolutely poor. The second poverty line was defined in terms of the internationally accepted threshold of US $ 150 per capita per annum. The proportion of population with an income level below this poverty line was estimated at 71% nation-wide and at 75% in the Hills. The third approach defines the poor as suggested by Michael Lipton—i.e., as those whose expenditure on food consumption absorbs 70% or more of total expenditure (Lipton, 1983). According to this calculation, two-third of the population were below the poverty line, 68% in the rural areas and 51% in urban areas.

In 1997, 45% of Nepalis were poor, but there was a variation between the different geographical regions. The number of poor people found across the ecological regions also gives an unbalanced picture. Accordingly, people below poverty line in the hills and plains (Terai) were 50% and 37% of the population, respectively. But the people residing in the mountains were as much as 63% below the poverty line. When analysing from rural–urban perspectives, 18% of the urban and 47% of the rural people have to survive under the poverty line. This reveals high poverty concentration in rural as opposed to urban areas (see CBS, 1996, In: Nepal South Asia Centre, 1998:128).

In Nepal, per capita consumption level has been treated as the criterion to determine size of people living below the poverty line, i.e., the determination of poverty on the basis of consumption, calorie intake received from food has been treated as the yardstick for measuring poverty. The Living Standard Survey conducted in 1996/7 has determined 2124 calories per capita per day as necessary. The per capita annual expense to purchase that calorie equivalent of food worked out to be NPR 2637 (NPC, 1998: 202–3). If the expenditure on non-food items is added to it, the per capita annual expenditure is estimated to stand at NPR 4404. Based on this assumption, the size of population living below the poverty line was 42% in 1998.

The NLSS survey in 2002/3 reveals that the distribution of poverty has significantly changed in its size and the features. As a result, 29.4 per cent poor live in the middle and eastern rural hilly areas where the population is also high. Accordingly, the percentage of the poor is 23.6 in the rural areas of the Western hilly region and 23.5 percent in the rural area of the Eastern Terai. Similarly, in the rural areas of Western Terai, it is 18.9 per cent and in the urban area it is about 4.7 per cent. According to the estimate, 7.5 percent out of the total poor dwell in the Himalayan region, 47.1 per cent in the hilly or Mountain region and 45.4 per cent in the Terai region. The detailed description of the above findings is presented in Table 3.8.

From the above picture of the poverty incidence in Nepal, the rural part of the country is much more vulnerable; however, there is also a significant number of urban slums, and unemployed persons in the urban areas. Therefore, the efforts to alleviate poverty should be judged in terms of the programmes, which are focused on those poor areas and the poor section of the society.

TABLE 3.8: Incidence of poverty below poverty lines by region

Region	*% of Total population*	*% of Poor*	*% of Ultra-poor*
As per Geographical Region			
Mountains	56.0	29.3	26.7
Hills	41.0	21.3	19.7
Tarai	42.0	28.7	13.3
As per Urban/rural Areas			
Urban area	23.0	13.2	9.8
Rural area	44.0	26.4	17.6
National average	42.0	24.9	17.1

Source: NPC, 1998: 203.

But a recent CBS survey report indicates an improvement in the level of poverty. Compared to the poverty level of the NLSS 1995/6 survey, the NLSS 2002/3 report shows a slightly improved poverty distribution picture. Accordingly only 31 per cent of total population are poor (MoF, 2005:129/30). However, the gap between urban and rural has not improved much.

ADDRESSING POVERTY: EFFORTS AND CHALLENGES

Tribhuvan Gram Vikash Karyakram (Tribhuvan Village Development Programme), an institutional effort, was introduced for the first time in Nepal in 1952 aiming for institutional development, social mobilisation, and attitude change particularly at the local level (Adhikari, 1982, 26–28). Planned economic development effort was started in Nepal in the middle of the 1950s. Since then, a total of eight periodic plans have already been completed, and currently the Ninth Plan (1997–2002) is underway. The first five plans (during 1956–1980) had given more emphasis to infrastructure development than to social development activities such as focusing on the poor and downtrodden section of the society. However, some of the notable activities during this period were the Village Drinking Water Programme, Hill Transport Development Programme, Remote Area Development Programme, Small Area Intensive Development Programme, and Praja

Development Programme, which were introduced during that time. However, their limited scale of coverage and lack of effectiveness for implementing these programmes, became the basic features (Adhikari, 1982, 18–24; Kayastha, 1986, 16). Only the goals of the Sixth (1980–85) and the Seventh (1985–90) plans were designed for fulfilling the 'basic needs' of the people (NPC, 1981; 1986). During the Eighth Plan (1992–1997) and the Ninth Plan (1997–2002), the emphasis was on the poverty alleviation issues (NPC, (1998). The objectives and resource allocations in each of the plan periods are presented in Appendix III.

POLICIES ADOPTED FOR POVERTY ALLEVIATION DURING THE 1990s

The government from the beginning of the 1990s started to show its commitment regarding poverty alleviation. The UNDP summarised from a number of sources, a statement of the general goals, strategies, and priorities of the government of Nepal in the following ways (UNDP, 1991):

- programmes to alleviate poverty to receive the highest priority. The requirements of women, children and economically and socially disadvantaged citizens will be paramount in determining the design of Nepal's development programmes;
- special attention to be given to improving people's access to safe drinking water, basic education and family planning so as to improve the quality of life;
- a concerted effort to be made to launch programmes that generate income among the rural poor;
- the promotion of forestry and environmental protection to feature prominently in HMG/N's plans, both as a matter of conserving and responsibly exploiting the environment, and as a means of providing income-generation opportunities for the poor;
- emphasis to be given to expanding the nation's production base. Productive sectors such as agriculture and industry will receive high priority in order to promote rural and urban income generation.

The decade of the 1990s has an important space for targeting the problems of poverty issues because the size of people under poverty is quite large. One of the major objectives set in the Eighth Plan (1992–97) was alleviating poverty. For this policies were directed to run self-targeted programmes for the poor. It has also given emphasis to increasing the access of the poor to productive resources, to arrange to award contracts of technically simple civil works to poor groups, to bring legalisation to remove social malpractice and create public awareness. The other contents of the policies adopted in this regard were enactment of legal provisions for the protection of those destitute and helpless against exploitation, initiatiation open dialogue for agreement with foreign governments for employment of Nepalese workers. It also emphasised creating employment in the non-agriculture sector through the food programme and to make institutional arrangements to monitor and co-ordinate poverty alleviation activities (for details also see NPC, 1992; 617–23).

It was realised that only a five-year plan could not be enough to reduce the huge size of poverty level in the desired extent. Therefore, government visualised a twenty-year long-term thinking during the Ninth Plan (1997/2002) planning phase. As a commitment the objectives and the focus to be given in the subsequent other three plans such as the Tenth (2002–7), Eleventh (2007–12), and Twelfth (2012–17) were also identified at that time. According to the plan document, the long-term development plan aims "to create a society that is cultured, modern development-oriented and endowed with skills through alleviating the prevailing wide spread poverty in the country" (NPC, 1997: 59). This shows that the poverty problem has been taken as the most crucial issue for at least two decades. Major macro-economic indicators projected during the four plan periods (1997–2017) are given in Annex IV.

Alleviating poverty is a objective during the Ninth plan (1997–2002) period and the following strategies have been adopted:

- all development activities under all the sectors of economy would be directed towards poverty alleviation;
- attention would be given to the agriculture sector which would play the leading role in poverty alleviation which provided maximum involvement of the people;
- emphasis would be laid on massive employment generation in industry, tourism, public works, transport, and service sectors;
- mobilise people's participation and create self-employment;
- social and economic infrastructure would be built and arrangements would be made for required productive resources and skill development;
- emphasis would be given to render primary health, educational, and drinking water facilities to improve the socio-economic condition of the deprived and weak communities living in the backward and remote areas attempting to achieve high economic growth;
- poverty programmes would be directed as per the *poor* and the *ultra-poor* categorisation of poverty;
- impact of the overall strategies would be rendered complementary to each other as well as co-ordinated and integrated manner;
- the poor group (which constitute 24.9 per cent) would be provided employment and income through sectoral programmes and assimilating them into the open market system; and
- for the ultra poor (17.1 per cent of the total population) including the backward groups and communities and women would be brought into the mainstream of socio-economic development by providing banking services and institutional assistance through social mobilisation and empowerment schemes at the local level (NPC, 1998: 204–5).

During the Plan period, the government brought an elaborate policy package to alleviate the poor section of the society. Some of the highlights are:

- high returning schemes such as livestock raising, and commercialisation and diversification of agriculture including intensive farming, will be given emphasis;
- some of the inter-related programmes of poverty alleviation and control of population should be implemented jointly or collaboratively;
- increment of public awareness through the literacy programmes and increase public investment for the study up to the middle grade of the students below poverty line;
- provide basic health facilities more extensively, particularly to the poor people and their children;
- ultra poor will be highly prioritised basically to the poor communities and their children;
- provide skill-oriented training for the creation of more employment opportunities abroad;
  - provide credit more easily;
  - launching of empowerment programmes for earning additional incomes;
- the deprived and the destitute will be provided special care for their development;
- women empowerment programme will be taken as part of the poverty alleviation programme;
- emphasis will be given to rural electrification annexing the irrigation and alternative energy schemes; and
- emphasis will be given to labour intensive technology and development of agro-based industries (NPC, 1998 : 205–6).

For the effective implementation of the poverty alleviation programmes the Ninth Plan planned for implementing different programmes, such programmes are grouped into sector-wise programmes, sectoral programmes and institutional arrangement programmes.

Sector-wise programmes are divided into *employment generation* and *development of human resource* domains. Both agricultural and non-agricultural employment has been emphasized to generate maximum employment.

Agricultural employment could be generated by creating infrastructure, providing credits, developing market networks, rural micro-cottage industries, "food for works". The government has also planned for the development of human resource to develop their skills to get jobs, which could help to generate employment in other places and self-employment. It also aims to carry out the programmes such as agriculture and forest, non-agricultural productive sector programme, infrastructure, social service, and population control (Ibid, 207–8).

Basically improvement in the farming system as visualised in the Agricultural Perspective Plan has given high priority to generate more employment and greater volume of production. The conservation and utilisation of forest is also planned to tie up with employment generation and maintaining ecological balance.

Similarly, the Ninth Plan also focuses on non-agricultural programmes tying up with agricultural programmes for improvement of the level of people and generating more employment. For this, priority is given to the establishment of cottage industries and adopting labour-intensive technology for the wider coverage of the poorer section of the society. In the same way, creation of infrastructure, expanding schooling opportunity, and family planning in an appropriate manner have been given special attention.

As some special classes or communities of society are more vulnerable, the plan also identified special programmes focusing on such communities. Some of the major programmes in this regard are: very backward remote areas without road access; deprived, ethnic, and down-trodden group; social and other oppressed group; landless rural family; families with small land holding; specific groups, urban poor, and unemployed, and social mobilisation programme. To cope with the poverty problem the plan has also identified institutional arrangement programmes such as poverty alleviation commission, poverty alleviation fund, poverty monitoring system, and geographic information system (Ibid, 209–10).

The plan emphasizes empowerment and social

mobilisation particularly to those of the ultra poor and the socially and economically deprived section of the society. For this, the government has focused on the role of grass-roots organisations and the NGOs to reach the poor communities.

A BRIEF ACCOUNT OF POVERTY ALLEVIATION ACTIVITIES IN NEPAL

The government has been carrying out some specific, focused programmes targeting poverty issues since the early 1970s. Among these programmes, some are related to infrastructure development, delivery of special food package, flow of production credits, providing employment and other community services, which are briefly presented below.

Subsidised Ration Distribution

This programme came in the early 1970s to provide special subsidised rations particularly in the hilly and remote districts. It aimed to market the excess production of the Terai and also to support the people of remote areas. The Nepal Food Corporation was created as an institution to take care of this scheme. Normally the transportation cost was subsidised up to the delivery points. On the recommendation of local administration, poor people were identified to deliver the food. Though the programme focused on the rural poor people of these districts, the services rather concentrated at the district headquarters and local market place and utilised by the employees working groups in these places (Koirala et al., 1992, 16). Due to the lack of efficiency and the mismanagement the programme was stopped in 1999.

Similarly, the Agriculture Input Corporation was created to distribute subsidised fertiliser to farmers. Various studies show that poor people could not benefit from such schemes because the poor are either landless, or if they have, mostly they have a small piece of dry land which may not be appropriate for the production and also they could not buy due to the cost factor. Often distribution could not match with the appropriate season (Ibid., 16–17).

Production Input Distribution

During the 1970s the government launched other programmes to benefit the poor section of the society, particularly the rural people. Production input distribution is one of the important ones. For this farmers were provided subsidised fertiliser through Agriculture Input Corporation. Though this scheme helps the farmers to increase agricultural production, the benefit went to the larger farmers rather than to the landless or marginal farmers. Apart from the credit programmes the government has given irrigation programmes to benefit farmers. It can also be found that irrigation programme has high priority for agricultural development since the planning efforts started in 1956. But the poor and small landholding farmers hardly benefit from irrigation programmes due to higher costs to run projects, unreliable input delivery mechanisms and feeble target extension programmes.

The government has designed credit programmes for the poor communities or small farmer including women, for enlarging their income level by giving some production input such as production credit to the small farmers and rural women to invest in their farm production. Such loans can be used only for purchasing agricultural inputs like seed, fertiliser, seedlings, animals, small-scale handicraft, shops, etc. The loan was given to both groups and individuals. To provide such loan the Agricultural Development Bank of Nepal (ADBN) initiated the Small Farmer Development Programme (SFDP) in 1975. The programme provides maximum NPR 30.000 to each individual to make an investment with a 16% interest. The target family or the groups are identified as defined in 4.5 section of this chapter. Altogether 205.000 persons in the 29.525 organised groups from 604 VDCs of 75 districts are included as the target population of the SFDP programme (Economic Survey F.Y 1999/2000). Due to the inability to offer enough collateral, high transaction cost for lenders and the complex lending processes of borrowers poor people hardly got any benefit from such credit schemes (Koirala, op cit.: 17–8).

Similarly, women were also provided production credit through a programme called Production Credit for Rural Women (PCRW) aiming to increase the income of rural women, enhance the status of women in the society, and improve the welfare of their families. This scheme has been in operation since 1981 and covered altogether 610 VDCs and 12 municipalities of 67 districts. Altogether 25,585 women got 37 million loans, and 179,160 women got different training such as family welfare, population education, nutrition, sanitation, leadership development by the end of 1999 (for details see Ministry of Local Development, 1999: 14–15).

Though this programme basically provides credit to farmers, the landless and marginal groups could not get benefit. The programme also could not visualise the entrepreneurial and marketing aspects, which are equally important for getting benefit. In recent days there have been many incidents of Maoist attacks at the office of SFDP, as the programme put its clients into the credit trap.

Integrated and Community Development Projects

Various integrated rural development projects have come to Nepal since 1975 via the grant/loan assistance of different donor agencies. These projects were much guided by area and sectoral development concepts, and they adopted a holistic approach focusing on the eradication of poverty particularly at the district level. It also attempted to implement the development programmes in a co-ordinated way. Basically this scheme intended to improve the quality of life of the people in the rural areas, particularly of the rural poor. Objectives of the IRDPs were to increase production and productivity, generate employment, create and strengthen basic infrastructure for local development, develop and strengthen social services, enhance institutional capability for sustained rural development, and raise the standard of living of the rural poor (Gurung, 1998: 10; Kayastha, 1986: 16). Of the total 17 such projects which were introduced in Nepal, nine had already been phased out and the remaining have been in operation in different districts.

Of the total 75 districts of the country, these IRD Projects covered 48 districts. Those projects created during 1975–81 were designed adopting sectoral and area development approach which covered agriculture, transport, health and nutrition, social service, public works, and water resources (Gurung, op.cit. 11). Despite its beautiful objectives, lack of co-ordination among sectoral line agencies, lack of motivation of implementing employees, over prescription of donor agencies' personnel, etc. became major hurdles in implementing the project activities successively. However, some infrastructure such as roads, irrigation canals, and institutional buildings were built (Ludwig, 1989; Pradhan, 1985). These projects were co-ordinated by the Ministry of Local Development and implemented through line agencies and their central ministries. Similarly, projects created during 1983–90 were mostly based on the decentralisation principle wherein district-based District Panchayat or the District Development Plan had the major role for implementing the project. Finally, the IRDPs initiated during 1990s are also co-ordinated by DDC, however, they are implemented through mobilising NGOs or the local-level community organisations. These projects aim at strengthening local-level and district-level institutional development and support a basic district-level infrastructure programme. Though the NGOs are encouraged to implement project activities such as education, health, and water and sanitation through infrastructure development activities and environmental conservation, their effectiveness has still been doubtful. Some of the identified problems are co-ordination between NGO and district-level governmental organisations, and also about the accountability and transparency of NGOs. Another problem is about monitoring when there is a direct link between donor and the NGOs.

Despite the importance of IRD projects and their contribution to infrastructure development, their contribution did not much benefit the poor people (Gurung, 1998; Koirala et al., 1992). Major problems were lack of commitment and co-ordination and also these projects were found to be rather costly, complex, and lacking in sustainability of the project benefits.

Food and Feeding Programmes

With the assistance of World Food Programme (WFP), the government distributed some food items to malnourished children, lactating and pregnant women, and also to some primary school children during the 1980s. Up to 1987, some 190,000 targeted population were distributed such food items; however, this programme could not continue and expand to the larger lactating communities. Another nutrition programme was initiated with the guidance of UNICEF. This scheme was implemented jointly through Ministry of Health, Education, Agriculture and Local Development. The objective of this programme was to fight malnutrition. However, the problem of co-ordination, and low spatial coverage (5 districts only) were two of the reasons for not being effective in helping the poor communities.

Employment Programmes

Food for Work programme with the help of World Food Program has also implemented to benefit the poor, as well as to construct infrastructure like roads. This programme was beneficial to those who really work at the field; however, the volume of food was not enough to accommodate the large number of unemployed labourers.

Skill-generating Programmes

The government has also made programmes to provide skill training to the unskilled masses by creating training institutions. CTEVT, Department of Cottage and Industry, including the NGOs such as UCEP, etc. have been providing such training; however, the capacity is limited (Guru-gharana, 1992: 102; Koirala et.al., 1992; 15)

Garib Sanga Bishweshwar Karyakram (GSBK)

Among various types of poverty alleviation programmes, *Garib Sang Bishweshwar Karyakram* (Bishweshwar Among the Poor Programme) is important. According to the Ninth Plan (1997–2002), 42% of the total population are poor, of which 24.9% are normal poor, and rest 17.1% are the more deprived who are termed as *ultra poor*. GSBK is designed to address this poorest section to support their livelihood. The programme is designed to cover all the parliamentary electoral constituency areas of the country (for details see Central-level Programme Implementation Committee, 1999). The main objectives of GSBK are as follows:

- encourage poor people to organise through the social mobilisation,
- enhance human resource development for improving social capital at the local level,
- collection and mobilisation of savings at local level, helping poor to access education, health, drinking water, agriculture extension, technology, market management, and marketing system,
- help poor approaching the credit financing institutions, developing indigenous skills and development of self-employment from small industries, helping to build relation with government, non-government, co-operative, financial, and private organisations,
- development of local level leadership and active civil society, empower for making independent by involving them in decision-making process,
- legalising the people's organisations and institutionalising them.

As an implementation strategy, 100 families of each of the 205 constituencies would be provided the benefit each year. For this, the programme would start from each VDC and/or Municipality ward of each of the 205 constituencies. Within a period of five years the programme would cover half a million poor families. Major activities under this programme are: building social mobilisation organisations, saving capital formation, basic and skill development training, basic education, basic health, work for self-employment and income generating, institutional credit, drinking water, irrigation, forest environment, appropriate technology and technical service, home for homeless, organisational decision making and control over resources, develop relations with governmental and financial institutions, NGOs and private level organisation, development of legal institutions (Ibid., 3–4). The selection of poor people will be among both men and women of poor families, children, helpless, disabled, deprived persons/communities, and other communities such as those who have in danger of losing their identity (Ibid., p. 4). This programme tries to categorise poor people on the basis of income, nutrition, employment, social, and other indicators of the families.

For implementing this programme a three-tier organisational structure has been developed. The Minister for Local Development works as chair of the Central Level Programme Implementation Committee (CLPIC), which develops the policy guidelines for implementation, co-ordinating, monitoring, and evaluation of the programme. District Level Co-ordination and Monitoring Committee (DLCMC) has to work under CLPIC headed by a Ministry of Local Development nominee who chairs the DLCMC . This committee is responsible for implementing the whole plans and programmes such as selection of VDC, target group, social mobiliser, NGOs co-ordination with local-level institutions, co-ordination with the CLPIC and other concerned institutions and communities (Ibid., pp 5–13). Agriculture Bank of the concerned district has to play vital role to implement the district level programme.

Though this programme started in 1998, it has still been in the process of institutionalisation, becoming a subject of discussion especially for the roles and co-ordination with local level institutions such as DDC, VDC, Municipalities, etc. Political parties other than the ruling party have been suspecting the smooth implementation of the programme.

Western Terai Poverty Alleviation Project

This programme has been operating since 1997 in the 419 VDCs of eight districts in Western Terai. The programme is intended for generating income and welfare of small farmers, landless, and poor village women, bringing a sustainable way for poor and small farmers, and institutional capacity development of the financial institutions of the project area. The project has targeted to provide loan and other facilities to 28,833 women, 935 community shallow tube-wells, 200 community shallow deep pump set construction, 200 private ownership roar pump installations, 2.050 km roadside plantation, 1.025 ha. plantation for fodder/firewood, and 29,000 people will get agriculture extension and skill-oriented training.

The programme has planned to implement different activities co-ordinating with different institutions such as credit service through Village Development Bank, shallow tube-well construction through Agriculture Development Bank, extension and skill training activities through concerned line agencies and DDC, community development activities through DDC and institutional development activities through the programme office itself (see Ministry of Local Development, 1999).

This programme is a governmental programme designed to manage in a collaborative way among different organisations such as Nepal Rastra Bank, Agricultural Bank, and concerned subject related ministries and the Ministry of Finance. However, the Ministry of Local Development has been playing a co-ordinating and implementing role. Project Steering Committee and Executive Committee as the central level at Ministry of Local Development should be responsible for the overall planning and implementation while DDC, District Project Co-ordination Committee, and concerned line agencies are related to implementing and co-ordinating the project activities with concerned agencies including VDC and users' groups at the grass-roots. At the grass-roots the VDC is and the users' groups are responsible units for implementing and getting the project benefits. The VDC is mostly concerned with forming the beneficiary group, co-ordinating the local group and the district level organisation, etc. while the users' groups have to identify their requirements, mobilise local resources and people's participation, maintain accounts, implement the project activities, etc.

Jagriti Women Income-Generating Programme (JWIGP)

This programme has been developed to bring the women into the forefront of development. This programme is basically intended to empower women by creating social awareness and involving them in income-generating programmes. The Ministry of Women, Children and Social Welfare works as the central co-ordinating organisation responsible for overall planning, implemention, monitoring, and evaluation of the JWIGP programme. At the district level a women social worker works as co-ordinator to co-ordinate the distric-level concerned agencies and the grass-roots VDC and Women groups.

This programme primarily focused on improving the economic standard of the backward women in the group and helping them in employment and income generation. Under this programme, 65,000 women of 940 VDCs are targeted to create awareness, provide skill development training, self-employment, public health and co-operative, and provide micro credit through Agriculture Development Bank for the generation of income. This programme is intended to narrow down the gender related issues particularly of its target groups in the country at large (HMG/N, MWCSW, 1999); HMG/N, MoLD, 1999: 29).

Though this programme is still in an institutionalisation phase, the political colour seen in the appointment of women social workers at the district level and the disagreement made by the other opposition parties have created some problems for the smooth implementation of this programme.

Enhancing Swabalamban for Poverty Alleviation in Arun Valley

This programme was started in Sahkhuwasabha and Bhojpur districts in 1998 for developing various infrastructures to create self-employment for developing a sense of independence. This programme also covers various programmes such as community development, awareness creation, income generation, and other social mobilisation programmes (Ministry of Local Development, 1999).

Poverty Alleviation Fund (PAF)

The government has created PAF as an independent organisation under the Development Committee Act 1956, which channels the resources to poverty alleviation activities in a co-ordinated manner. The objectives of this fund are to support programmes designed by the poor; to mobilise local and foreign resources; to facilitate and co-ordinate the programmes under government, NGOs, and the private sectors, etc. towards poverty alleviation. This programme also facilitates the self-employment, skill development programmes, and micro-credit programmes to the target groups in a co-ordinated manner. It also provides soft loans to the NGOs for carrying out poverty alleviation activities. The PAF also carries out research regarding poverty and poverty mapping and develops a monitoring mechanism at the local, district, and central levels. Initially the government has allocated NPR 100 million to create the fund (Ministry of Local Development, 1999: 26–27).

POVERTY ALLEVIATION PLANS AND PROGRAMMES: A REVIEW

Both positive and negative features can be found in the plans and programmes that are directed for poverty alleviation in Nepal. There is a positive indication of the poverty alleviation plan and the programmes during the Eighth Plan (1992–97). During this period the level of poverty decreased by five point. It was 49% in 1992, which came down to 42% in 1998. During the plan period some of the development institutions such as the number and scope of NGOs has overwhelmingly been expanded from 1200 in 1992 to 20,000 by the end of 1999. Apart from this, Acts and Regulations of the local bodies such as VDC, DDC, the municipality and the Local Self-Governance Act 1998 and Regulations 1999 have been enacted to empower the local-level institutions.

Apart from this the government has made a commitment to implement the Agriculture Perspective Plan (APP)—a 20 year plan covering a period from 1995 to 2015. APP includes agricultural programmes such as development of co-operative societies, agricultural and rural credit, poverty alleviation credit, female farmer development, small farmer development, and these projects have directly supplemented poverty alleviation efforts. This plan also aims to increase agricultural growth, increased factor productivity; commercialising and diversifying agricultural production, and developing both short-term and long-term strategies to alleviate poverty and achieve significant improvement in the standard of living through accelerated growth and expanded employment opportunities (Agricultural Projects Services Centre, 1995: 3–4).

Protection and utilisation of forests by the forest users' group has also helped to alleviate poverty by fulfilling the demand for energy sources. The forest development programme implemented by the forest users' group, who were activated under community forest and other rural development projects, has buttressed poverty alleviation endeavours. Projects like micro and small hydro and alternative energy development programmes like biogas have also been found helpful in poverty alleviation. The other areas of activities are physical infrastructure development, increasing access of the poor to productive resources, education and training, social extension programmes, population programme, employment generation, food security programmes for the background community towards alleviating the poverty problems (NPC, 1998).

To support the governmental priorities, the approaches and strategies were modified and adopted for programming assistance to Nepal's agricultural, forestry, and natural resources development, for example by FAO (1991). For this four major 'strategic programmes'—policy analysis and planning, developing sustainable farming systems, management of natural resources and environment, and alleviation and food security—were instituted. Similarly the World Bank (1990) has also published 'relieving poverty in a resource-scarce economy,' which places great strategy in conformity, broadly, with the government's stated objectives, priorities, and approach. (Seddon, 1995:301). In the same way a majority of the foreign NGOs are also moving towards a similar recognition of the government's priorities for development and its commitment to decentralisation and 'popular participation' through local groups and non-government organisations as a key element in the official development strategy.

On the other hand, there are plenty of discrepancies that do not help with regard to poverty alleviation activities in Nepal. One of the basic problems is faulty allocation to the basic requirements. For example, the whole of the education budget inclusive of regular and development expenditure for the current FY 1999/200 represents only 13.2% and that for health sector is only 5.6% of the total. It is therefore necessary to rearrange the budget allocation to adequately fund the social sector programmes. It is possible through adopting more decentralised, participatory approaches to development, by making prudent economies and reducing unit costs, by charging users for the benefits they receive. However, the implementation could not be very effective and also could not continue up to the required extent. Some projects, which had promising features were directed towards poverty alleviation, however, the size and coverage of such projects were rather small, and replication in other parts seems doubtful. However, how far the target population—those who have been suffering from poverty—actually get relief from such changes could be a question of debate.

Effective government implementation of policies is lacking due to lack of accountability, transparency, rule of law, and also the lack of political and administrative commitments. Rampant corruption, mismanagement, and lack of effective implementation of development programmes are other reasons why poor people could not realise fruits of development. Therefore foreign aid channelling through both government and NGOs is also under question. It has been difficult to understand how it flows and what it is used for, though such supports are believed to be for livelihood improvement of the poor people (Panday, 1999: 11).

In connection with the local development programmes,

some of the problems for effective implementation are: lack of co-ordination in programme implementation among different agencies, misuse of resource, duplication of programmes, weak management due to the lack of timely monitoring and supervision, lack of information, and lack of trained manpower in local development efforts. Therefore, institutional development, development of management capacity, promotion of economic and technical capacity, increase in the productivity of the programme, etc. are some of the important issues regarding local development (NPC, 1998: 241–242).

A look at the situation to date reveals that poverty alleviation efforts have not been broad, effective, or focused on the poor and the ultra poor. The number of the poor covered by the targeted programmes stands minimal compared to the total number of poor people. The programmes targeted at the poor do not seem to be successful as they are externally operated and lack active participation of the poor. The targeted groups have not benefited from such programmes as the real poor could not be identified and those programmes could not reach areas with high poverty ratios. There is a lack of information at the local level regarding many programmes run by the government and NGOs. Because of lack of public awareness, these programmes are unable to bring about expected improvement upon the socio-economic condition of the poor. Besides this, such programmes are extremely scattered at the field level, and their effective monitoring is very difficult. As a consequence, output is very low as compared to investment.

Participation of the people in the mainstream of development also holds an important role for mobilising human and other resources for the development of the country. Such participation could be possible through economic, institutional, political, and administrative and institutional decentralisation (Gurugharana, 1996a: 31–46). The democratic environment since 1990 has been broadened for the people's participation; however, the absence of democratic values and concentration of resources at the centre are becoming problems. Due to the infrastructure and procedural constraints, including the lack of information flow about market opportunity, people's participation through the free market mechanism is limited. Only capable and informed people have room to expand their opportunities.

Apart from these, there are other negative factors. Political instability, lack of political consensus, lack of discussion on issues rather than political action, lack of implementing capability, lack of accountability and trustworthiness on the part of both political and administrative staffs are some of the important problematic issues for alleviating poverty. Garib Sanga Bisheswar and Mahila Jagriti Karyakram are some of the cases of differences among the political parties regarding implementating mechanism. Due to the corruption both at the political and administrative level, the implementation of the plan/programmes could somehow be difficult. Resource constraints and values/cultures of the people also often become problems toward this issue.

Lack of strong commitment on the part of policy formulation and implementation is also a reason for the ineffectiveness of poverty alleviation programmes in Nepal. The National Planning Commission makes policy, which is implemented by the sectoral ministries. The common problems occurring during implementation could be: first, the implementation of the plan policies and programmes depend upon the annual programmes and the allocations decided by the Ministry of Finance, which often contradicts or de-emphasises the national policies. Second, it also depends on foreign aid as more than 50% of the development budget is covered by foreign loans or grants. It often gets donor's priority rather than the country's needs. Third, the changing priority of the government/political parties in power for implementing the policies and programmes creates difficulties. Apart from this, corruption both at political and bureaucratic levels also creates plenty of discrepancies between words and the deeds. Frequent changes in national plans, policies, and priorities; lack of grass-roots participation in the developmental process; political instability; centralisated decision making; aid dependency and foreign influence; lack of local resource mobilisation; and weak institutional capability to implement development initiatives are other hurdles in implementing the poverty progrmmes.

Although government agencies, NGOs, and private organisations are active in poverty alleviation activities, due to the lack of co-ordination, and cross-flow of information among these agencies, duplication in programmes, lack of mutual co-operation and spatial imbalance in distribution of programmes is evident. In totality, causes like failing to attain spectacular growth in GDP, not assimilating the poor in programmes seeking growth in production, the poor not having easy access to opportunity and facility and a say in the decision making have stood as challenges.

It can be concluded that the government has given its focus on alleviating poverty both by bringing favourable policy changes and also introducing different target-group oriented programmes. However, lack of commitment both at political and administrative levels, and also the co-ordination problem among governmental and non-governmental organisations, have become the major hurdles in this endeavour. Some other challenges as highlighted by Ministry of Finance (2005:138/9) are as follows:

Since attempts to reduce poverty cannot be expedited without developing agriculture sector in a sustainable manner, there is an obvious need to develop this sector for raising both the production and productivity.

Due to excessive concentration of non-agricultural sector activities in the urban areas with its minimum impact in the rural areas, it has been very difficult in establishing inter-sectoral linkages in the economy.

Since Human Development Indicators and Human Empowerment Indicators in terms of Nepal are very low, there is still a great challenge to improve these social dimension related indicators.

Poverty Reduction Programmes, so far, have not been effective as expected. According to the second NLSS 2003/04, the population living above the poverty line in the year 1995/96 has slipped below that line by 20 per cent. This indicates that the poverty reduction programmes have not been effective.

The Gini Coefficient in FY 1995/96 was 0.34, but it is estimated to have gone up to 0.41 in 2003/04. As the Gini Coefficient moves towards the value of unity, it implies that the gap between the rich and the poor has widened. It shows that inequality between the rich and the poor is increasing in Nepal.

END NOTE

1. The present size of loan is NPR 21.946 million, i.e., per capita loan volume is NPR 9.975,56. (*Source: Nepal Samacharpatra*, 9 Aug, 2000).
2. A person is defined as currently active if he or she is either employed for at least one hour during the previous seven days, or has a job attachment if temporarily absent from work, or is available to work if work could be found (for details see CBS, 1999: 25).
3. NRB (1988) defines the size of landholding as: *large farm size* = holding of land more than 5.4 ha. in Terai and 1.04 in the Hills and Mountains; *medium farm size* = 2.73 to 5.4 ha. in Terai and 0.52-1.04 ha in the Hills and Mountains; *small farm size* = 1.03 to 2.73 ha in Terai and 0.21 - 0.52 ha in the Hills and Mountains; and *marginal farm size* = up to 1.02 in Terai and up to 0.21 ha in the Hills and Mountains (NRB, 1988 in Nepal South Asia Centre: 117).

4

Growth and Policies of NGOs in Nepal

The modern form of NGO movement in Nepal came into existence after the middle of the 20th century; however, momentum for faster expansion has taken place since the early 1990s. The government of Nepal has considered NGOs as development partners while on the other hand, people (particularly those suffering from poverty, illiteracy, poor health and other forms of socio-economic problems) are also expecting efficient roles and better services from the NGOs. In this context, questions may arise: how far policies support expanding NGO activities with these hopes and expectations of the government and the people; are there any problems with NGOs to work as development partner; how the NGOs are administered. These are some of the issues often raised with regard to NGOs' role in Nepal. This chapter deals with these issues covering traditional welfare services, growth and function of modern NGOs, governance of NGOs, and NGOs in national development policies.

A BRIEF ACCOUNT OF TRADITIONAL WELFARE SERVICES IN NEPAL

The Eastern philosophers, especially those of South Asia, took an important role in propagating the ideals of social services within society. Religious epics composed many thousands of years ago have also produced a number of examples of social service rendered by the rulers and the people. The history of social welfare service in Nepal is as old as the society itself. Such actions were very much guided by the philanthropic feelings (Tiwari, nd: 7–8). Factors creating such social actions were basically initiated by the philosophy of religious values. Such values became a part of the daily life of the people as well as the governance principles of the society. Therefore the philosophy of administration was based on *dharma shashtra* (religious principle). Such *dharma shastra* always inspires the people for *paropakar* (helping others particularly the needy people without any self-interest), which ultimately becomes a necessary part of human life for living within the society more cohesively and happily. Even at the present time, such belief among the people can be found as *paropakar nai sabaibhanda thulo dharma ho* (helping others without self interest is the biggest religion), *sewa nai dharma ho* (Service is religion), etc. in the day-to-day living.

The traditional mode of social functions covers a diverse range of activities, including creating social and physical infrastructures. Supports for *marda and parda* (during sorrows and happiness) for the neighbouring and the needy people in the society, providing food and shelter to the helpless travellers, rendering treatment services to the sick people, mobilising local resources, creating public awareness, etc. were some of the examples of social welfare functions. The other forms of such welfare functions were constructing or renovating *pati/pauwa* (public residences/inn), *kuwa/dhara* (public wells/taps) or *chautara* (shading trees on the road side), temples/monastery/ mosques, and roads/bridges for the public utilisation. The basic motivations for involvement in the welfare functions were self satisfaction, assuming eternal peace after death, and establishing *kirti* (fame).

For the sake of delivery of such services, people both individually and in groups within the community or outside the community, practised getting involved in a voluntary way. *Guthi*[1] can be taken as one of the important and most popular social institutions created even before the unification of Nepal in 1769 (Subedi, 1984: 69–81; Nepali, 1965: 192–94; Dahal, 1986: 254). As a social institution, *Guthi* became the backbone of the local economy too (Regmi, 1978). The other forms of social organisations created in those periods were *parma* (labour exchange group), *dhikur* (credit group) (Chand, 1991). Parma system for working in the field or repairing houses is still in operation particularly in the rural part of Nepal. Apart from these, similar type of people's organisations which were created within some of the ethnic communities were *bhejas* among Magars, *chumlung* among Rai and Limbu, *nangkhur* among Tamangs, *nogar* among the Gurungs and *bolawanegu* among the Newars, *dharma phanchayat* among Thakali, etc. (Lama, et al., 1992: 85; Bhattachan, 2000:74; Pokharel, 2000: 58).

Apart from these traditional institutions, the individual roles performed by different actors were also equally important for the delivery of such services. Among them *dhami jhakris* (faith healers) are the most commonly rooted in the Nepalese society. They play the role of medical practitioner and on many occasions they also provide other occupational counselling. On top of that, they also contribute to social learning for building and maintaining moral values among the members in the society. Such roles have been played by others and are also called *janne, jharphuke, guruba, lama,* etc. in different social settings of Nepal. Though scientific validation of such practices has yet to be documented in a precise form, one can observe the high level of trust in their services in the Nepalese society. As these practices are still deeply rooted in the cultures and social values of the society, some of the modern NGOs and also the health delivery centres have attempted using them as social motivators particularly on building health awareness (i.e., delivery of health-related messages to the people at the grass-roots).

Apart from these, *lami* (match makers) also play crucial roles for arranging marriages among the boys and girls in the society. Even at present, more than 70% of the marriages are held on arranged basis in which these *lami* play significant roles, and many people still have great reliance on such services. They normally provide their services voluntarily; however, the benefited parties sometimes provide gift in cash or in kind for their services.

Various reasons contributed to the sustainability of these traditional institutions and practices in the Nepalese social system. Some of the features behind their existence and sustenance during many centuries could be:

- community based,
- no official or legal recognition,
- voluntary membership,
- leadership based on seniority,
- extensive use of local resources,
- concern and priority to help disadvantaged,
- individuals, families,
- small group size,
- less formal structure,
- no formal rules and regulations,
- decisions made through mutual consultation and agreement,
- extensive use of indigenous knowledge, and
- effective and sustainable (Bhattachan, 2000: 74).

All these informal social institutions created in the ancient period or even in the medieval period were due to the social affiliation, family lineage, ethnic identity, etc. They helped to mobilise community assets, motivate the people, and to implement social welfare programmes (Shah, Indra Bikram et al., 1986: 5). Both the social institutions and the social actors could be found working as a 'social insurance' (Platteau, 1991) and in real terms considered as 'social capital' (Putnam, op.cit.) in the Nepalese society.

In this way one can easily say that the social service practices in Nepal have been developed in a philanthropic way for keeping the peace and prosperity of the society and better living conditions. It has also contributed to developing brotherhood and sisterhood within the community, which developed a culture of religious tolerance, social satisfaction, and economic and political independence during the whole history of the country. Many countries in the world fight against the social stratification, religious identity, and economic supremacy; however, Nepalese society always relied on mutual understanding, mutual co-operation, and self-sustenance of the people and the society. Though such traditional welfare activities would have been playing important roles, their limited minuscule size, diverse functional nature, and limited resource base were not enough to combat the modern socio-economic milieu (Maskey, 1998: 74–75). However, the traditional role and approach of the NGOs were motivated by 'welfare orientation' and were confined mostly towards philanthropic sectors and activities and the interest of their involvement in such activities was 'social service'. It is also equally true that the scope and degree of effectiveness, including the sustainability and reliability of the traditional practices of these traditional social institutions, have not been explored sufficiently.

DEVELOPMENT OF MODERN NGOS IN NEPAL

Growth of Modern NGOs in Nepal

The creation of modern social organisations for the delivery of services other than the government had came in to Nepalese society only during the second quarter of the twentieth century. It was a Herculean task, following the *Rana rule*[2]—feudalistic government. As only 4% of the people were literate and industrial infrastructure was nearly nil during that time, this situation called for more action for socio-economic development, particularly to bring about social consciousness and service delivery more extensively from sectors such as private and non-profit other than the public sector. The situation was not only likely to be in favour of breaking such situation for bringing social awareness, but also helping the self-sustenance of the poor people for improving their livelihood. However, it was not easy to create social welfare institutions in those times. Some of the important reasons are: first, due to the strict control of the government assuming a probable threat from the informed citizens, and second, there was an absence of social workers for working with new spirit and understanding.

In such a context, the modern concept of social service was materialised for the first time by establishing a social organisation named Shree Chandra Kamadhenu Charkha Mahaguthi in 1926, with the objectives of providing shelter and training for the destitute and the disabled (Ghimire, 1998:3). In a way this organisation was established with an inspiration of the Gandhi Movement launched in India as a part of the Quit India Movement (Maskay, 1998: 75). After 20 years, *Paropakar Sanstha* came as the second modern organisation in Nepal aiming at providing medical service to victims of natural calamities and people in difficult situations (Paropakar, 1998). The entrance of modern NGOs into Nepalese society and the careful look from the government's eye came in side by side. Other social organisations were established such as *Nepal Aurvedic Sangh* (homoeopathic centre) in 1950, and *Tharu Kalyankarini Samiti* (community organisation for the socio-economic upliftment of Tharu ethnic group) in 1950 (Ghimire, 1998:3). Social organisations created before 1951 had mostly been founded to address community development, health and awareness building, and improvement of livelihood. The ruling elite during that period feared that their interests would suffer if people became educated and their socio-economic conditions improved. The government was not in favour of the proliferation of such institutions and it was naturally difficult to create a working environment. Despite the immense roles of these social organisations, their vision of socio-economic development, the momentum could not take place due to the harassing and non-co-operative approach of the government from the very initial days of their emergence.

The process of creation of modern NGOs in Nepal started in real terms only after the establishment of democracy in the early 1950s. Some of the early established NGOs were Tuberculosis Control Association (1952), Marwari Sewa Guthi (1954), Madan Prakashan Guthi (1954), Kabya Pratisthan (1954), Family Planning Association (1959), Rotary Club (1960), Nepal Red Cross Society (1960), and Nepal Children's Organisation (1963). These organisations were basically created for the delivery of community welfare, development of literature, protection of orphans and abandoned children, and health and family planning (Ghimire, 1998:3). Introduction of

Panchayat polity[3] in 1960 again had brought some problems to the smooth growth of NGOs in Nepal. There was always suspicion and feelings of mistrust on the role of social organisations expecting people's involvement in the political action in the name of social welfare organisations. However, the involvement of the Royalties in some of the NGOs such as Nepal Children's Organisation, Nepal Red Cross, Nepal Disabled Association, etc. somehow brought a wave of people's participation in this sector. Consequently, some three dozen modern NGOs came into existence during the 1951–75 period in the area of health services, creation of awareness, imparting skill development training, and delivery of other community services which were basically based on voluntarism and committed for relief including other forms of social welfare services.

In 2000, the NGO sector has become one of the fastest growing sectors in Nepal, particularly after the political change in 1990. There are over 25,000 registered NGOs all over the country. Out of these NGOs, 8,825 are affiliated with *Social Welfare Council*[4] *(SWC)*, a government bureau for looking after NGOs. The number of such affiliated NGOs has still been growing and reached 18,126 by the middle of 2005 (see Table 4.1). There could be an uncounted number of different unregistered groups for civic action, which might have long historical backgrounds. Due to the absence of proper recording systems, it is difficult to get the precise number of NGOs in Nepal.

Table 4.1 shows that, in a way, NGOs mushroomed during the 1990s in Nepal. In 1977, there were only 37 NGOs affiliated with Social Service National Co-ordination Council (SSNCC), which grew gradually up to 220 NGOs including 52 INGOs in 1990. Out of these registered NGOs, those affiliated with Social Welfare Council (SWC) were 576 in 1992, and 5978 in 1997 (NPC, 1992:718; 1998:700).

The question may arise as to why the number of NGOs mushroomed during the 1990s when they have also been becoming the agenda of debate among policy makers, academicians, practitioners, and the beneficiaries at large. Some

TABLE 4.1: Patterns of NGO Growth in Nepal

Year	*No. of NGOs*	*Remarks*
1926	1	First modern NGO established in Nepal
1951	4	At the time of establishment of democracy in Nepal in 1951
1977	37	At the time of NGO Governing Act introduced in Nepal in 1977
1990	220	At the time of restoration of democracy in Nepal in 1990
2000	8825	Within a decade after restoration of democracy in Nepal
2005 Mid-July	18,126	The current size of SWC affiliated NGOs in Nepal

Source: Chand, 1991; Rademacher & Tamang, 1995: 34; Ghimire, 1998; SWC, 1999; 2000; 2005.

of the reasons for this fast growth of the NGOs in Nepal could be as follows:

A. Social reason: Naturally, people have some sort of desire or interest or seek roles to contribute to society which could provide them with a kind of self-respect and social importance within the society. For this, NGOs could be the best possible institutions as interested people can easily create or join an NGO. In this way, the creation of NGOs has been considered the best easiest and possible means for socialising and involving in social welfare institutions. This process contributed for the faster growth of NGOs in Nepal.

B. Economic reason: Educated people might have been lured to create NGOs for two reasons. First, faster growth of INGOs in the country and the enactment of the new Social Welfare Act for taking the local NGO as a compulsory requirement for working partner of INGO helps to expand the number of NGOs. Many NGOs were created as DONGOs to implement their activities and formalising local counterpart (Shrestha, 1994). However, there were some others, which were real partners for working in the country with the new vision. Secondly, the Eighth Plan (1992–97) and also the local development agencies such as Village Development Committee

Act 1992, District Development Committee Act 1992, Municipality Act 1992 made room for the NGOs as development partners for carrying out development activities. Accordingly many NGOs including the GONGOs were created. However, others were simply created as followers or imitators expecting better salary, relation with government people and foreign people, scope of going abroad, facility of modern communication means, etc. for joining or creating NGOs in Nepal.

C. Political reason: Though the economic condition of the country was not sound to provide economic benefits to the large number of masses, the restoration of multiparty system in 1990 created an environment of addressing plenty of expectations and hopes, particularly among the youth. The party leaders, however, have to make assurances to provide employment to the unemployed voters and the party supporters. Creation of NGOs could have some scope for employing some of them, which could be the easiest possible means. Many of them were created for election purposes. Similarly, the *Parliamentary Election Area Development Fund*[5] has also been channelled through such NGOs/clubs. Expectation of money during the election time and building good relations with the leaders of local people, particularly the youth, also become a strong reason of rapid growth of NGOs in Nepal.

D. Other reasons: Simplifying legal framework for NGO registration and renewal process, rising self-interests among different social forces, environments created by both national and international socio-political interests were also reasons for the rapid expansion NGOs in Nepal during the 1990s. A large variety of groups such as user groups, sports clubs, religious sects, pharmacists, tea-stall owners, civil servants, construction contractors, libraries, trusts, non-profit companies have also been registered as NGOs due to the absence of other laws for governing such activities. The other reason could be that the NGO registration/renewal and affiliation records have not been up-dated in time (i.e., the non-functioning or dead NGOs once affiliated with SWC, their records have remained there).

Types of NGOs in Nepal

Classification of NGOs helps to understand the nature and function of NGOs and to develop NGO-related policies and operational plans. However, to some extent it may also give a distorted picture of complex realities and relations of such classification (Tvetd, 1998: 24). In Nepal, classification of NGOs can be found still in confusion. The present NGO governing act *Sangh Sangstha Ain 2034* (Organisation and Association Act 1977), does not clearly specify the types of functions, roles, registration and operational process of the organisation and also of the association in different ways. The act provides liberty that all kinds of organisations other than public or for-profit can be registered and termed NGOs. Therefore, confusion arise in Nepal whether NGOs should be classified according to the type of their functions or by their size and coverage and amount of resources that can be generated or mobilised by this sector. However, few studies attempted to categorise NGOs on the basis of the objectives and functions in Nepal.

In 1985, the Integrated Development Society (IDS) made an attempt to classify the NGOs as per the nature of their functions. According to the IDS report NGOs were classified into three categories. The first group falls under socio-cultural group, which are related to social, cultural, religious groups. The second group falls under community services. The nature of functions of NGOs under this group is integrated community services. The third group falls under economic group, asset creation groups, labour exchange groups, and credit exchange groups fall under this category.

Similarly, PACT (1987) classified NGOs into two categories such as social services and transitional. The first one related with social service delivery, whereas the second related to social services and some development promotion, mixed services delivery and development promotion, local development promotion, sustainable local development promotion, sustainable and geographically extendable development.

South Asia Partnership Nepal (SAP/N) also divided NGOs into seven types, such as social (philanthropic, relief, etc.), sectoral (health, education, etc.), community development (e.g., rural development, intermediate, etc.), income generation (user groups, etc.), research and development, target oriented (women, children, population, environment, etc.), activist groups (human rights, etc.) (SAP-Nepal, 1988). The Social Service National Co-ordination Council also categorised NGOs into six groups such as community development, child welfare, women service, religious, youth, and disabled and helpless. (SSNCC, 1989; in Dhakal, 1989: Appendix D, i–vi).

Chand classified NGOs a local, regional, and national basis. According to him a local NGO should have at least 21 regular members with Nepalese Rupees[6] (NPR) 10,000 financial regular sources having at least NPR 50,000 seed money. A regional NGO should have 151 persons with NPR 151,000 financial sources and NPR 200.000 seed money. Finally, the national-level NGO should have 501 members with NPR 500,000 financial sources and NPR 500,000 seed money. (Chand, 1991: 46). In the same line the Canadian Centre for International Studies and Co-operation (CECI) studied the potentials of Nepalese NGOs and classified them into four groups both on the basis of functional specialisation and size of the NGOs. Accordingly there were local, self-help NGOs, local service NGOs, regional/national NGOs, and professional NGOs (CECI, 1992: 2–3).

Finally, at present Nepalese NGOs can be categorised into two groups. The first can be a national or local entity registered as an NGO, and the other is an international NGO (INGO) which is registered in their respective countries and working abroad in Nepal.

National NGOs

NGOs in Nepal are of different sizes and functions. Normally these organisations are registered in District Administration Office and apply for *affiliation*[7] *with SWC*. Many of them have very few activities, simply celebrating annual conferences and occasional meetings, while others are actively working with diverse activities. However, information regarding NGOs' roles, functions, resource mobilisation status and working capacities is lacking. On the basis of registration and renewed records, and the progress reports submitted in SWC, Nepalese National NGOs are categorised into ten groups. They are: community and rural development, urban slums improvement, empowerment of women, improvement of environment, delivery of public health, irrigation, health

TABLE 4.2: Function-wise NGOs in Nepal

Functional Area of the NGOs	*Number of NGOs*	*%age*
Community development	10285	56.7
Youth activities	3064	16.9
Women service	1577	8.7
Environment protection	1023	5.6
Moral development	487	2.6
Child welfare	603	3.3
Health service	408	2.3
Handicapped & disabled service	387	2.1
Educational development	230	1.4
Aids & drug abuse control	62	0.4
Total	18.126	100

Note: Figure in percentage is rounded up.
Source: Social Welfare Council Office Records (2005).

FIGURE 4.1: Percentage of NGOs by nature of activities

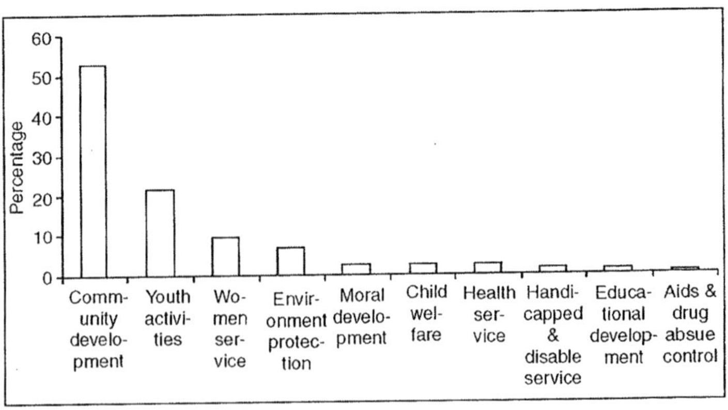

education like AIDS and drug abuse, youth activities, and development of moral values (SWC, 1999; 2000). The number of NGOs according to their functional classification is given in Table 4.2. (also see Figure 4.1).

The above information shows that community and rural development activities, youth activities, environment conservation, and women development related activities were the most preferred activities which help creation of more NGOs in these sectors. These activities are important for the development of the country particularly for rural development. However, there is more funding possibility from INGOs, donor agencies, and the government in these sectors, which NGO entrepreneurs to create such NGOs in the country. NGOs related to moral development, child welfare, and health service comprise a little more than 2% each of the total. While the remaining handicapped services, educational development, and aids and drugs control related NGOs altogether comprise less than 3% of the total SWC affiliated NGOs in Nepal. The role of NGOs in the national development process is discussed.

International Non-Government Organisations (INGOs)

As stated earlier, INGOs are registered as voluntary organisations and working abroad. Churches and the missionaries were the early initiators for working in developing countries. When international donor agencies such as World Bank and the Western countries started to use the NGOs as a channel of aid, various organisations of this kind were formed and started working in the developing countries as INGOs. Normally, INGOs are an important institutional mechanism for providing direct financial support, financing sector support institutions, increasing political space, creating feedback links from voluntary organisations to donors, and building development partnerships (see Brown and Korten, 1989). However, sometimes deliberate intervention in the socio-economic, and political values in the developing countries were also noticed through these NGOs (Terje, 1998). But in developing countries such as in Nepal, the role of INGOs has been increasing both in number and volume of activities.

In Nepal, INGOs can work after making the *agreement*[8] with the concerned governmental authorities. The first organisation of this kind was United Mission to Nepal (UMN), which has been working in Nepal since 1954. Of the total INGOs working in the country, only two-third are affiliated with SWC. On the basis of the roles and functions of INGOs they can be categorised into different groups. According to a PACT study carried out in 1987, some of the INGOs were working as operational, others were as donor/intermediary, and some others were playing both roles. Of the total 34 INGOs studied during that time 10 were classified as 'operational', 14 as 'donor/intermediary', and 3 were working as both (PACT, 1997).

According to recent information, the involvement of INGOs is found in eleven different types of activities (see Table 4.4). A total 84 INGOs affiliated with SWC up to 1999 while in the middle of 2005 the number has shot to 126. Of the total 84 INGOs nearly one-fourth are working for health and community development, while 17 work for community development. Similarly, 14 INGOs support child welfare and orphanages, 11 eye care service, and 10 are for educational support.

TABLE 4.4: INGOs and Their Functional area

No. of INGOs	*Area of Activity*
20	Health & community development
17	Community development
14	Child welfare/orphanage
11	Eye care service
10	Education
4	Disabled service
3	Water and sanitation
2	Agriculture
1	Women & community development
1	Housing
1	Dental service

Source: Calculated on the basis of SWC 1999 office records.

Four INGOs are related to disabled service, three to water

and sanitation, two to agriculture, and one each to women and community development, housing and dental service. The above information shows that health, community development, child development, eye care, and educational awareness are the most preferred areas of activity. These INGOs are from different countries and have different capacities (see Annexure V).

The INGOs are also classified in other ways for the purpose of recognising and arranging support services. This classification is based on three main indicators: volume of funding, NGOs conforming to the rules and regulation of the government, and working directly or with local NGOs or user's group (SWC, 1998). Many of the INGOs prefer to go directly into implementation, however, preference is given for taking the local NGOs as their implementing partners, which could help sustainability, cost-effectiveness, and genuine participation.

The role of INGOs came into hot discussion the 1991 seminar/workshop for direct implemention at the grass-roots development programmes. The reasons behind this were the negative effects for the institutional development and professional development of local NGOs. Therefore the workshop suggested that:

- foreign agencies should not be allowed to directly implement grass-roots development programmes independently,
- INGOs must work with/through counterpart Nepalese NGOs, and
- even those foreign agencies who have been direct implementers should actively work towards gradually handing over the entire running of the programme to their Nepalese counterparts with a time-frame of 5 years (NGO Federation in Nepal, 1991, in Maskay, 1998).

This was reflected in the Social Welfare Act 1992 when it was enacted a year later. It clearly states that any INGO interested in working in Nepal should be affiliated with SWC and must have local NGO(s) as working partner(s). The intention of this provision is to promote the working capacity of local NGOs and to control the direct value transfer of INGOs to society. Seeking donors'/INGOs' money is something like hunting. Sometimes donors themselves create NGOs for promoting their programmes, which are called DONGOs (Riker, 1991: 43); however, mostly they are directed at implementing INGOs' own interest and often make them parasite NGOs. In many cases INGOs themselves are experimenting their philosophy rather than committing to systematic development of the country. There is also a situation of mistrust and lack of confidence between the INGOs and NGOs. However, it is difficult to bring all INGOs under the SWC (the NGO governing body) due to its present weak legal provision and the weak institutional arrangement of SWC. Those which are affiliated with SWC do not always have pure social service motives. In this context, Nirmal Pandey, NPC Member (Social Sector) commented on the role of INGOs that they are not transparent about their agendas, roles for the development, real size of amount delivered to the country has become an issue (Pandey, 1999: 8–9). Similar views can be found in others too. INGOs basically from the Western countries have been used "mostly for their own political interest, selling own technologies and goods, providing own skilled/unskilled manpower, and spreading Christianity" in countries like Nepal (Bhattachan, 1999: 21–22). It indicates that due to the INGOs' hidden interest society would lose more than gain. The objective use of INGOs and the possible effects of social costs are also important issues regarding INGO functioning in Nepal. However, INGOs' role especially in creating health awareness and health delivery services, has been giving a positive indication. INGOs have also been helping to alleviate unemployment problems by providing a few hundred jobs to unemployed educated urban folks.

GOVERNANCE OF NGOS IN NEPAL

Legalising the NGO Sector

Naturally, a clear legal arrangement is necessary for NGOs. In Nepal, traditional social organisations were not registered, as most of them were created on the basis of mutual trust and understanding; they were small and most of them were formed on the basis of primary contacts, often within the homogenous communities. It was difficult to create social organisations in an organised way because of the absence of legal provision and also the negative attitude of the ruling class. For this, the interested people have to make a request to the Prime Minister, who was naturally difficult to reach for common citizens.

Even after establishment of democracy in 1951, there was a severe lack of legal and institutional provision, which could guide, facilitate, co-ordinate, and control the NGOs in the country. The *Societies Registration Act, 1959* was the first independent initiative taken by the government to institutionalise social organisations. This act spelt out the domain, *modus operandi* and functioning procedures of the social organisations to some extent; however, due to absence of a one-window system, NGOs could be registered from different governmental departments as per the sector discipline of the social organisations (Maskay, 1998: 135). There were some other acts and regulations such as National Directives Act 1962, Foreign Currency Exchange Act 1962, *Muluki Ain* 1962 (Civil Laws), and Company Act and Regulations 1965, which were also concerned with the functions of social organisation. The constitution of the Kingdom of Nepal 2019 (1962) prohibited creating political organisations and the effects of this constitutional provision went to the creation of NGOs, suspecting NGOs' possibility for becoming involved in politics. The government became very conscious of granting permission for the creation of any social organisation, which affected the smooth growth of NGOs in Nepal.

During the 1970s it was realised that there was an urgent need for a one-window policy for the operation of social organisations for more enhanced and effective functioning of the NGOs. As a process the government, in association with the national-level social workers, started to have a dialogue and conducted different seminars such as in Rampur, Chitwan in 1971, Mujhelia, Janakpur in 1974, and again in Mujhelia, Janakpur in 1976. These seminars concluded and suggested the role of social organisations, need of a governing body for the social organisations, and classifying them in accordance with their functional discipline and sectoral affiliation. Identifying such problems, a separate Act to govern social organisations was suggested along with the creation of a central organisation for co-ordinating and facilitating the social organisations scattered in the country, which could help in classifying, prioritising, and assessing the NGO programmes. That could be helpful in maintaining accountability and developing a system of the flow of financial aid, maintaining their accounts and audited on a regular basis including for maintaining the code of conduct for social organisation (Chand, 1998: 49–50; 1991: 33–34; Maskay, 1998: 77–78). Apart from the above reasons, a need for quantity outreach and quality work, bringing more professional manpower in the social service sector, human resource development opportunity in NGO, co-ordinating institutional arrangements were also highlighted.

It was also obvious that a new and more comprehensive act was necessary because of two broad reasons. First, the existing social organisation was working in a disintegrated way. There was no uniformity in rules and regulations regarding NGO operation in Nepal, which made it difficult to co-ordinate, facilitate, and to administer the NGOs communities. Second, due a change in funding policy of the international development agencies such as World Bank and the Western governments, the NGOs were seen as the channel of aid for NGOs/INGOs for creating and working in the country which called for effective legal arrangements. The scope of probable funding from these Western INGOs/development agencies naturally gave some momentum to the growth of NGOs in Nepal. In this context, two important legal provisions were made in 1977 for the institutionalisation of the social sector in Nepal. Enactment of *Sangh Sangstha Ain 2034* (Organisation and Association Act 1977) and *Social Service National Co-ordination Council Act 1977* (also called *Samajik Sewa Ain*) were therefore considered the important endeavours in this regard.

After the restoration of a multiparty system in 1990, there

was a big cry from the NGO/INGO communities for enactment of a new act particularly addressing the new role of the then SSNCC for governing NGOs. The first elected government after 1990 also showed its firm commitment to bring about a change in NGO dynamism by liberalising the NGO-led rules and regulations. As a result *Social Welfare Act 1992* replaced the Social Service Act 1977. Apart from this, some other acts, among them Village Development Committee Act 1992; Municipality Act 1992; District Development Committee Act 1992, Local Self-Governance Act 1998 and Local Self-Governance Regulation 1999 have been enacted. These acts also gave more room for the NGOs in the local development planning process and in the implementation of local development projects. Similarly, some other legal provisions toward this endeavour are Children's Act 1992, Co-operative Act 1993, Natural Disaster Relief Act 1993, and Handicapped Protection & Welfare Act 1993.

Sanga Sanstha Ain 2034 (Organisation and Association Act 1977)

The Sangh Sanstha Ain 2034 (1977) covered all voluntary institutions. This act enables the registration of all kinds of voluntary organisations other than governmental or private organisations. The act also clearly states that the proposed organisation should not be profit oriented. According to the main provisions of the act, at least seven persons (citizens) can create a social institution. They should apply in the district administration office[9] (which is the implementer of this act) attaching a statute of the proposed organisation. The statute should specify the name, objectives, address, organisational and management provision, authority, responsibilities, and code of conduct of the executive committees, and financial sources and its operations. The application should also include the names, addresses and occupations of those members subscribing to it. Normally persons who were interested to create an NGO must submit prior approval from the SSNCC office for registration. This system was continued up to 1991; however, the Sanga Sanatha Act has not specified any such provision. But after 1991 it has full-fledged authority to register, renew, or take other necessary action of such social organisation.

The act also made a provision of renewal system of the organisation. For this, each organisation should submit an annual progress report and annual financial audit report to the CDO office to renew the registration for another term. This office has the discretionary authority to renew the organisation from one to five years.

The CDO office can also take action against the misconduct or misuse of the NGOs property. Though the CDO office could monitor and evaluate the functioning of NGOs activities, it has not been in practice due to various reasons. However, most of the CDO office concentrates only on registration and the renewal process rather than assessing the NGOs' activities. In a bigger district like Kathmandu, an officer with an assistant are deputed, whereas almost all other districts manage with an assistant employee with regard to NGO functions. Therefore, the role of CDO office is passive as it is confined only to registration and renewal of the NGOs.

Social Service National Co-ordination Council Act 1977

The Social Service National Co-ordination Council Act 1977 was created to avoid duplication in the activities of social organisations and with a view to bring about uniformity in the national and international NGOs. It was also entrusted with co-ordination of the local and an international funding and grants and with formulating a policy programme to be implemented throughout the nation in a transparent and co-ordinated way. This organisation was supposed to work for the promotion, facilitation, co-ordination, monitoring, and evaluation of the activities of the non-governmental organisations in Nepal. SSNCC implements its activities through different six committees. They are: Community Service Co-ordination Committee, the Youth Activity Co-ordination Committee, the Health Service Co-ordination Committee, the Child Welfare Co-ordination Committee, the Women Service Co-ordination Committee, and the Hindu Religion Service Co-ordination Committee. On the basis of their activities, NGOs were categorised under one of the co-ordination committees. The role of the SSNCC was to work as an umbrella organisation for all the NGOs working in the country. Chand writes, "mechanism that was conceived through the formation of these committees was largely directed to maintain co-ordination right from the grassroots till the national level. The programmes being undertaken by each individual NGO, were made to be transparent, largely because there was linkage through the committee and their programmes were frequently supervised and monitored both by the co-ordination committees and also by the Council" (Chand, 1999: 161). The committee mechanism of NGO management had somehow helped the then SSNCC to operate and co-ordinate NGO functions.

As the role of SSNCC was pervasive, it was also difficult to co-ordinate the different nature of governmental departments and the different nature of NGOs/INGOs. Her Majesty The Queen was appointed to head it (CECI, op.cit. 1992, 8).

An important positive aspect of the legal system and working practice of SSNCC was that the compulsory reporting system, particularly of the foreign resources channels through NGOs must be endorsed in SSNCC's account. It helped to make the NGOs' accounts more transparent and also to facilitate monitoring the NGOs' activities more objectively. It also helped to prevent negative effects such as spying and evangelisation activities, which could displace local values and cultures.

On the other hand, some negative factors contributed to controlling the smooth growth of the NGOs in Nepal. One of the biggest problems realised during the SSNCC period was getting prior approval from this office for their registration. It was not practical to take pre-approval from the Kathmandu-based SSNCC for a person(s) of the district. Therefore the NGO workers at the grass-roots and NGO sector specialists felt that there was a deliberate attempt to restrict the growth of NGOs, as the registration required time-consuming screening procedures (Rademacher, 1995: 14). Further, NGOs were not allowed to focus on development issues, which could sensitise the people to challenge their status quo in the social and political power structure (CECI, 1992: 8). Therefore social organisations could not be created smoothly, despite the acts's including voluntary organisations serving the physical, economic, and intellectual development of the Nepalese people. During that period, mostly the Kathmandu-based elite was creating NGOs. Of the total NGOs established in Nepal, around 70% were working in Kathmandu and the rest in the district headquarters. Many NGOs were what Korten (1991) calls GONGOs, as they existed with the full confidence of government. In order to avoid excessive government control, some NGOs circumvented these acts by registering as non-profit research institutions under the 1964 Company Act (Lama et.al. 1991:3). It was simply because the government was always suspicious about the NGOs on political grounds, multiparty political activities by these NGOs being the most dreaded aspect. These all led to severe criticism of the SSNCC and to a new vision regarding the roles and scope of its functions.

Social Welfare Council Act 1992

The restoration of a multiparty political system in 1990 gave a congenial atmosphere for the proliferation of NGOs in Nepal. As said earlier, the Social Welfare Council Act 1992 came by submerging the previous Social Service National Co-ordination Council Act, 1977. According to this act the Social Welfare Council was constituted as a governmental bureau to look after the NGO affairs in Nepal (for details see HMG/N 1992;1993). The present act eliminated the practice of pre-approval of NGOs before registration in the CDO office and opened the door for interested people to create NGOs and work accordingly. This new provision created a favourable environment for creating NGOs in Nepal because:

- Interested people could register any type of NGO in the CDO office after completing certain prescribed formalities, i.e., registration does not require any recommendation or prior approval from any other institute(s).

- Due to the enactment of local bodies act (such as DDC Act the Municipality Act and VDC Act, etc.), there was sufficient 'political space' for the NGOs to stretch their activities and to focus on development issues, which could sensitise people to challenge their status in the social and political power structure (Chand, 1998: 54).
- The process of channelling foreign resources through NGOs has been simplified, i.e., the donor INGO can transfer its resources to the local partner more conveniently.
- The affiliation process was made easier, and it was mandatory to complete the process within a three-months period.
- The scope of mobilising local manpower and resources together with foreign resources has been made easier (Dhakal, 2000: 90).

Despite these positive features, after the enactment of the SWC Act 1992 and some of the lacking aspects are identified. The flexibility in creating NGOs helped for easy proliferation, however, there was still no mechanism for making the NGOs more responsible and accountable to the target beneficiaries and the state. Similarly, the over-flexibility of legal provision provided a leeway to the NGOs not make their activities transparent. NGOs could not be directed as per the need of the society and the country; rather, over-discretionary power made a threat for NGO anarchism. The legal provision also could not foresee the *modus operandi* for the efficient use of resources and also the better co-ordination among the NGOs and the local development agencies for shouldering the development process.

Social Welfare Council (SWC): New Manager of NGOs

After the enactment of Social Service Act 1992, SWC established a new manager of (I)NGOs replacing the existing SSNCC. The Social Welfare Council Act entrusted SWC as an autonomous body responsible for promotion, facilitation, co-ordination, monitoring, and evaluation of the activities of the non-governmental social organisations in Nepal. It is also responsible for the extension of its supports to the government in the matters of developing the NGO sector policies and programmes of the nation and to implement them in a co-ordinated way. Apart from these, the council also delivers training to the NGO workers and provides small grants and back-up supports to the local/national NGOs affiliated with this organisation. It also creates the necessary environment to link the local NGOs with the international NGOs and assists in developing partnership between them for the implementation of their activities (see Box 4A).

Box 4A : ROLE AND FUNCTIONS OF SWC

- Promote, facilitate, co-ordinate, monitor, supervise and evaluate NGO activities;
- Provide possible assistance for the establishment, promotion, extension and strengthening of NGO activities;
- Function as a co-ordinating body between HMG and NGOs;
- Advise and suggest to the government in the formulation of plans, policies, and programmes related to social welfare and service sector;
- Establish trusts or funds for social welfare activities and encourage others to do the same;
- Conduct training, undertake studies and research on social welfare subjects;
- Do the physical verification of NGO assets;
- Undertake necessary measures for the execution of the aims and objectives of the act;
- To avoid duplication and maintain co-ordination among various social organisations;
- Enter into agreement or contract with foreign and international agencies; and
- Make an effort in procuring national and international assistance and use it judiciously.

Source: Social Welfare Council Act 1992, Article 9

To perform all these functions the act provided for three important bodies—SWC Council, SWC Management Committee, and SWC Secretariat. A 19-member Council is the supreme body, meeting once in a year to discuss and approve the policies, plan, programmes, and budgets. The Ministry for Women, Children and Social Welfare the SWC Council, while the other members are either are appointed by the government or from among the organisational representatives as per the Council Act (for details see Annexure VI).

A 7-member Management Committee, also chaired by Chairperson of the SWC Council, normally plays an executive role and meets monthly to implement SWC activities. SWC Secretariat implements the SWC plans and programmes. The Member-Secretary works as executive head of the SWC Secretariat. The Secretariat is responsible for co-ordinating Ministry of Women, Children and Social Welfare, other concerned functional line ministries, and the Planning Commission at the one end, and the affiliated NGO/INGOs to the other end. The Secretariat is organised with four departments: Planning and Programme Department, Monitoring and Evaluation Department, General Administration Department, and Financial Administration Department. The organisational chart of SWC is given in Figure 4.2, and the organisational structure and manpower status of the SWC Secretariat are given in Appendix V.

FIGURE 4.2: Organisational Structure of SWC

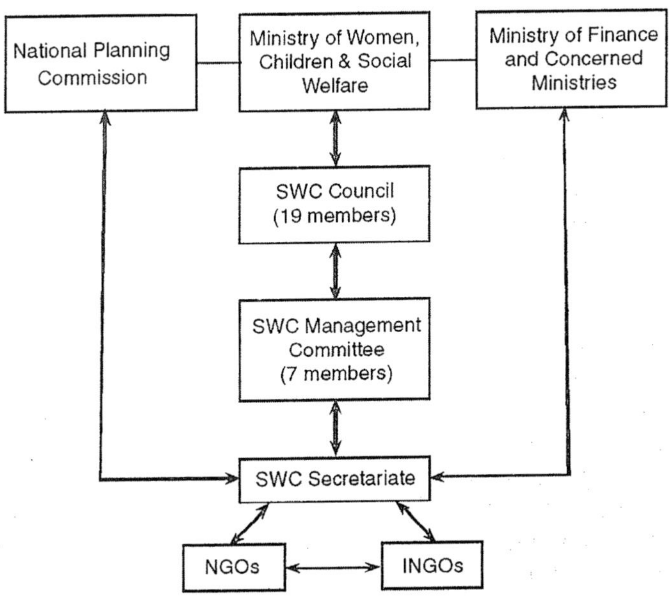

Though the SWC is expected to play a dynamic role in co-ordinating and managing the NGOs in Nepal, some problems have made the SWC less effective. First, the Member-Secretary is the executive head and one of the important actors for the execution of SWC programmes who is appointed by the government on the basis of a political decision. According to the SWC Act, the Member-Secretary is appointed for a four-year period; however, it has always become a subject to the understanding with the government and often with the Ministry for Women, Children & Social Welfare. The selection of this post has often been based on political affiliation and connections to the power centre rather than professional competence. None of the Member-Secretaries could complete their tenure during the period of the 1990s.

Second, as numerous affiliated NGOs/INGOs have been increasing, a competitive work force at the SWC has not been harnessed. As a result the role of SWC has become rather a witness for making an agreement between SWC-NGO or SWC-NGO-INGO. In an interview with R.N Gupta (Gupta, R.N, Plan Makwanpur Manager, Interviewed on 22 Oct., 1999), an INGO executive expressed the role of SWC as a "post office" which has no creative role. As the role of SWC is just a registration department, it cannot monitor the function of NGOs, which led the NGOs to become more anarchic. Due to the ineffective role of the SWC, NGOs are not becoming transparent and accountable for their work.

Third, the roles of Ministry of Women, Children and Social Welfare (MoWCSW) and the SWC have not been clearly defined in the SWC Act, leading to misunderstanding. Due to the lack of proper understanding, both institutions often perform similar functions such as providing support to the same or different NGOs for similar functions. Apart from this, many of the ministries and line agencies also provide resources without co-ordination with SWC, which often leads to waste of resources and duplication of activities on the one hand and on the other a higher volume of cost for managing the NGOs.

Apart from these problems, the SWC itself has been suffering from operational shortcomings in such as monetary and human resources. Around 120 personnel are not enough to monitor and evaluate the 8825 NGOs and 91 INGOs scattered in different parts of the country (interviewed with Dr Tika, 14 June, 2000).

Ministry of Women, Children and Social Welfare: A Central level NGO Governing Office

The Government of Nepal has created a central-level department—the Department of Labour and Social Welfare, in 1972 to regularise the social welfare functions. The need of the labour issues and social welfare issues at the central level organisation was felt necessary. This lacuna was filled by the creation of the Ministry of Labour and Social Welfare (MLSW) in 1981. In fact, the creation of this ministry can be taken as an important step towards institutionalisation of the social service sector in the kingdom. Basically this institution has to work for long-term and short-term planning, policy formulation and strategy development, implementation of the plans and the policies, and monitoring and evaluating the plans and programmes carried out by this ministry and other concerned agencies (see HMG/N, Ministry of Labour and Social Welfare 1995). In a process of administrative change government has reorganised the number of ministries and their functions in 1995. Among these changes, the nature and the volume of functions of MLSW was changed. Accordingly the Labour part was dropped and Women were added as Ministry of Women and Social Welfare (MoWSW). This ministry has to take responsibility for the women's component in the planning, policy-making, implementing, and monitoring and evaluating its overall functions. In 2000, the scope of this ministry was again broadened. As there was a need to address the child-related issues which is also an important part of society, the government has decided to establish a ministry-level organisation for this cause. As a result, the name of this ministry has changed to Ministry of Women, Children and Social Welfare (MoWCSW). Social Welfare Council (previously SSNCC) has to work under this ministry. According to the Social Welfare Act 1992, the minister of MoWCSW works as

TABLE 4.5: Central-Level Organisations for Facilitating NGOs in Nepal

Name of Organisation	*NGO-related Function*	*Operational Channel*
Ministry of Women, Children & Social Welfare (MoWCS)	Planning, policy making, implementation, monitoring & evaluation	Through SWC Through selected NGOs
Ministry of Finance (MoF)	Facilitation & control, duty-free status, and tax exemption	Through SWC
Ministry of Education (MoE)	Facilitation for education-related (non formal education) NGOs	Through District Education Office Through selected NGOs
Ministry of Health (MoH)	Facilitation for health-related NGOs	Through SWC Through selected NGOs
Ministry of Labour (MoL)	Facilitation and controlling working visa for expatriates	Through SWC
Ministry of Local Development (MoLD)	Facilitation and co-ordination to local development/community development-related NGOs	Through DDC, VDC, municipality Through selected NGOs
Ministry of Population and Environment (MoPE)	Facilitation to social mobilisation and environment awareness creating NGOs	Through selected NGOs
Ministry of Home (MoH)	Registration/renewal of all NGOs, Facilitation to drugs-related NGOs	Through CDO Office Through selected NGOs
Ministry of Foreign Affairs (MoFA)	Facilitation and control of formal visa	Through SWC
National Planning Commission (NPC)	Approval & co-ordination of NGO activities with the national development plan/programmes	Through SWC

the chairperson of the governing body of SWC. Under his/her recommendation, the government appoints a Member Secretary including other appointee(s) of the council. This ministry has to perform the enactment process of SWC. The MoWCSW has the responsibility for the approval of annual plan, programmes and budget of SWC, approval of the general agreement carried out between SWC and the INGO, monitoring and evaluation of SWC functions. In 1997, the ministry created a district-level Child Development Centre in each of the 75 districts for working child-related functions.

Apart from this ministry, there are other organisations directly or indirectly related to the management of NGOs in the country. Some of these organisations are Ministry of Finance (MoF), Ministry of Education (MoE), Ministry of Labour (MoL), Ministry of Health (MoH), Ministry of Local Development (MoLD), Ministry of Population and Environment (MoPE), Ministry of Home(MoH), Ministry of Foreign Affairs (MoFA), and National Planning Commission (NPC). The role and functions regarding the NGOs of these central-level organisations are briefly presented in Table 4.5.

Table 4.5 shows that various ministries have been involved both in planning and implementing NGO activities; however, inter-ministry co-ordination is the main problem. Different ministries—such as Ministry of Women Children and Social Welfare, Ministry of Home, Ministry of Local Development, Ministry of Population and Environment, Ministry of Education, Ministry of Health—also implement their activities through selected NGOs. How these activities can be implemented more effectively in an economic manner has often become a problem. Different sources indicate that there is a practice of creating NGOs or channelling such grants through respective District Development Committee on the basis of political affiliations or other relations with the concerned ministries.

NGO FEDERATIONS: SELF-GOVERNING ENTITIES

The democratic environment gave an impetus to both NGO proliferation and NGO unionisation. Along with this, the idea among NGO leaders and members of social organisations to build solidarity among themselves under an umbrella outside the government-sponsored SSNCC also took shape. Maskay thinks the reasons behind this unionisation were the increasing involvement of NGOs in development work in various spheres of national life, which gave rise to the issue of autonomy for them to work unfettered.

Second, they started making an explicit demand for increased share of public funds for the people-oriented projects in which they were involved (Maskay, op.cit: 91–92). Apart from this, to put pressure on the government to protect social organisations and social workers from the increasing defame, and also development of a sense of partnership among like-minded NGOs were other reasons for creating such associations.

So there are different NGO federations created after 1991. Among such federations, the NGO Federation of Nepal (NFN, 1991) the National Federation of Nepali NGOs (NFNN, 1991) and the NGO Coalition/Nepal 1991 (Rademacher & Tamang, 1995: 39–40) which were created to develop networking among national/international NGOs & governments mutual co-operation and developing NGO ethics. Other like-minded NGO leaders also formed some coalitions or networks such as Association of the Development Agency of Nepal (ADAN), Child related NGO network, Federation of Dalit-related NGOs, etc. Among these various self-governing NGO associations, NGO Federation came as the biggest one with more than 1400 members. Some of the major functions of the federation are as follows:

- to create a stable NGO policy environment for safeguarding the working autonomy of the NGO sector of Nepal;
- to develop and enforce an "NGO Code of Conduct" among member NGOs to make them more accountable, transparent, and trustworthy so as to foster the positive image of Nepali NGO sector; and
- to promote and develop capacity-building activities for empowerment of the member organisations in

management field, which will help them to have a clear vision on their programme/project goals, objectives, planning, designing, and implementation (NGO Federation of Nepal, nd).

The objectives set by the NFN are as follows:

- to act as an advocacy and pressure group organisation for its members;
- to develop and conduct management-related capacity-building activities for its members;
- to encourage and initiate activities to develop strong linkages with relevant agencies or organisations;
- to initiate, followup, and enforce self-regulating activities for its members; and
- to identify major issues and problems, and promote sustainable development on the basis of democratisation, government initiative and community self-help.

This is also a process of institutional identity and for preparing to promote NGO ethics and professionalism and are ready to put themselves under strict official and public surveillance. It was also for developing their capacity and promoting self-reliance. However, these federations were empowering themselves rather than developing capacity to take greater roles and responsibility to reach the target groups. These federations were often linked to certain particular political parties, which is against the basic norms of "non-political or political neutrality" value for being an NGO. Apart from this, NGO associations could not maintain transparency and accountability. Instead of obeying the existing legal provisions regarding the financial transparency, these associations were found against the governmental legal enforcement efforts (see *Kathmandu Post*, 1999; *Kantipur*, 1999; *The Rising Nepal*, 1999; *Gorkhapatra*, 1999; *Samacharpatra*, 1999). In this way they are working as trade unions rather than helping to build a system for efficient operation and good co-operation.

NGOS IN NATIONAL DEVELOPMENT POLICIES

NGOs as Development Partners

Planned economic development effort was started in Nepal since 1956. Since then, nine periodic plans have already completed and the Tenth Plan (2002-07) is underway. The first five plans (1956–1980) had given more emphasis to infrastructure development. Only the Sixth (1980–85) and the Seventh (1985-90) plans were designed for fulfilling the basic needs of the people (NPC, 1981; 1986). Though the role of NGOs was not highlighted in the major objectives of the Sixth and Seventh Plan documents, the social sector was emphasised by their implementation mechanism.

During the Eighth (1992–1997) and the Ninth Plan (1997–2002), emphasis has been given to poverty alleviation issues. As poverty alleviation is a huge task for public sector organisations, the government has been considering the NGO sector as a development partner to shoulder the developmental efforts of the country. The interim government during 1990/91 announced a 13-point national policy regarding NGOs. Some of the important highlights were:

- SSNCC should co-ordinate NGOs, INGOs, and HMG and should provide technical supervision, follow-up activities of the programmes, inspect the financial and physical condition of the NGOs on a regular basis;
- SSNCC should facilitate and provide approval to the transfer of technical and financial assistance;
- NGO/INGO should be registered with SSNCC and their plan, programme, forms of assistance, and quarterly progress report, etc. should be submitted;
- SSNCC should evaluate NGO activities and submit the half-yearly and annual report to the Ministry of Labour and Social Welfare and Ministry of Finance, and
- NGOs' annual income/expenditure should be audited by the registered auditor and submitted to the SSNCC, which should be submitted to HMG with the comments (Maskay, 1998: 85–86).

Though this policy suggested some positive guidelines for (I)NGO projects, reporting system, monitoring and evaluation, and the role of SSNCC and the concerned agencies, the then-government's tenure was over and the new government brought out more elaborate policies with regard to NGO functioning in Nepal.

NGO Policy since 1992: A Breakthrough in Governmental Roles

In view of the catalytic role of NGOs in breaking the stumbling block of poverty, the government of Nepal recognised the NGO sector as development partners. That is, NGOs could both complement and supplement the government in carrying out development activities and delivery of basic services. However, the problems facing the NGO sector, highlighted in the Eighth Plan, were:

- Policies, acts, and rules to protect, promote, and encourage NGOs were lacking;
- The government imposed greater controls rather than allowing the NGO to run independently;
- Vague administrative procedures and lack of co-ordination; and
- Urban concentration of NGOs (NPC, 1992: 718–719).

To overcome these problems the following policies were adopted during the Eighth Plan (1992–97):

- Mobilisation of social organisations in the field of social and economic development, as they are more effective from the points of view of cost, flexibility, motivation and dynamism;
- Extension of NGOs to remote and rural areas from privileged areas to perform creative and innovative works of public importance;
- Encouragement of INGOs to run their own programmes through local NGOs;
- Involving the NGO sector actively in social and economic activities at the local level in co-ordination with and under the guidance of district development

committees, municipalities and village development committees;

- Introduction of a 'one window system' to make government decisions with regard to NGO function;
- Encouragement of NGOs to empower weak and helpless people, classes, and communities of the society to lead a life befitting human standards, on increasing the participation of women in development, on developing the appropriate technology, its transfer and use, and on conserving the environment;
- Strengthening the management capability of the NGOs in rural and remote areas through the partnership with INGOs;
- Organisation of information, data, and communication regarding NGOs; and
- Developing an effective monitoring and evaluation system (NPC, 1992: 719–721).

On the basis of policies developed in the plan, the area of partnership from the NGO sector was decided. Some of these important activities were community and rural development, urban slums improvement, empowerment of women, improvement of environment, delivery of public health, irrigation, health education like AIDS and drug abuse, youth activities and development of moral values, and the transfer of technology. Apart from this, commitment was also made to develop the local/national-level NGOs' capabilities, simplifying the rules and regulations for the easy functioning of the NGOs, and also introduction of an effective monitoring and evaluation system of the NGO works in the country (NPC, 1992: 569–572).

In view of the host of problems such as mass illiteracy, poor health, and lack of income and employment opportunities, the Ninth Plan (1997–2002) has set a single objective of 'poverty alleviation'. To achieve this goal the government has considered the NGOs as development partners. Commitments have been made for the mobilisation of NGOs in a way to make their works complementary to the development activities carried out by the government. The important contributions made by NGOs in the socio-economic development are objectively identified, and the nature, scope, resources, and capabilities of such NGOs have been categorised and co-ordinated with the local self-governance system. NGOs are encouraged to work in backward communities and especially in underdeveloped, remote regions, and also to expand their activities toward those regions and communities. They are motivated to work as facilitators vis-à-vis local institutions including District Development Committee (DDC) and Village Development Committee (VDC), educational institutions, and various community organisations and consumers (NPC, 1998: 101–102)

Apart from the above policies adopted in the Ninth Plan, the long-term concept for the role of NGO operation has also been introduced. The comparative ability of NGOs is planned for use on a long-term basis for the empowerment of the people and the people's organisation and creating conducive working environment. This can help to achieve the goal of sustainable social, economic, environmental, and institutional development, and encouraging them to actively participate in the development process

To achieve the objectives of NGOs as development partners, the following policies have been set for the plan period 1997–2002:

- Improvement of policies regarding the ambiguity of Acts regarding registration and working procedures;
- Involvement of NGO policy and programmes for poverty alleviation and socio-economic development;
- Development of appropriate policy and criteria for classifying NGOs according to their area of activity and geographical region;
- Involving the NGOs in mobilisation of internal resources, training, sharing of experience;
- Mobilising INGOs in building up the capability of NGOs on the basis of their specialisation;
- Adopting a one-window system to bring about simplicity in administration to further enhance the effectiveness of resource mobilisation from the INGOs;

- Adopting institutional development of monitoring and evaluation systems of NGOs activities,
- Taking special steps to honour the contributions of NGOs to national development;
- Encouraging the competence of NGOs in building up capability and efficiency of the local bodies in accordance with the decentralisation policy; and
- Making institutional arrangements to mobilise NGOs in remote areas (NPC, 1998: 753–754).

There is much similarity in the policy contents of the Eighth and Ninth Plans. Commitment has been made for facilitating and enhancing NGOs/INGOs to carry out development activities. In the Ninth Plan, a long-term concept for the role of NGO operation has also been introduced. In the long term the NGOs are to empower the people and the people's organisations and to create a conducive working environment. This can help to achieve the goal of sustainable social, economic, environmental, and institutional development, and to encourage them to actively participate in the development process.

However, some of the problems and challenges for the effective role of NGOs during the Ninth Plan (1997–2002) were:

- Ineffective monitoring system,
- Difficult to regularize NGO/INGO working,
- Lack of transparency of their activities, and
- Difficult to bring their activities in a one-door system (NPC, 2002: 545).

To make the role of NGOs more effective the Tenth Plan (2002–07) aims "...to develop non-governmental organisations, community based organisations and civil societies as partners of poverty eradication and sustainable development programmes by activating them in the sectors of community development particularly related to health, education, environment management and moral development as well as in the activities of increasing awareness of the targeted groups, such as, children, women, disabled, senior citizens, youth, backward class, ethnic groups and downtrodden communities" (NPC, 2002:545).

The Tenth Plan adopted two major strategies to make NGO/INGOs partners for their meaningful contribution in the socio-economic development of the country. For this, procedures for effective coordination, M/E system for their works would be simplified, and code of conduct would be developed to make them more responsible and transparent. It also aimed to motivate and implement INGOs' resources only through local institutions including local NGO, CBO and the local bodies as a part of local planning process (NPC, 2002:546).

Implications of the NGO Policies Adopted 1990 onward

The implications of the NGOs' roles can be seen in the local planning processes and resources mobilisation that have directly or indirectly effected the livelihood improvement of the target beneficiaries.

A. NGOs' roles are onsidered at local development planning process

The enactment of Village Development Committee Act 1992, Municipality Act 1992, and District Development Committee Act 1992 had given wider roles to NGOs in local development. These acts were submerged in Local Self Government Act 1998, which also provides much wider room to incorporate NGOs in the local development planning process. According to this Act (1998) and the Regulation (1999), the role of NGOs begins from the ward level of the Village Development Committee and Municipality level. Accordingly, the VDC/Municipality Ward Committee Member can consult the NGOs for the possible projects in the ward from VDC and also help users' group and NGOs for formulation and selection of project(s). Apart from this, the VDC and also the Municipality can ask annual projects from Ward Committees, users' groups, and NGOs. The reasons behind this co-ordination by the VDC/Municipality with HMG, NGO and donor agencies in the following matters during the planning of their programmes include:

- to eliminate duplication of similar project activities;
- to maintain complementarity between DVC/

Municipality and NGOs;
- to promote users' role in the development activities run both by NGOs and the local development agencies;
- to adopt the best possible ways for providing maximum benefit to the villagers; and
- to schedule different programmes in a proper way (HMG/N, 1998).

Normally, the VDC/Municipality develop their development programmes, which could be funded by the following sources:

- VDC's own fund,
- DDC's grants,
- Grants-in-aid of HMG, and
- NGOs funding (ibid).

Any NGO can work in a village setting in three conditions. First, an NGO can work in a village with its own resources or the resources managed by oneself. In such a case, the NGO should inform the concerned VDC/Municipalities about the nature, volume, and type of activities including the number of beneficiaries, etc. Second, the NGO can also work in any local area in a participatory way with the VDC/Municipalities (i.e., both NGO and the concerned VDC/Municipality can share the project cost and develop an understanding of project implementation). The implementation in this situation depends upon the conditions agreed upon between both parties. The third provision is that an NGO can work simply as a contracting agent. In this case, the NGO should submit a proposal to the VDC/Municipality or DDC to implement certain activities as per the terms of reference agreed by the concerned parties (HMG/N, MoLD, 1999). The VDC/Municipality—NGO collaboration process is shown in Figure 4.3. Apart from this, the VDC/Municipality should try to promote the NGOs for project formulation, selection, approval, implementation, monitoring, and evaluation and maintenance of the activities for running the VDC.

Similarly, the Local Self-Governance Act 1998 has also addressed the role of NGOs in the planning process of the

FIGURE 4.3: VDC/Municipality–NGO Project Formulation/ Implementation Process

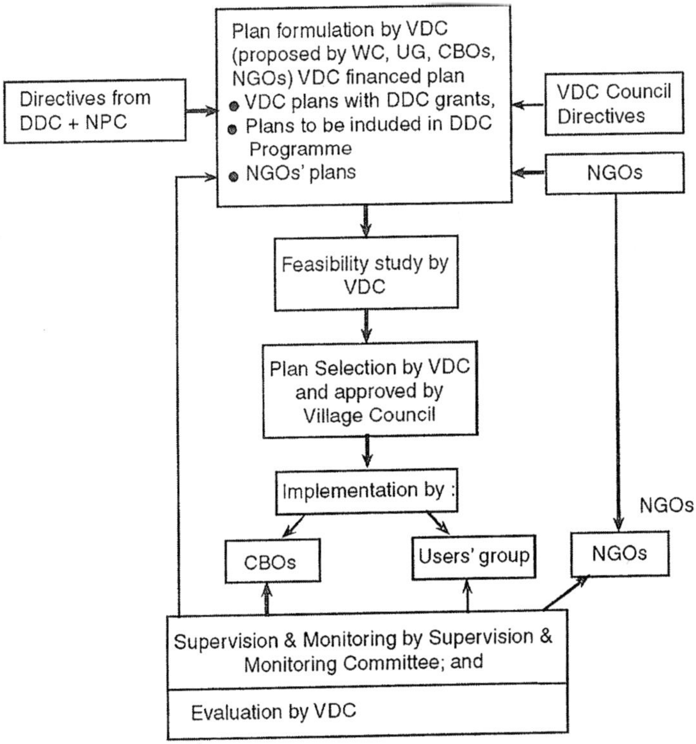

district level plans and their implementation (see Figure 4.4).

According to this act, NGOs are involved both in the plan formulation and implementation process. The involvement of NGOs in district plan formulation and implementation is shown in Figure 4.4. Accordingly, an NGO representative is invited for the participation in the *Yojaya Tarjuma Goshti* (plan formulation seminar) organised by the DDC. This meeting is normally held annually during the end of November.

Again, NGO representatives of the concerned *Ilaka*[10] level are also invited for the participation of Ilaka level plan formulation meeting. This meeting usually held at the end of January.

The Local Self-governance Act (see HMG/N, MoLD, 1998)

FIGURE 4.4: NGOs in District-level Plan Formulation and Implementation Process

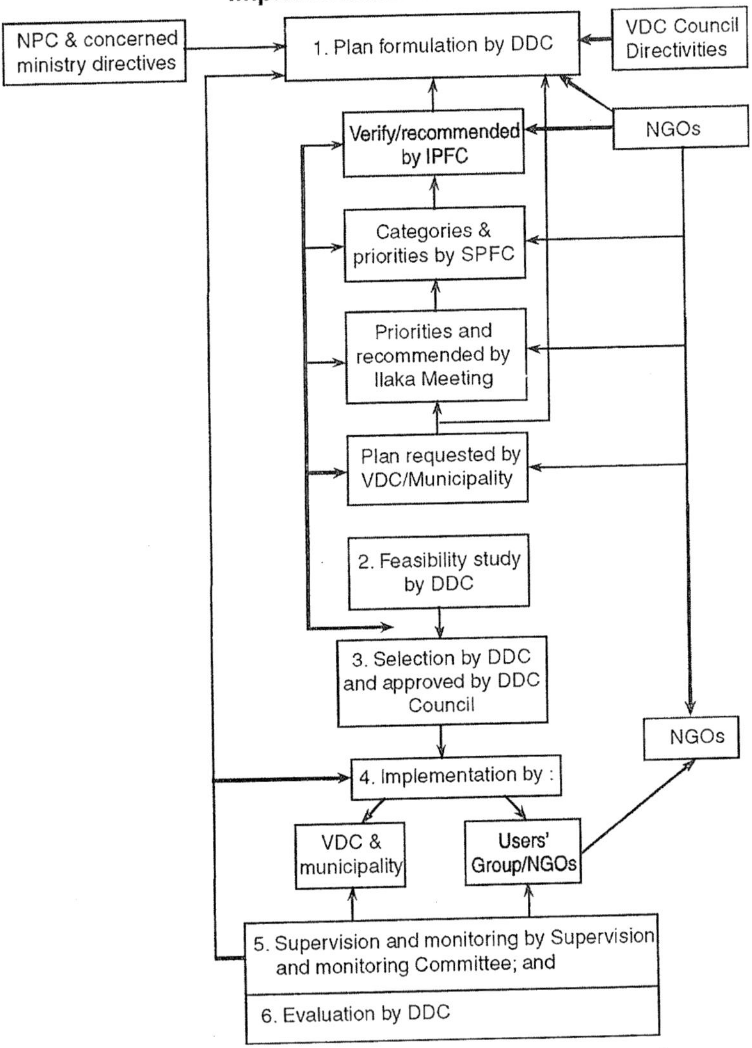

also provides an opportunity for the NGO representative as a full-fledged member of Subject-wise Plan Formulation Committee (SPFC) and also of Integrated Plan Formulation Committee (IPFC). The SPFC categorises the district level and central level plans and prioritises these plans and submits them to IPFC and to DDC, while the IPFC verifies all plan documents and recommends the selection process and ultimately forwards them to the DDC Council for approval. Apart from the involvement of NGOs in the process of plan formulation, they are also involved at the plan implementation stage. Normally NGOs implement their activities from their own source of income. In this case, the NGO simply informs the DDC about their type, nature, volume of activities, and the number of beneficiaries. But NGOs could also implement DDC projects both in partnership (sharing the project inputs) and as implementing agents like at the VDC/Municipality level. Implementation is normally carried out as per terms of reference (TOR) agreed by the both parties.

This provision broadens the working space of NGOs particularly at the local level and in seeking real partnership both at the plan formulation and implementation level. However, some problems still could be found in NGO operation at the local level. First, the Local Self-governance Act 1998 does not specify the legal treatment if any NGO does not work under/with VDC or DDC/Municipality. The (I)NGOs are governed by the Organisation and Association Act 1977 and Social Welfare Council Act 1992, which do not specify any provision regarding working with the local development agencies. Second, the participation of NGOs at the VDC/Municipality and also at DDC largely depends on the political connection of the respective parties with the respective local authorities, which either corrupts or politicises NGOs.

B. Resource MobilisationThrough NGOs

The pattern of resource mobilisation through NGOs during the 1990s has been significantly increasing in Nepal. Major funding through NGOs are made from the following sources:

- local resource mobilisation;
- NGOs' earnings such as public subscriptions, and membership fees;
- governmental line agencies budget;
- parliamentary area development funds; and

- international donor agencies, embassies and INGOs funding.

The policies developed during the 1990s also gave heavy importance to people's participation. As a result the enactment of local development agencies manifested this commitment. Users' groups, local CBOs, and the NGOs are mostly entrusted for implementing the village-level plans. In this context it is natural to expand the local resources mobilisation. Communities usually could participate in NGO programmes with cash, kind and labour sharing. Projects related to drinking water and construction of school buildings were found more felt-needs. Generally around 40% of the total cost of drinking water project and school construction projects were covered from local beneficiaries in Nepal. However, it is difficult to estimate the volume of local participation in the whole NGO sector in the country. The other sources of earnings of the NGOs could be entrance fees and membership renewal fees. Mostly,

TABLE 4.6: Allocation of Governmental Resources Through NGOs

Organisation	*Programme*	*Amount (in NPR)*
Ministry of Home	Drug abuse control	4.5
Ministry of Population and Environment	Environment-related awareness creation	4.5
Ministry of Women, Children and Social Welfare	Children, women, & old people-related activities	6.0
Ministry of Local Development	Community development	2.5
DDC, VDC/Municipality	Various nature of activities	N.A.
SWC*	Various nature of activities	4.5
Parliamentary area Development Fund**	Various nature of activities	132.5

Source : Concerned office records.

Note: * the amount delivered through SWC covers only the NGO promotional grants.

** Part of this amount also channelled through users' groups and local school, health post, etc.

the local community-based organisations generate funding from some sort of cultural programmes and sometimes selling lotteries; however, information regarding the NGOs' earning is also greatly lacking.

Similarly some of the line ministries also channel their budgets through NGOs to implement some of their activities. During 1999/2000 the following amount was delivered through different ministries and agencies (Table 4.6).

INGOs and the donor agencies have stood as the major contributors to the NGOs in Nepal. The size of such grants over the last few years gives an increasing trend. The total grants as committed in the general agreement between SWC and different INGOs are given in the following Table 4.7.

TABLE 4.7: INGO Grants through SWC

*Fiscal Year**	*Amount (NPR in Million)*
1999/2000	1,192,7
1998/99	1,089,3
1997/98	693,4
1996/97	401,0
1995/96	508,0

Source: SWC Office Records.
Note: * Nepali Fiscal Year covers a period of July 15–July14 of the next year.

The amount given in Table 3.7 gives an account of general agreement. As given in Appendix V, different categories of activities are funded by INGOs. These activities are community development, eye care service, child welfare/orphanage, and women and community development. Other activities are health and community development, disability, water and sanitation, agriculture, education, housing, and dental service. Almost 47% of the total INGO grants were delivered to child welfare and orphanage efforts, while community development and health and community development got around 31% of the total grant money. Activities such as education and agriculture development bag only around 6%.

The resources spent by several of these organisations are not officially reported. According to SWC source, the total annual budget of these INGOs is NPR 6 billion for the year 1999–2000. Similarly, UNDP's various development co-operation reports list only 28 INGOs with their level of expenditure in the year 1998 totalling US$ 17.5 million (see Ministry of Finance, 2000). However, various unofficial estimates show that around NPR 4 billion has been spent every year in the country through them. It demonstrates that very few organisations are officially recorded and the resource flow of majority of the NGOs/INGOs is unaccounted for (Ibid, 47–48). However, there is a suspicious environment about the total resources funded by the NGO sector, because the resources spent by several of these organisations are not officially reported. SWC records are far from being complete, and there is no other authentic source in the country.

The major contribution of NGOs in Nepalese society can be openly said to be adult literacy. The other areas of contribution from the NGO sector are health and sanitation, family planning, poverty alleviation of the marginal people (see Ghimire, 1999b). Almost 80 per cent of the eye care services are provided by the non-government run hospitals.

SOME ISSUES OF NGO POLICY AND ITS IMPLEMENTATION

As stated earlier, plan documents have given NGOs/INGOs a meaningful role by recognising them as partners in national development in mobilising and implementing the resources at the grass-roots level. After bringing the development policy statements into the Eighth and Ninth Plan some positive changes can be found in Nepal. As an effort the government brought SWC Act in 1992 for governing the NGOs more effectively. The act made a provision of INGOs/donor funding through the local NGOs (i.e., channelling their resources through local NGOs).

The local development act also gave room to the NGOs to work in the local area in a mutual way for the development of the local area and the community. Another important aspect is encouraging the local NGOs to work more aggressively with the partnership of INGOs/donor agencies in their target areas. It gave a fertile environment for the proliferation of NGOs in

Nepal. However, the status of NGOs themselves is at a crossroads, and the country also could not take much benefit from the huge number of NGOs. The present issues regarding the NGO functions in Nepal can be seen in the following areas.

The concept of development through NGOs has become like a "wild-goose chase" game due to various reasons. First, problems come on the part of government. The government should confirm that development through NGOs is a right paradigm of development. If the answer is yes and work as a partner ensues, then it should be specified; the nature, type, and volume of NGO activities and the target area and the population NGOs have to deliver the services. In this case, NGOs could be free to manage and operate their activities. If NGOs are set free to choose whatever activities they like, then NGOs can hardly play the role of development partners. The plan-documents during the 1990s show that the NGOs would be mobilised particularly in the rural areas; however, in practice the concentration of NGOs was mostly found in urban areas (see Table 4.8).

TABLE 4.8 Geographical Coverage of NGOs in Nepal

Description	*Rural*	*Urban*	*National*
No. of NGOs	2,648 (30)	6,177 (70)	8,825 (100)
No. of people living	19,140,000(87)	2,860,000(13)	22,000,000 (100)
No. of people per NGO	7,228	463	2,493

Source : Calculated on the basis of: SWC, 1999; 2000; and estimated size of population by the year 2000.

Note: Figures are rounded up. The figures in parenthesis are percentages

The table shows the concentration of NGOs in the urban areas. Even the government grants delivered through the NGOs are concentrated in the urban areas, which is against the spirit of NGOs' policies specified in the Eighth Plan (1992–97) and Ninth Plan (1997–2002) (see Dhakal, 1999; 1999:311 and also see SWC, 1998a; 1998b; 1998c).

Study shows the lack of proper co-ordination between governmental and non-governmental organisations, which may be working with the same beneficiaries for the same nature of problems but co-ordination may be established on political grounds rather than on developmental issues (Dhakal & Ulvila, 1999: 15–17).

Another issue is that government has not been properly informed, particularly of the INGOs' funding but also about their hidden interests (Pandey, 1999), due to lack of proper monitoring and assessing systems. In such cases, the NGO management capability of the government should be enhanced. The present SWC, which has been suffering from the weak institutional arrangements including the intervention from the politics is hardly able to monitor and evaluate the total affiliated 8825 NGOs and 91 INGOs. SWC is working as a "post office" (Gupta, 1999) rather than a management agency.

Second, other problems come from NGOs. The most commonly blamed issues against NGOs are that they are indulging in politics, or business or often both in the case of Nepali NGOs. INGOs may be spying, secretly promoting their business, or working as religious conversion (Ghimire 1999a; Bhattachan, 1999: 21). One of the great issues of NGOs is the question of good image in the society. With regard to the role and performance of NGOs, debates are going on about the credibility of NGOs, type and coverage of NGO activities, and also of their working methodology. The non-transparent practices, weak institutional linkages, inadequate management capacity, insufficient planning practices, and unaccountable mode of involvement have subjected this sector to criticism as it does not work according to the actual mandate nor the strategies to involve NGOs. Thus, although there is a mushroom growth of the NGOs, due to the lack of proper guidelines there is a lot of confusion regarding the working relationship of the NGOs within the system (Kanchan Lama Verma: nd). Rademacher believes that "It is difficult, if not impossible, to get a clear picture of the intentions and performance of every new NGO. It is also unwise to automatically liken a larger NGO population to a surge in 'people power' enthusiasm, the newer NGOs must first prove that they are genuine and effective" (Rademacher, 1995: 34–35).

The NGO leaders were often found getting involved in what Bhattachan termed 'Pajero NGOs', 'Briefcase NGOs', Suitcase NGOs, 'Green Dollars NGOs', 'Family NGOs', etc. (Bhattachan. 1998: 15) while Ghimire commented that "government officials consider NGOs to the illegal claimants to their monopoly on corruption and therefore criticise them. Business people view NGOs as fashionable, modern industries where without investment or risk high profits can be made. For the general public, social organisations are considered as another government office or a playground of the shrewd, powerful, rich urban folk. For intellectuals, they are not more than begging bowls"(Ghimire et.al nd., in Rademacher, 1995: 32–33).

Apart from these problems, there is also a danger of losing social characteristics due to the over-dependency upon INGOs as the local NGOs often work simply as followers rather than with a voluntary spirit (see Panday, 1999b: 11) and also lose their "autonomy" and "alignment with donor's priorities" (CECI, 1992). Therefore, NGOs try to keep their financial transactions secret. Often the NGOs are constituted within the family, relatives, or a few like-minded persons. The organisation often led by a single person domination is also another NGO characteristic. Some of the influential people of NGOs have been bringing millions of Nepalese Rupees without informing the government (Ghimire, 1999b). The saddest aspect is that people have been made dependent and compliant instead of independent and relying on their own power. In this way people are losing their self-confidence and most importantly, the spirit of voluntarism, which had been a social practice in the Nepalese society in the form of 'social capital'.

In this context government should review the existing policy to address problems like these and to enhance the implementation capability of the policies for enhancing development through NGOs a better option.

END NOTE

1. *Guthis* were the social institutions created both before and after unification of the country in 1769. They were basically for

performing funeral, wedding, and religious ceremonies including construction and/or repairing the temples and other public infrastructure. Community contributions basically in land grant and sometimes in cash as well were the basic sources for the regular operation of *Guthi*. Such *Guthis* were classified into three broad categories, namely *Raj Guthi* (created by official or national trusts), *Chut Guthis* (semi autonomous status), and *Niji Guthi* (managed solely by the Guthiyars (Guthi members). Some of these traditional *Guthis* are still in existence and performing as usual.

2. The Rana family ruled over Nepal from 1846 to 1951 as de facto King in a feudal and autocratic manner. They were always suspicious of social institutions and educated people because they thought educated people could be a threat to the continuity of their family rule.
3. Panchayat as a party-less political system was introduced in Nepal in 1960. The constitution of the Panchayat system did not consider any political organisation and work as in the multiparty democratic system or in a single-party system. However, the system was constituted as a three-tier system (village/town level, district level and national level) where people can contest the election in an individual way. The constitutional provision gave the king absolute power. (For details see HMG/N, 1962. The Constitution of the Kingdom of Nepal 1962.)
4. Social Welfare Council (SWC) is a governmental bureau for co-ordinating, facilitating, and controlling the NGOs/INGOs working in Nepal. This body was created in 1992 under Social Welfare Council Act 1992. Before constituting this body the Social Service National Coordination Council (SSNCC) was conducting these functions during the period 1977 to 1992. The SSNCC was merged into SWC after enactment of Social Welfare Council Act 1992. For details see section 3.4 of this chapter.
5. The government of Nepal provides a sum of NPR one million per annum for each parliamentarian as a *Parliamentary Election Area Development Fund*. Altogether there are 265 parliamentarians in Nepal. Though this fund is channelled through District Development Committee, it should be expended as per the decision and direction made by concerned parliamentarians. The practice is that such fund flows through users' group, NGOs, Clubs, etc. which are often formed by the workers/supporters of concerned parliamentarians and also their respective political parties. For details see Parliamentary

Election Area Development Fund Implementation Directives 1998.

6. Nepalese monetary unit is called *Rupaiya* (Rupees). The abbreviation can be written as NPR.
7. NGO may not be required for affiliation with SWC just for the sake of being a legal entity. However, affiliation with SWC becomes mandatory when any NGO takes external support from the INGOs or other donor agencies. Affiliation also becomes a precondition for receiving grants from the SWC including other functional ministries.
8. Any legally registered INGO can work in Nepal by either making an agreement with the concerned line ministry or with SWC. In the case of affiliation of INGO with SWC, two agreements—general agreement and project agreement—should be made. A general agreement is made between SWC and concerned INGO and project agreement is made between SWC, local partner NGO, and the INGO. Before making such a project agreement it is mandatory to take prior consent from the concerned line ministry, National Planning Commission and the Ministry of Finance about the nature and type of function, facilities and condition of expatriates, etc. (For details see Social Welfare Act/Regulations 1992, General Agreement/Project Agreement between SWC and the concerned INGO/NGO documents). This study is based on those INGOs which are affiliated with SWC and working as partners with the national/local NGOs.
9. District administration office (Chief District Officer's Office), which is popularly called CDO office, is a governmental department under Ministry of Home. This office has been established in each of the 75 districts.
10. According to the Local Self-government Act 1998 each district is divided into different areas called *Ilaka. Ilaka* is constituted for DDC electoral purpose. Depending upon the population and VDC/Mumicipality size of district there could be 9 to 17 *Ilakas* in a district. Each *Ilaka* elects an Ilaka-Member who works as a DDC member. The act also made a provision of *Ilaka Level Discussion Meeting* in course of formulating Ilaka level plan to incorporate at the DDC annual plans (for details see Local Self-governance Act 1998).

5

NGOs' Interventions for Addressing Livelihood

This chapter deals with the empirical studies of two NGOs—PLAN International and Backward Society Education (BASE)—working in two village settings—Markhu Village Development Committee and Hekuli Village Development Committee, respectively. This chapter introduces the general background of the study area, which is followed by a presentation of the livelihood situation and the organisational landscape of the sampled area. Similarly, it discusses the case study of NGOs emphasising the organisational and management structures and their objectives, including the area of activities. On the basis of objectives and programmes, livelihood issues are analysed regarding the output of their operational programmes. Finally, it discusses the major issues with regard to the case NGOs and their roles for improving livelihoods.

GENERAL BACKGROUND OF THE STUDY AREA

Location: The two study areas—Markhu VDC of Makwanpur district and Hekuli VDC of Dang district—lie in mid-hills of central Nepal and mid-western Terai of Nepal, respectively (see Map 5.1). These locations typically represent two distinct ecological areas where agricultural production is the dominant livelihood portfolio. Markhu VDC is one of 43 VDCs in Makwanpur district, which falls in 13th *Ilaka*. This VDC has a mountainous terrain ranging from 1.500 m to 2.300 m above sea level. The land is covered mostly by *Bari*[1] and the jungle. The VDC is divided into two parts by a seven-kilometre long lake[2]—the reservoir of Kulekhani Hydroelectricity power plant. Markhu is connected by a dirt road to Hetauda—the headquarters of Makwanpur and Kathmandu—the capital city of Nepal some 60 kilometres from both sides.

Hekuli Village Development Committee is one of the 39 VDCs lying in 6th *Ilaka* of Dang district. The landscape is plain and below 500 m from the sea level; however, the river/stream belts are at the lower level than the other parts of the VDC. This VDC is a plain; however, low land at the bank of local *Kholas*[3] is mostly irrigated, and uplands are mostly dry. Around 35 per cent of the total land covered by forest, which is managed by local communities. Hekuli is connected by a dirt road with Tulsipur and Ghorahi—district headquarters of Dang, which is 450 kilometres from Kathmandu—the capital of Nepal.

People and Society: Traditionally, in Nepal, people have lived in villages in a clustered way on the basis of their caste, culture, and religious homogeneity. On this basis different settlements can still be found, particularly in the rural areas of the country. Altogether there are 17 settlements in Markhu and 19 in Hekuli which are clustered mostly on the basis of ethnic identity (Dang DDC, 1995). However, administratively both VDCs are divided into nine wards each (see fn.3). The 1991 Census accounted the total population in Markhu and Hekuli VDC as 3.077 and 8.512 respectively. The ethnic composition of the people in these villages also shows a microcosm of the Nepalese socio-ethnic picture. Both villages comprise multi-ethnic social construction. However, Tamang is the dominant ethnic group in Markhu, and accounts for 50% of the total population, while Tharu (also called Chaudhari considered indigenous group of the area) is the dominant group in Hekuli, comprising 58% of the total population (see Table 5.1). Apart from Tamang, other communities such as Newar, Brahmin/Chhetri, and Magar have also been living in the Markhu VDC area. Most of the people in Markhu have been living in this area for many generations. Similarly, Brahmin/Chhetri, Sanyasi, Damai/Kami, Magar, Newar, and Gurung also have been living in Hekuli.

FIGURE 5.1: Map of the Study Areas (Markhu VDC - at the top, NEPAL—at the centre, and Hekuli VDC— at the bottom)

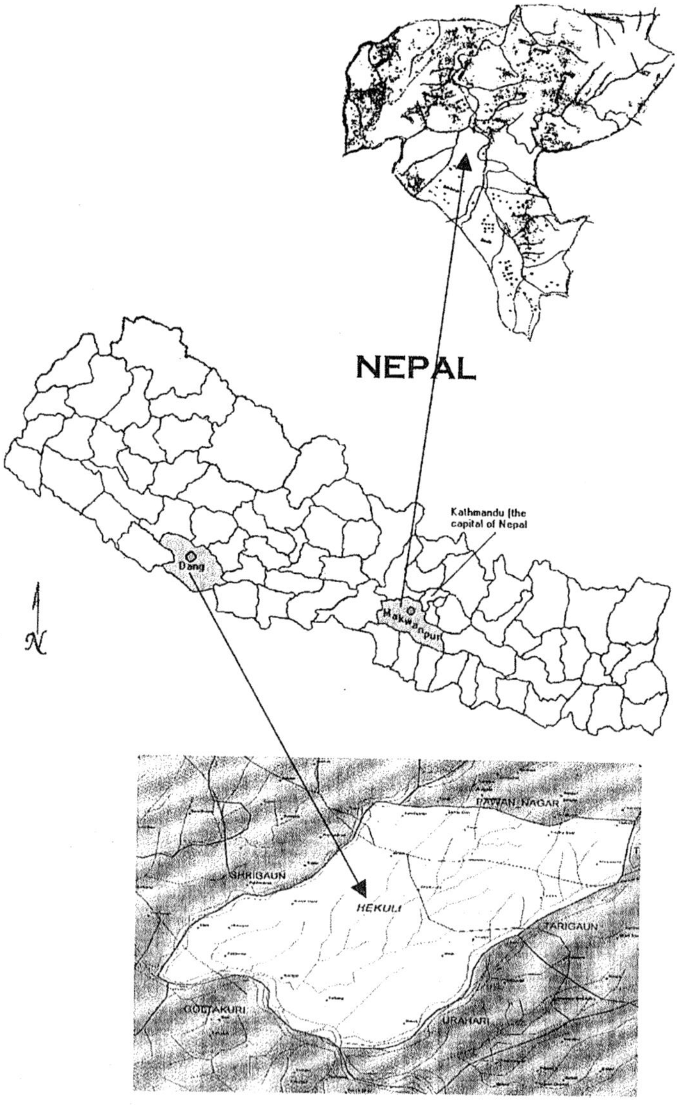

TABLE 5.1: General description of population/household in Markhu and Hekuli

Description	Markhu VDC		Hekuli VDC		Total
No. of households		606		1139	1,745
Total population		3077		8512	10,257
Average family size		5.8		7.5	
Ethnic composition (in percentage)	Tamang	50	Tharu	58	
	Newar	22	Brahmin/ Chhetri	29	
	Brahmin/ Chhetri	20	Sanyasi	6	
	Magar	7	Damai/kami	4	
	Others	1	Others	3	

Source: Population Census, 1991; Dang DDC, 1995.

Tamangs basically rely on Buddhism, however, both Hindu and Buddhist cultural practices are common in many castes and difficult to distinguish among different community groups of Markhu. The major rituals are commonly celebrated. In Hekuli also, the different castes share these festivals; however, Tharu community celebrate *Maghi*[4] more importantly. Whatever their religious practices, the people of these villages also live in a family structure within a society. The husband becomes the head of the family but wife (mother) also plays this role if she becomes a widow or in the absence of the husband (father).

LIVELIHOOD SITUATION OF THE STUDY AREA

The sample survey gathered information regarding household assets such as land ownership, size of livestock, employment of the household members, quality of house, availability of electricity and drinking water facilities, etc. Livelihoods approach (Carney, 1998); Farrington, et al., 1999; Ellis, 2000) places a lot of emphasis on assets, particularly on identification of assets possessed by the poor as it plays a great role in their better living. In a society where agricultural farming places an important role, land is normally considered the best asset. Therefore, categorisation of people has been based on the size of their landholdings in both Markhu and

Hekuli. However, other forms of assets are also important both for utilising the land and ultimately for making better livelihoods.

Occupation and Livelihood in Markhu: Agriculture is the mainstay of people, though it has been becoming more and more difficult to maintain household consumption. The estimated average size of family land holding in Markhu is 11,47 Ropani[5] (approximately 0.57 hectares) which is quite a small piece to maintain an average family size of 5.8 persons (see Table 5.2).

TABLE 5.2: Landholding Status in Markhu

Description/ Asset group	*Low-income group (landless or family less than 10 Ropani (0.5 ha) land size)*	*Medium-income group (family 10 Ropani to 30 Ropani) (0.5-1.5 ha land)*	*High-income group (family with 1.5 ha or more land size)*	*Total*
Sample size	68 (65%)	28 (27%)	8 (8%)	104 (100%)
Major source of income	A: unskilled labour B: agriculture	A: agriculture B: labour, business	A: agriculture B: service, business	
Per family average landholding	5.37 ropani (0.26 ha)	18.96 ropani (0.95 ha)	37.13 ropani (1.86 ha)	11.47 ropani (0.57 ha)
Per family Bari/Khet (paddy %)	Bari: 0.24 ha Khet: 0.02 ha	Bari: 0.88 Khet: 0.07 ha	Bari: 1.78 ha Khet: 0.07 ha	Bari: 0.53 ha Khet: 0.04 ha
Per family livestocks (number)	2.5	3.5	5	2.96
Per family Poultry (Number)	3.5	4.5	7	4.04

Source: Household Survey, February, 2000).

The lower income group comprising 65% of the total households, own only an average of 0.27 hectare land, while the medium income group posseses 0,95 ha land and the higher section with 1,86 ha of average size of land. Most of the land in Markhu was only *bari*, as the Kulekhani Hydro project submerged the paddy fields of most of the families. It led many people either to migrate to other parts of the country or shift to other locations, normally upland within the VDC and live more marginally. Therefore, the people lack *khet*[6], which has many times more productivity power than *bari*. Average size of *khet* of Markhu people was only 0,04 ha. So the people have to rely only on *bari* which is subject to good weather for production. Maize, therefore became one of the major staple foods for their consumption. In Markhu, major agricultural products are maize, millets, mustard, and rice. However, local farmers cultivate vegetables such as potatoes, onion, radish, cauliflower, cabbage, garlic, beans, tomatoes, pumpkin, *sag*, and other varieties of climbers. Some of the leading local farmers have been commercialising vegetable farming and also horticulture farming such as pears, plums, lemons, etc. Apart from these, people have also been supplementing their household incomes by rearing livestock—buffaloes, cows, goats, and chickens—which could contribute to their household consumption and making organic manure for the field and for cash. A few families have also become involved both in fish farming and traditional fishing. However, the majority of the people have not been involved in such new ventures. This situation compels the Markhu people to seek alternative income sources for their livelihood. Due to the shortage of educated/trained manpower, most of the teachers, and governmental employees come from other parts of the country. For most of the year many men from most of the communities registered in the village are working and living in Kathmandu and other urban centres as far as Kolkata and Delhi supplementary income (Dhakal & Ulvila, 1999). Often older boys are with their fathers in urban centres. Therefore the resident population of Markhu is predominantly female.

Occupation and Livelihood in Hekul: In the past, the size of population was small in Hekuli and the area of arable land was plenty for cultivation, which made the people self-sufficient. The malaria eradication efforts of the government after the 1950s made this area better for living, which led to immigration, from Hills to the plain land Terai. Slowly, the migration process and faster growth of population, and also the land distribution system made bigger differences between rich and poor in Hekuli. Normally, the mainstay of Hekuli is agricultural farming; however, the farming system has become more difficult and challenging. Among such difficulties the size of land is becoming smaller and smaller. In Hekuli, too, two types of land—*khet* and *bari*—are considered the most important asset for the villagers. The lowland beside the local *Kholas* are irrigated for the whole year, while the uplands are either seasonal *khet* or *bari*. Though the land is fertile, irrigation has been the major problem in the dry season. However, the important crops produced in Hekuli are rice, wheat, lentil, and mustardoil seeds. People who have irrigated land also plant vegetables such as potatoes, onion, garlic, beans, tomatoes, cauliflower, cabbage, radish, pumpkin, *sag*, and other varieties of climbers. Some of the lead farmers have been starting vegetable farming as cash crops; however, most of the villagers are confined to traditional crops. Rearing livestock—buffaloes, cows, goats, and chickens—both for their household consumption and also for organic fertiliser in the field and for making cash is a common social practice.

The present ownership of land shows that some people are rich and possess large amounts of land and the others are poor and marginalised or even landless (see Table 5.3 for land-ownership portfolio of the people in Hekuli). Many people such as Tharus and some others who migrated and could not manage their living are distinctly becoming poor.

The average size of family landholding is less than 5 *katha*[7] (0,16 ha). Only half of their land is *khet* and rest *bari*. Such poor people make up 41.4% of the total people of Hekuli, which is around the national poverty level of 42% (see Table 5.3).

Among them, 70% are Tharu, and the rest are from other communities. The output from this small piece of land to maintain an average family of 7.5 members is absolutely insufficient for survival; these peoople can obtain a maximum

TABLE 5.3: Landholding Status in Hekuli

Description/ Asset group	*Low income-group (landless or family less than 10 katha) less than 0.5 ha land size)*	*Medium-income group (family 10 katha to 2 bigha) (0.5-1.5 ha land)*	*High-income group (family more than 2 bigha land) (family with 1.5 ha or more than land size)*	*Total*
Number	43 (41.4%)	45 (43.3%)	16 (15.3%)	104 (100%)
Per family average landholding	0.5 katha (0.16 ha)	21.72 katha (0.72 ha)	63.3 katha (2.11 ha)	21.2 katha (0.71 ha)
Major source of income	Main: agriculture labour, Secondary: agriculture	Main: own agriculture Secondary: labour + other employment	Main: own production Secondary: business+ other employment	
Bari/Khet (paddy %	50% dry land khet 50%	41% dry land 59% khet	23% dry land 77% khet	
Livestock (number)	2	4	8	
Poultry (Number)	3	5	8	

Source: Household Survey, April 2000.

two to five months' food supply from their own production. Illiteracy, poor health, and poverty are the basic characteristics of these poor people. Therefore, unskilled labour could be the most dependable option for family survival, but this is also very seasonal. Therefore, the poor people employ their school-going children to supplement their family income to survive. Such labour most often could be the agricultural labour, which is often called bonded labour or the *Kamaiya*[8]. These Kamaiyas have mostly been from this group. Rich people usually hire such labour. A livelihood picture of a Kamaiya[9] is given in Box 5A.

Box: 5A KAIMAYA GRAM CHAUDHARI'S LIVELIHOOD SITUATION

- No. of Family: 7 (husband, wife, 3 daughters, 2 sons)
- Living in a small thatched hut at the bank of Chiregard khola
- Property status: landless, however, occupied 4 katha public land
- Occupation: working as Kamaiya since childhood
- Annual family income: 45 muri rice and a pair of clothes for each working person
- (Gram earns 25 muri of rice, his wife 5 muri, first son (14 years old) 6 muri, daughter (12 years old) 5 muri, and second daughter (10 years old) earns 4 muri rice annually)
- Never attended ALC classes run by governmental/NGOs
- Never sent the children to school
- Never taken any amount of loan from the banks/NGOs-saving groups
- Loan taken: (Rs. 7,000) from local Zamindar for house construction
- Mostly rely on local faith healer *(guruwa)* & sometimes buy medicines from local medical shop for medical care.

Source: Based on the interview taken with the Gram Chaudhari. Interview was taken on 04. 19.2000 by the Researcher himself.

The medium income group, which constitute 43.3% are marginal farmers who hold 21.72 katha (0.72 ha) land per family. Among them 62% are Tharu. (see Table 5.3). The land possessed by this group is of somewhat better quality and bigger size than that possessed by the poor, which is at least three times smaller than the size of richer group. Subject to the weather this group can maintain their daily necessities.

The richer group constitutes only 15.3% of the total population in Hekuli; their average landholding size is 63.3 katha (2,11 ha). Both Tharu and non-Tharu represent the equal size of 50%. These people having bigger landholdings are called landlords or *Zamindars*[10]. This section of society is educated and has a better livelihood. The Land Reform Act 1964 discouraged the hoarding large amounts of land and attempted to gain tenancy rights; however, it was also not very effective in such areas due to ignorance and less bargaining power of the poor people.

Livestock farming represents also important village assets. Usually livestock are used for tilling land (ox and male buffalo power); cows and buffaloes are used for producing such power, and for milk and for fertiliser. For the purpose of meat piggery, poultry, and goats/lambs are commonly reared. Compared to rich people, the poor again have fewer of such assets that could supplement their income for livelihood.

Ranking Problem: Different problems make human life difficult. Such problems range from income generation to health and hygiene, drinking water, the schooling system, etc. To identify the problems facing the villagers for meeting their livelihoods four groups—two in Markhu and two in Hekuli—met (see Table 5.4). Drinking water was taken as the most important problem at both places of Markhu, while fertiliser in the case of both Rawat Gaun and Hekuli of Hekuli VDC.

TABLE 5.4: Problems in Markhu and Hekuli Rank Order

Group	*Markhu VDC**		*Hekuli VDC***	
	Problems	*Rank*	*Problems*	*Rank*
A	Bhirkharka Ward No. 6		Rawat Gaun Ward No. 3	
	Drinking water	1st	Fertiliser	1st
	Registration of local school	2nd	Employment	2nd
	Seeds/seedlings	3rd	Irrigation	3rd
	Road access	4th	Seeds	4th
B	Bajrabanth Ward No. 4		Hekuli Ward No. 8	
	Drinking water	1st	Fertiliser	1st
	Market	2nd	Skill training	2nd
	Fertiliser	3rd	Seeds	3rd
	Seeds	4th	Electricity	4th

Source: Dhakal and Ulvila, 1999; Hossain and Dhakal, 1999.
Note: * The sessions were conducted from 8–9 November, 1998.
** The sessions were conducted from 7–8 July, 1999.

On the other hand, the second ranking covered quite diverse fields. School registration and the market ranked second in Markhu A and B respectively, and employment and skill training were in Hekuli A and B, respectively. Need of seeds/seedlings were also given either 3rd or 4th rank in all the four groups. In Markhu A, road access, and in Hekuli B electricity placed 4th (Table 5.4). It shows that, for livelihood all kinds of assets, natural, human, financial, physical, etc. made some problems one way or the other. In this context, the type of organisations and their functions are briefly presented in the following section.

ORGANISATIONAL LANDSCAPE IN THE STUDY AREA

The role of social groups, institutions and organisations for grass-roots development is important and vital, as assets alone cannot produce anything. Traditionally the size of population was small and the social demands were not much, (i.e., there were only a limited number of socio-economic problems, particularly in village settings). People in society try to manage their living both individually and with their community-based organisations. Government had very limited roles with the communities. The growth of people, expansion of more demands due to the learning process and demonstration effects, and also the environments created to address the dissatisfaction of the people brought more socio-economic problems in the societies like Markhu and Hekuli. Such a situation calls for more service delivery agencies to fulfill the demands of the society. Institutions can process and design strategies to cope with the shocks and the negative trends and select the activities to be implemented for bringing about a desired output.

Different types of organisations were found created and working in both the Markhu and Hekuli study areas (see Table 5.4). These organisations range from governmental, non-governmental, community-based traditional, and private organisations.

Government Organisations

The grass-roots development process started in Nepal only after the establishment of democracy in 1951. During the 1950s there were only 55 village development centres, 10 seed development centres, 4 veterinary development centres, and five dairy development centres in different parts of the country. The others were just 292 post offices, 2,000 primary and 165 secondary schools, 94 health centres and 578 co-operatives (Poudyal, 1984: 139). From the beginning of 1960s the government realised that due to the lack of local institutions

TABLE 5.4: List of Governmental, Non-governmental, Private, and Community-based Traditional Organisations in Chronological order.

Name of org.	*Markhu VDC*	*Hekuli VDC*
Government organisation	1963 VDC 1965 Health post Schools* (secondary school 1 primary school 5) 1975 Post office 1975 Electricity office 1975 Police station 1975 Nepal Bank Ltd 1984 Small Farmer Dev. Programme 1984 Agriculture Service Centre 1984 Veterinary Service Centre 1992 Fish development Centre□ *Total number of government organisations are 16*	1963 VDC 1974 Health post Schools* (secondary school 1 primary school 5) 1974 Sajha (Co-operative) 1981 Post office 1984 Agriculture Service Centre 1984 Veterinary Service Centre 1984 Police station 1998 Rural Development Bank 1996 Telephone service installation *Total number of government organisations are 14*
Non-government organisation	1992 Community Support Association of Nepal 1993 Indrasarobar Fisherman's Association 1995 PLAN International Makwanpur 1996 Centre for Self-help Development (CSD) 1996 Satteswari Youth Club 1996 Indrasarobar Youth Club	1991 Backward Society Education (BASE) 1991 Chandra Smriti Youth Club 1992 Social Upgrade in Progress Education Region 1994 Chure-mahabharat Sewa Samaj and 1995 Janakshiksha Samajik Sangh
Community-based traditional organisation (inddigenous)	Maruwa guthi, See guthi, Mahalaxmi Guthi, Tamang Ghedung Forest users groups #	Matam Forest users groups (1991 onward)#
Private organisation	Local shops, fish farmers, bus service	Local shops, tile factory (cottage level), bus services

Source: Dhakal & Ulvila, Marko, 1999; Hossain & Dhakal, 1999, Concerned Office.

Note: * The schools were established at different times; however, most of the primary schools were established in 1990s (for details see Dhakal & Marko, 1999; Hossain and Dhakal, 1999).

These Forest Users' Groups were entitled to manage a jungle near the village. The group members comprise the whole village irrespective of caste and ethnicity (see also fn 37).

¤ Inland Development Research Centre (IDRC) had started an experiment on fish farming in Indrasarobar Lake since 1984. When the experiment proved successful Fish Development Centre was established 1992 to facilitate the fish farmers.

local development efforts could not be implemented. As a consequence, around 4,000 grass-roots organisations[11] at different villages, towns, and districts were created. Apart from this, government has also started to create different institutions such as agriculture extension offices, financial institutions, post offices, health centres, schools, police stations, etc. It shows that the government has introduced a concept of the delivery of basic health, education up to secondary level, agriculture extension services, communication services, and a required volume of security to the people at grass-roots level. Most of the line agencies have their district-level offices, and some others such as agriculture, health, post office, and police, have at *Ilaka* level service centres or sub-centres. These offices could provide necessary extension and security services to a specified pocket. Normally these centres should serve three to four VDCs.

Village Development Committee (VDC): In both Markhu and Hekuli more than a dozen governmental organisations exist for providing services. Among these organisations the Village Development Committee (VDC) is the important (see HMG/N, MoLD, 1998; 1999). It is a political/administrative organisation, which has been considered as the foundation of decentralised spirit of the governing system in Nepal. This institution also is taken as a mechanism for the *inclusion*[12] minorities and women, particularly in grass-roots development. It is constituted both by locally elected and a government-recruited employee. Some of the major functions to be carried out by the VDC are as follows:

- plan (both annual and periodic plans), design operational calendar, and implement the plans and programmes/projects,
- co-ordinate other governmental offices, NGOs, users' group, and private organisations which have the programmes at the respective VDC,
- maintain co-ordination with neighbouring VDC and DDC and concerned district-level line agencies,
- mobilise local people/resources into the development process of the village,
- monitor and evaluate village-level projects,
- identify the persons to provide social securities,
- settle village disputes, provide recommendations in different occasions, etc. (HMG/N, 2055: 17–20).

To perform village development activities each VDC gets an annual block grant of NPR 500,000 from the government. The government also provides the social security grants[13] for distribution, collect local land tax of the VDC area (HMG/N: 2055, 21–24). Apart from this, the VDC can generate income by imposing different taxes, and charges for application or recommendations. In both VDCs, apart from the VDC chairman, a government-appointed employee has to work as VDC secretary and a VDC-appointed a technical assistant and a runner also work in the VDC.

In both Markhu and Hekuli the VDC have programmes for constructing foot trails/road development, drinking water projects, and support the salary of four school teachers in Hekuli and one in Markhu. These VDCs have mostly confined their activities to functions such as issuing recommendations to the concerned persons, distribution of Social Security, collecting land tax, etc.

Despite the VDCs' important role in the local area, they often suffer different problems. Some of these problems are:

- politicisation of VDC activities,
- lack of sufficient resources to carry out VDC activities,
- lack of employees to carry out their activities as each

VDC normally has two employees, a secretary and a technical assistant, who are confined to regular administrative works,
- lack of legal space to have effective roles for co-ordinating other institutions working in VDC level, and
- lack of the role of civil society to help/persuade VDC for its effective roles.

The VDCs encounter such problems, which make the working of the peopleless effective.

Health Post: A Health Post is established both in Markhu and Hekuli. The health situations of Markhu and Hekuli are similar to other villages of the country. The most common diseases/health problems found in both study areas were worm infection, skin diseases, pneumonia/chest infection, amebiasis/giardiasis, cough and cold, fever, gynaeological and obstetric problems, and eye infection (concerned Health Post office records; also see COSAN, 1997). Malnutrition and unhygienic conditions are a major cause of these illnesses. These health service centres provide both curative and preventive services such as delivery of health awareness regarding AIDs, nutrition, pregnancy, primary care, distribution of contraceptives, immunisations, etc. The number of out-patients in a day averages 20–25. During the field visit there were few health personnel such as a Health Assistant, an Auxiliary Health Assistant, a Midwife (ANM), a Village Health Worker (VHW), and the administrative staff like a clerk, two peons and a sweeper in Markhu Helath post, and a Health Assistant, Auxiliary Health worker, and two other peons working in Hekuli Health Post.

Normally, the health post could not meet the demand for medicines and sometimes there is a shortage of health-personnel. The annual volume of some important medicines supplied from the government is sufficient for just 15–30 days (PLAN 1999). The health post generally provides primary care to the patients; beds for the patients, pathology services, instruments, and the doctors were all lacking. However, some co-operation can be found between these Health Posts and

NGOs working in these VDC for the delivery of health services. Therefore, people frequently use *Dhami Jhakri* (faith healers). Because of the tradition, orthodoxy, and also accessibility, people often rely on the traditional mode of treatment practised by local *Dhami/Jhakri*. In the PLAN project areas in Makwanpur, the number of traditional healers is many times larger than that of the modern medical personnel. Around 100,000 people reside in PLAN International Mawanpur Project areas (including Markhu), where about 1200 such faith healers have been providing their services (PLAN: 1999, 45). It shows that only 83 people could be the ratio between each faith healer, whereas each health assistant has to serve 20,000 people in this area.

Gurubas are the most trusted local medical practitioners in Hekuli VDC. Before introducing the modern health care unit, Guruba were the only relied upon agents for common treatments; however, their role is still important, and when people become sick or bitten by a snake generally they approach these *Gurubas* for the treatment. Dependency on *Gurubas* for treatment of human beings and also for domesticated animals is a very common phenomenon in Hekuli. There are *Ghar Guruba* and *Deshbandi Gurubas*. The *Ghar Buruba* delivers home services, and *Deshbandi Guruba* serves an area. Altogether there are some 30 *Gurubas* who have been providing their services in Hekuli.

The voluntary nature of service delivery and easy accessibility are among the leading reasons for relying on these faith healers. They have been playing a crucial role for advising on health matters and also on change in occupation, adopting new technology, etc. People usually make a first attempt with these *Dhami/Jhakri* for their treatment. If their cure fails they still seek *'thulo jhakri'* (a noted healer). If it still does not work, then only do the patients attempt allopathic medical treatment. It could also be possible that the patient is taken to a modern health service place when the case becomes extremely bad and the health personnel become helpless for treatment. Despite this, people often have more trust in their traditional service mechanisms, the scientific validity has yet to be proved and orthodoxy become the dominant factor of the choice of faith healer practices in the rural Nepal.

School: The literacy rate in Nepal is also one of the lowest in South Asian countries. In Markhu VDC, there are six primary schools and one Lower Secondary School[14]. Among them some of the schools at Khadpukhel and Bhirkharka are not registered with the Government Education Department and running as *open schools*[15]. Some of the wards such two, seven, and nine lack even a primary school. It is estimated that the maximum distance to reach a nearest primary school is around a two-hour walk for the children of these areas. The literacy rate in Hekuli VDC is around 30%, which is lower than the average national standard of 47%. Of the total six schools, five primary and a secondary school are located in different villages of the Hekuli. Among them, one was a privately managed primary school, an English in Mirauli village. Most of the primary schools in this VDC have been established a few years' back.

In Makwanpur district 54% of boys and 33% of girls are enrolled in schools. Of the total enrolled students, 35% of boys and 60% of girls drop out before completing primary school while around 82% of boys and 86% of girls drop out before completing high school (PLAN 1998). Schools normally provides services only to those enrolled, but those who are not enrolled—the dropouts and the illiterates in society—are not covered by these schooling services in the society such as in Markhu and Hekuli.

Agriculture Extension Office: As stated earlier, agriculture is the mainstay of people in both Markhu and Hekuli. So the government has created agricultural extension offices such as agriculture and veterinary service centres in both Markhu and Hekuli (Dhakal, 2000d).

The agriculture service centre provides agricultural extension services—selection and plantation of demonstration fields, distribution of improved seeds like rice, maize, and wheat to the leader farmers (generally one farmer in each of the VDC). It also distributes vegetable seeds and fruit saplings in subsidised price, delivery of information regarding production technology, insecticides/pesticides, and fertiliser utilisation to the farmers of the command area. This office also launches special production programmes (crop and/or vegetables) in certain pockets. A Junior Technician (JT) employee related to agricultural was deputed to each of the Agriculture Service Centres in Markhu and Hekuli to deliver such services.

Similarly, a veterinary office established in both places provides treatment services, counselling, technical supports, training, distribution of fodder seeds/seedlings, creation of fodder nursery including facilitation related to animal husbandry (i.e., treatment of sick animals), and technical services. It also assists the villagers for getting high-breed of livestock such as cows, buffaloes, pigs, goats, etc. Generally the services disseminate information regarding hybrid animals, animal diseases and precaution measure, recommending the farmers for buying improved breeds, and providing treatment services to the farmers. A junior-level animal husbandry technician is deputed to deliver such services in each of Markhu and Hekuli centres.

Apart from these offices a Sajha (co-operative) in Hekuli was established in 1974 to deliver chemical fertilizer and also improved seeds (e.g. wheat, rice, vegetable, etc.) to the farmers. The co-operative works along with other agricultural extension offices in the VDC. In Markhu, the government has created a Fish Development Centre (FDC) to provide training to fish farmers and potential fish farmers as well as help in marketing.

These governmental offices—Agriculture Service Centre, Veterinary Service Centre, Sajha, Fish Development Centre—have to play crucial roles, particularly regarding agricultural production and induce new technologies in this field. However, the bureaucratic mentality of the employee, limited size of workforce, limited scale of activities, lack of innovativeness, etc. all make the delivery of services inefficient. People who had access these offices could get more benefits than the people who did not. Therefore, the poor people have little chance to get benefits.

Postal services: In both Markhu and Hekuli, Post Offices are created as part of the government postal services, which provide better opportunity for using postal service to the people. As per the governmental plan to provide telephone services in all the VDCs of the country (NPC, 1998, 586–587), rural telephone service has also been established in Hekuli and also a neighbouring VDC of Markhu. The telephone service has provided to the VDC; however, it has been in operation by a private person in an operational contact system on a commercial basis. Normally people get services whenever they require them.

Financial institutions: The government has created various institutions to provide financial and banking services to the people. Small Farmers' Development Programme (SFDP) in Markhu and Rural Development Bank (RDB) in Hekuli are among such institutions, which focus on small farmers and poor communities, particularly women. Both SFDP and RDB provide production loan only for small farmers and landless. SFDP provides maximum NPR 30,000 both individually and in group to a small farmer for which the credit taker should produce house, land, project itself, or sometimes the group as collateral. The big farmer(s) who asks for more than NPR 30,000 should contact the Agricultural Development Bank located in Palung and Bhimfedi; the Nepal Bank Ltd. (NBL) in Markhu; and the Agricultural Development Bank, Rastriya Banijya Bank or Nepal Bank Limited in Tulasipur in the case of Hekuli. These banks are located only few kilometers far from the study areas.

Normally in each village 5 to 25 members could form a group, and the loan taker should produce a recommendation from the group asking for loan from SFDP. Each member should save some amount every month. The SFDP provides credits on livestock, fisheries, food grain, and vegetable production and cottage industries on the recommendation of the group. Total number of SFDP groups in Markhu VDC was 13, with 59 members. The SFDP has invested NPR 1,151,000 in Markhu (SFDP Office Records, Bajrabarahi, Makwanpur, 1999). On the other hand, RDB provides only in group-collateral, which should be paid back in 50 instalments within a year. A group of five women could make a group to be eligible for contacting RDB and getting the loan. When the bank recognises the group, the members are provided nine days of training about saving, credit, and the role of the groups and individuals and account operation, etc. All the group members meet on a weekly basis in their respective centres for saving both the individual and group amounts, asking for credits, payment of weekly instalments, etc. Up to the study period, out of 90 members 87 have taken loans from this bank for different types of production and business activities. Compared to the 16% per annum interest charged by the SFDP, the RDB interest is higher with 20%; however, both of the banks pay only 9.5% interest for individual/group savings (RDB Office Records, 2000). Compared to the SFDP, the RDB lending process is easier. As the credit group members and the bank staff meet every week, it helps for the follow-up and monitoring. However, the bank source revealed that the people still don't have banking habits and the schemes for investments. Due to the lack of follow-up process, the SFDP was somehow failing to collect its credits. Apart from such problems the new social/political problem (Maoist problem) has created more problems for the activities of these banking services.

Non-Governmental Organisations in the Study Area

After the restoration of multi-party democratic system in Nepal in 1990, people at many villages such as Markhu and Hekuli had an opportunity to be acquainted with many new organisations. Among these organisations, PLAN International (an INGO), other NGOs like Center for Self-help Development (CSD), Community Support Association of Nepal (COSAN), Tamang Ghedung Sang, Sattswari Youth Club, Indrasarobar Club, and Indrasarobar Fishfarmers' Association (IFA) are the important ones that came into operation in Markhu VDC. Similarly, in Hekuli VDC, five NGOs such as Backward Society Education (BASE, 1991), Chandra Smriti Youth Club (1991), Social Upgrade in Progress of Education Region (SUPER, 1992), Janashiksha Social Association (1994), and Chure Mahabharat Sewa Samaj (1995) came into existence (*Source*: District Education Office, Dang, 2056; Dang DDC, 1995. Among them PLAN International in Markhu and BASE in Hekuli have been the important ones with more resources and activities[16].

Community-based Organisation

Guthis: The Nepalese rural society has developed and existed over many centuries. The system of co-operation is traditionally known as Marda and Parda. Such co-operations are based on voluntary delivery of services, which still can easily be found in rural communities. Such community-based organisations have been in operation only on the trust and understanding within the communities. Such organisations in Markhu as (see Guthi, Mahalaxmi Guthi, Tamang Ghedung, and Maruwa Guthi) all are the indigenous forms of social institutions. Normally the people exchange their help with other members of the society, who expect reciprocal help. In funerals especially, both maternal and paternal relatives contribute grains and money to perform the functions. In all the Tamang villages—Sarbang, Khadpukhel, Dalsingpakha, Sanomakhu, Chhardar, Nayagaun, and Sikarigaun—when a member of their community dies the neighbouring community, particularly the paternal and maternal relatives, help the victim's family[17]. Similarly, the Newar community of Bhirkharka, Taumat villages and Markhu Bazaar also perform such celebrations by creating such as Guthi and Mahalaxmi Guthi, which are traditional institutions that existed among them (Dhakal & Ulvila: 1999, 13). The members of the Guthi should contribute rice, maize, and money as per the requirement and decision made by the Guthi committee. The head of the Guthi is elected unanimously from the community, and they come mostly from the senior members of the community. This Guthi performs funerals and also manages festivals, local temples, mitigation of community disputes as well. Similarly, Brahmin/Chhetri of Bajrabanth also exchange such supports through the Maruwa Guthi within their communities. They have made a small trust from the members of their community. Of the total community members, two of the trusted persons have a joint bank account to operate the financial account of this Maruwa Guthi. For every funeral case they collect NPR 10 and a mana of rice (about a kilogram rice) from every house to support the victim family. Trust and respects are the basic features running such guthis.

In Hekuli, the Matam, a traditional community leader, works as an agent of the traditional social institution. The Matam co-ordinates and mobilises the local people for local development initiatives including mitigation and justice, and is the most trusted local service delivery agent. Matam, also called Aguwa or the leader, plays the leading role of the community particularly within Tharus in Hekuli. The villagers elect the Matam on an annual basis during the annual Maghi celebration. Though Matam is an individual, he works as an institution. He works on the basis of trust and understanding, and mostly co-ordinates the local communities and also works with the outsiders (individual/organisation) representing the community. Sometimes they also need to solve the problem of local conflicts. To a great extent bringing about social peace and order is also the responsibility of the Matam (see Hossain and Dhakal, op.cit.).

Forest Users' Group (FUG[18]: The forest in Nepal covers total 5,518,000 hectares, which accounts for 37% of the total land in the country (Forest Development Master Plan 1988). During the 1960s to 1980s, deforestation was quite high due to corruption at the government level land also lacking assets and choices, open access to Nepal's natural resources has provided the poor with the only feasible short-term mechanism for survival. This deforestation process affected Nepal's agriculture in a negative way, i.e., the land suffers from a chronic nutrient deficiency (Dahal and Dahal 1993, ii–iii). Therefore, during the early 1980s, the government of Nepal realised that the consumers and the communities can better conserve and manage the forests. Since then, beneficiaries have been encouraged to managing a piece of forest, which should be recognised by the concerned district Forest Office. There are over 8000 FUGs all over the country, of which 245 are in Dang district (DFO Dang Office records, 1998) and 295 in Makwanpur. In Hekuli VDC, there were nine different FUGs in operation, which were created by the local villagers. The community-managed forest comprises 270,94 hectares, from which almost all families of Hekuli have been getting benefits (see Hossain and Dhakal, 1999). Similarly, the total number of such FUGs in Markhu VDC were 21 and the area of land handed over to them for managing was around 369,47 hectares (see Dhakal & Ulvila, 1999: 10–11).

The FUGs mobilise the beneficiaries for plantation, conservation, and utilisation of the forest resources in a voluntary way because forest resource is the most important resources both for fulfilling household fuel (90%) and livestock fodder requirements in Nepal. It is also equally important for construction material for making houses and largely for balancing the ecology. Therefore the importance of forest comes as the felt need of the people. FUGs are the grass-roots level community organisations, people in both Hekuli and Markhu place high value for these institutions.

Markets and Private Services

The creation of markets plays an important role in bringing people into the market mechanism and widening the opportunities for the sale of what the people have or the purchase of what they need. Markhu and Simlang bazaars are the main administrative and business centres of Markhu. There are a few dozen shops and lodges/restaurants in the place, however, some small grocers can be found in most of the villages of Markhu VDC for the supply of consumer goods. Due to the daily public bus services to Kathmandu and Hetauda, and also other means of transportation, the people of Markhu have better access to the bigger markets. Some of the nearest local markets for vegetables, seeds/fertilisers are Taukhel, Bajrabarahi, and Bhimphedi within the adjoining VDCs.

On the other hand the people of Hekuli normally fulfil their daily consumption of goods and agricultural inputs such as fertiliser, improved seeds, pesticides, insecticides from the private shops created by local entrepreneurs within the VDC areas. Such shops in Hekuli have been created to generate non-agricultural income, to use idle labour, and also to get loans from local financial institutions. These private shops are scattered in different settlements of Hekuli such as Baibang, Padumpur, Rawat Gaun, Dandachi, Laubasta, Mirauli, Kumalgarhi, Chakhora, Hekuli, Sukadeva, Salaura. However, they can also access bigger markets such as Tulsipur Bazaar or even Ghorahi Bazaar. Privately run bus services and other means of transportation make possible easy access to other parts of the district and also to other parts of the country.

Despite the importance of a market mechanism, it often becomes difficult to apply, particularly in the case of poor people who have only unskilled labour to sell and purchase the rest of the things for their livelihoods. Rich and more informed people get more benefits from private markets and services. How to link up the poor people in the market-mechanism and benefit them has been a challenge in these areas.

NGOS AND THEIR AGENDAS FOR LIVELIHOODS: TWO CASE STUDIES

As stated earlier, Markhu VDC where PLAN International and Hekuli VDC where BASE have been working were studied to assess their activities in relation to the livelihood improvement of the beneficiaries. In this section the general description of the NGOs case and their activities are assessed.

Case Study One: PLAN International

General Background of PLAN International: PLAN International was founded as a "Foster Parents Plan for Children in Spain" in 1937. It works as an international humanitarian, child-focused development organisation without religious, political, or governmental affiliation (PLAN International, 1996: 3). Child sponsorship is the basic foundation of the organisation. PLAN International plays a mediating role between a child in need and the foster parents who would help that child. In other words PLAN tries to address the difficulties and opportunities of the children in need and also explores the generous persons to carry out this need. Though children are the entry point, PLAN implements its activities both through individual families and the communities. It has been working in more than 40 countries in the world, and has a donor base in almost 20 nations (PLAN, 1996: 1–7).

PLAN International has been working in Nepal since 1978. Up to 1992, it was confined within the Kathmandu Valley, the capital city of Nepal. PLAN started to give its concerns to other parts of the country only after 1992. It has been launching its programme activities in Bhojpur, Morang, and Sunsari of Eastern Nepal since 1992, and some other districts of Central Nepal (Makwanpur, Rautahat, and Bara) since 1995. The mid-western and far-western districts such as Banke (1994), Salyan (1995), and Bajhang (1997) have also been covered by the PLAN activities. Of these total districts, PLAN programmes from Kathmandu and Salyan have already phased out in 1998 (PLAN: 1999, 1). PLAN International Nepal supports more than 48,000 foster children and their families (*PLAN Familie*[19]) of which 9,000 children of their families are in Makwanpur (PLAN International Makwanpur, 2000: Terms of Reference, Feb 3, 2000).

Major activities carried out by PLAN International in Nepal cover five broad domains—health, learning, habitat, livelihood, and building relations (see Table 5.6).

TABLE 5.6: Domain of PLAN Activities

PLAN International, Nepal	*Health:* Preventive health measures, training health manpower, organising health camps, institutional supports *Learning:* adult literacy class (ALC), early childhood development (ECD), supports for extra school teacher, open school, school supplies, and construction and maintenance of school building *Livelihood:* skilled/vocational training, saving, seeds/sapling distribution *Habitat:* drinking water, toilet construction *Building Relations:* relation building between foster child-parents.

Source: PLAN, 1999.

Institutional Arrangement of PLAN International in Nepal:

PLAN International Nepal, as a country office, plays the key role in co-ordinating and launching PLAN activities in Nepal. It co-ordinates with PLAN International Head Office in London, and other concerned donor agencies abroad, Social Welfare Council (SWC) and other concerned governmental departments in Nepal, and its implementing district-level programme offices (see Figure 5.1). PLAN International provides general guidelines and financial supports, while SWC is mainly responsible for facilitating, co-ordinating, and monitoring of all the INGOs/NGOs such as PLAN International (also see Chapter 3). The PLAN International district office has to play important roles to implement PLAN activities in every programme districts. The district office co-ordinates the PLAN country office and the cluster offices of the concerned district. It also co-ordinates district-level line agencies and NGOs that have to work with PLAN International district office. Cluster offices are the main pillars of PLAN International at the grass-roots level. The clusters are responsible for implementing PLAN activities at the field level (see Figure 5.1). Normally, the PLAN secretariats created at country office level, district programme office level, and cluster level are responsible to plan carry out the PLAN International's activities. The country office comprises both expatriates and local employees, while district programme offices and concerned cluster offices are equipped with local employees among the technicians and generalists.

PLAN International does not implement any activity directly in the field. It implements through NGOs, local community-based organisations, local schools, health posts, women's groups, and users' groups, etc. As a process demands or requests should be submitted to the concerned cluster office from the communities through users' groups, women's groups, or other organisations. The field motivators, communication facilitators, Junior Technician of Agriculture (JTA), and other field workers of PLAN normally help to make such requests. The cluster office makes feasibility studies and forwards its recommendations to the district office. The district collects such proposals from different clusters and forwards them to the

FIGURE 5.1: Organisational Structure and the Function of PLAN International in Nepal

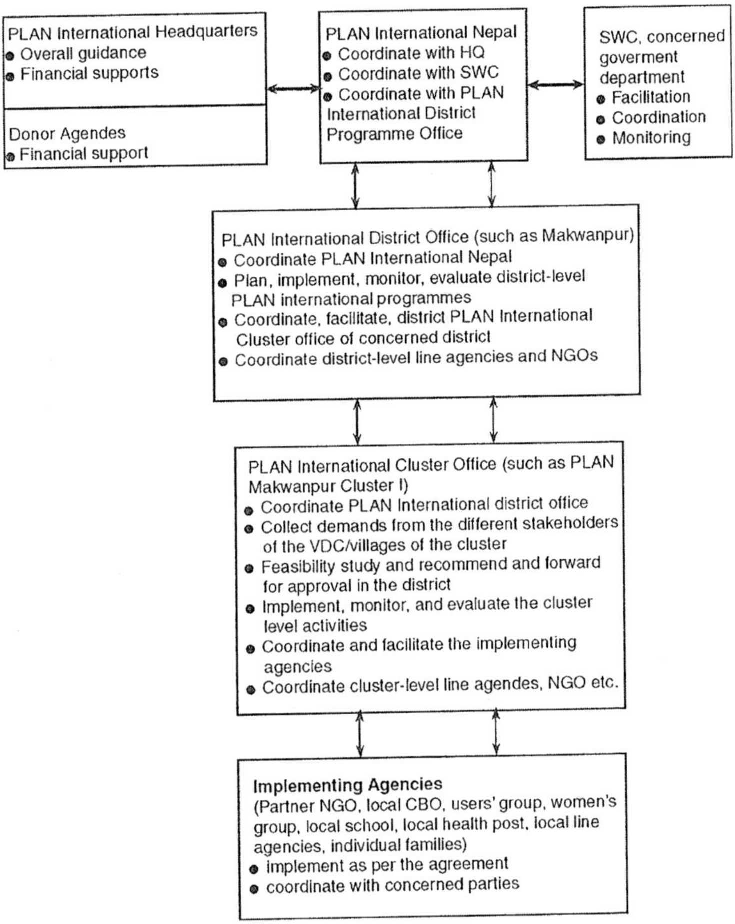

country office with its recommendations. The country office collects all such proposals and forwards them to PLAN International Headquarters and also to concerned donor agencies for funding. After getting the funding approval, the proposals come back the same route up to the cluster office for implementation. Finally, when PLAN office receives such proposals it implements the activities through NGOs, CBOs, users' groups, in some cases through governmental field units such as local health post, school management committees, Village Development Committees, and also with District Development Committee. The country office and district office also call for proposals for the operational contracts.

PLAN International in Markhu: PLAN International has been working in Makwanpur district since 1995, covering 17 VDCs of northern hill areas. These VDCs were grouped into four clusters where Markhu has placed in the Cluster[20] (PLAN International, 1999, 14–15). At the outset, PLAN International made a thorough survey in Markhu by employing different tools such as social and resource mapping, Venn diagram, seasonal analysis, flow chart, and well-being ranking to find out the livelihood situation of the people. On the basis of this information, PLAN International designed various nature of activities and implemented in its project areas (PLAN International Makwanpur, 1995). According to this survey, 325 households were identified as poor and vulnerable families who should be regarded as PLAN Families (FC family) for support (Ibid). Though the FC families can be considered as target groups of PLAN International, in some cases non-FC families can also be found included in PLAN International activities.

To implement the cluster-level activities, PLAN deputed 16 different administrative and technical personnel. They have to implement, co-ordinate, monitor, and facilitate the PLAN activities in its cluster VDCs. PLAN International implements its activities through local NGOs, schools, users' group, women's groups and sometimes the local VDC.

The nature of PLAN International activities and the institutional mechanism for implementing these activities in Markhu are given in Table 5.7.

Case Study Two: Backward Society Education (BASE)

As an NGO, BASE was created in 1991 with the vision "BASE's vision for creating an exploitation-free civil society" (BASE, 2054 B.S.: 4). This organisation has been working mainly with the Tharu community of Western Terai since its

TABLE 5.7: PLAN Activities and its Working Partners in Markhu

Nature of activities	*Name of implementing agencies*	*Target group*	*Remarks*
School repair Sports materials support Educational tour of the school students ECD classes running ALC, Chelibeti class, after school programme School teacher support	Users' group, Satteswari club Satteswari club Satteswari club Women's group COSAN, Tamang Ghedung Sang Concerned school	FC + non-FC family	For some reasons Tamang Ghedung Sang was discontinued after 1997.
Mobile clinic running Medicine support Distribution of contraceptives Health personnel Toilet construction Drinking water projects	Local HP + own staff, HP HP + own staff PLAN staff Individual household Users' group, SOUND Nepal	FC + non FC family	
Seeds/seedlings distribution, Tailoring/bamboo work training Organisation/leadership training, Famine ration distribution	PLAN staff + Women's group, Indrasarobar club PLAN staff + DDC, VDC	FC family members COSAN	
Saving/credit	CSD + Women group	FC + Non-FC	CSD was discontinued after 1998

Source: PLAN International, Cluster-I Markhu Office records.

establishment. The programmes, especially the non-formal education (NFE), started with the Tharu community soon after the establishment of BASE. Gradually the organisation expanded its activities in various programmes related to education (i.e., Kamaiya support, women development, income generating, health, and institutional development. Presently, BASE activities cover some 671 villages of 73 VDCs in six districts in Western Terai such as Dang, Banke, Bardia, Kailali, and Kanchanpur including a hilly district—Salyan (Chaudhari, 1998). Total number of membership affiliated with BASE were 137,272 of which 77,105 were male and 60,161 female (Chaudhari, 1998).

BASE is the largest NGO in Hekuli, where it has been working since 1991 (see Table 5.8). However, there were other smaller NGOs like Social of Great in Progress Education Region (SUPER) and Chure-Mahabharat Sewa Samaj, which are either non-functional or with limited activities. This study therefore focuses on the role of BASE, as it was the only NGO found managing development initiatives. Up to this year, BASE has expanded its programmes over six districts—Dang, Banke, Bardiya, Kailali, Kanchanpur and Salyan. Most of the BASE programmes have been focused on Tharu communities, however, some were for other poorer sections too. According to the BASE Program Guidelines, it has the following objectives:

- to implement different income-generating activities for backward communities;
- to mobilise the optimum level of local resources;
- to develop local indigenous technology and local skills;
- to run programmes for educating and creating health awareness;
- to organise the people for fighting for their rights;
- to involve in social mobilisation (BASE (2053B.S) (1996: 3).

Table 5.8 shows BASE's activities.

The head office and the training centre of BASE is located at Chakhoragaun in Hekuli VDC. However, all functional business runs from their programme office in Tulsipur Municipality. In Hekuli VDC there is also an area office, a hostel for rehabilitating Kamaiya children, and a health clinic of BASE, located in Rautgaun and Chakhoragaun. According to

TABLE 5.8: Functional Area of BASE Activities

Area of Activities
Education programme Organise non-formal education, arrange technical education, help for enrolling school children, run child development programmes, help for social development.
Income-generation programme Work for capital formation, conduct saving and credit program, train in animal husbandry, poultry, etc. initiate and help local handicrafts, establish village bank and co-operatives
Health programme Distribute contraceptives for family planning; arrange immunisation camps; create health awareness regarding AIDS, sanitation diseases, primary health care; manage drinking water facilities, run community clinic.
Sanitation programme Emphasise village sanitation, plantation and control of soil erosion, training to introduce community, improved stove.
Other programme Social mobilisation for anti-Kamaiya practice, social mobilisation for child labour, girls' trafficking, women empowerment, legal advocacy, etc.

Source: BASE (1996: 21–23).

the BASE official source, the BASE Village Committee with the help of BASE area office provides the following services in the Hekuli VDC:

- services in education (i.e., adult literacy and advanced classes);
- health service delivery (i.e., provides contraceptives, organises immunisation camps, create health awareness among the villagers);
- improved seeds distribution (i.e., distribute vegetable seeds);
- construction of wells for safe drinking water; and
- feeding and lodging facilities to some 15 kamaiya children.

BASE has been getting financial and technical support to run its programmes from different donor agencies and INGOs abroad such as Danida, Save the Children Federation (USA); MS-Nepal; UNDP; The Asia Foundation; PLAN International; etc. (Chaudhari, 1998). The details of donor and INGO funding is given in Annexure VIII. In a way BASE has been one of the largest NGOs for mobilising foreign resources.

Organisational structure of BASE: The General Assembly of BASE is the supreme body which forms the Central Committee. The Central Committee nominates Central Management Team, where the Project Director works as the chief executive or administrative head. Under Central Committee, there are six District Committees. Under these District Committees there are 16 Area Office[21] located in different places.

FIGURE 5.2: Membership Organisational Structure of BASE

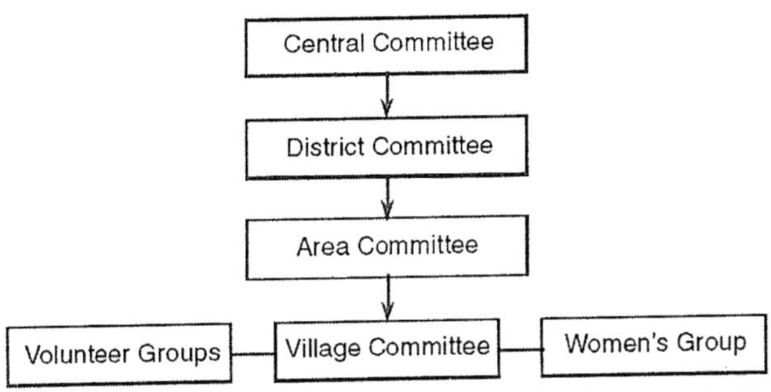

Area Offices (seven in Dang; one in Banke; two in Bardia; two in Kailali; two in Kanchanpur; and two in Salyan) work under District Committees. Village Committees are the grass-roots organisations at the village level working under the supervision of different Area Offices. In every village BASE has created different volunteer groups and also women's groups. Volunteer groups are supposed to help the village committee on different occasions as and when needed. As women can play important roles both in family and in society, BASE encourages them to form such groups. These groups should activate and motivate the women in village to participate in BASE activities.

Theoretically, BASE Village Committees collect proposal(s)

or the local people contact with the village committee for the support. The Village Committee assesses such proposals and recommends to the Area Committee. The Area Committee recommends again to the respective District Committees for decision or recommendation to the Central Committee. The Central Committee makes the final decision in favour of or against the possible projects. But in practice the Management Team is the key body, and plays the key role in designing possible projects. The project office plans, implements, co-ordinates different committees, arranges training, monitors, and supervises the operational activities. This office comprises different departments such as Education & Awareness, Health, Kamaiya Support and Advocacy, Finance and the General Administration, which are headed by different directors and the coordinators to look after the concerned activities.

BASE has created institutional arrangements for planning, programming, implementing, monitoring and evaluating its activities. The institutional framework of programme managemnt is given in Annexure D. The total number of employees working with BASE is 183 at central, district, and local offices.

BASE programmes in Hekuli: In Hekuli BASE has different activities ranging from Kamaiya advocacy, kamaiya rehabilitation, training of women's group members, mobilisation of health facilities, literacy programmes, and skill development programmes. Apart from these, BASE has trained the Village Committee and Area Committee members at institutional development activities in Hekuli (for details, see Appendix IX).

ANALYSIS OF THE LIVELIHOOD IMPROVEMENT PROGRAMME

Various forms of assets such as human capital, physical capital, financial capital, social capital and natural capital are important for a smooth livelihood of the people (Ellis, 2000; Swift, 1989; Maxwell and Smith, 1992; Reardon & Vosti, 1995; Mosher, 1998). The efforts of a single organisation or a single sector may not be enough to cater to all such assets to the needy people and improve their livelihood. NGOs as the grass-roots organisations and direct attachment with the people their roles could be crucial to uplift livelihood of the people at the grass-roots. How PLAN International in Markhu and BASE in Hekuli have been helping the targeted people and expanding their livelihood opportunities is discussed in this section.

NGOs and the Improvement of Human Capital of the People

Human capital is an important factor in poor people's lives as they can use their own labour. Consciousness-raising has been the centre of development strategy, which can help broaden their income-generating abilities for a better livelihood. The usefulness and effectiveness of human capital heavily depends on the education, training, and healthy condition of the people (Carney, 1998). The present literacy rate in Nepal is around 47% while the illiteracy rate in the rural areas of the country could be more than 70%. In this context, the programmes and the activities directed towards this endeavour could naturally be a commendable effort. However, the effectiveness and efficiency of such efforts is also equally important. In this context both Markhu and Hekuli VDCs were approached, discussed with both PLAN and BASE field level employees, and also interviewed with the target group members.

Literacy classes: The literacy and educational programmes carried out by PLAN in Markhu and BASE in Hekuli during 1998/99 are given in Table 5.9.

Both the NGOs try to deliver educational and literacy services. Both organisations place educational awareness as an important function of their organisation; however, the District Education Office in both Makwanpur and Dang and DDC office in Hekuli also have literacy classes. BASE takes it *"first sight in education"* while PLAN also focuses both on child enrolment, development of schooling system, and adult literacy classes. PLAN ran two types of classes: one, *Bal Kaksh*[22] for those below 15 years, and adult literacy classes for those who are above 16 years old. Apart from this, in Markhu, school

TABLE 5.9: PLAN International & BASE educational activities in Study area

	PLAN International (Markhu)	*BASE (Hekuli)*
Educational Activities	School repair, furniture support	Advance I class for 90 persons,
	Sports materials support annually	Basic class for 60 persons
	Educational tour of the school students	Study support for 10 girls
	ECD classes running at 6 places (120 children)	Campus student support for 5 students
	ALC & after school programme 180 persons	Development of literacy teaching learning materials in Tharu language
	School teachers' salary support for 4 teachers	Stationery and dress support to the school going 42 Kamaiya children

Source: Office records of PLAN International and BASE.

teacher support, school building repair/furniture supports, and Early Childhood Development (ECD) classes were the important ones. In connection with these services people in Markhu were found happier at least to join literacy classes and were also provided school repair, furniture supports and the supports for the salary of school teacher[23]. In connection with ECD classes, PLAN International has been providing dress and food for the children and also a salary for a teacher and her assistant. The objective of preparing the children for enrolment in the primary school and making free guardians look after them can also be taken as a positive approach.

Similarly, literacy classes were taken as the most important activity to break illiteracy, including the promotion of school enrolment and higher education supports, to the people of Hekuli. To increase enrolment, BASE also provided stationery and school dress to 42 Kamaiya children in Hekuli who have been enrolled in school. Apart from this, BASE also provided special supports to ten girls and five campus studying Tharu students.

Effectiveness of educational activities: The basic course of literacy classes in Nepal is developed by the Ministry of Education and has two parts—Basic and Advance of six months. Both NGOs adopted these courses; however, PLAN International-sponsored NGO—Community Support Association of Nepal (COSAN)—developed a course *"Navajagaran"*, and BASE has developed *"Pashchim KO Ful"* based on government developed literacy course and practical situation of the project area for the implementation. As Tharu speak their own mother tongue, teaching and learning materials of literacy classes using the Tharu language, their common dialects, cultures, etc. can be a positive step with regard to awareness building in the village setting. Apart from this an effort was also made by PLAN International in Markhu introducing Tamang language in literacy class to make more understandable and interesting in Tamang community; however, the respondents didn't find it useful due to the dialectical problems[24].

Of the total respondent[25] only 25% of adults got fair benefit from the literacy classes run under these NGOs, while 35% (36 from Markhu and 34 from Hekuli) benefited slightly from the literacy classes run by these organisations (see Table 5.10). Similarly, 20% of the total respondents were not benefited, as they could not participate due to various reasons, while 18% don't know about the literacy classes. Only 3% have developed good understanding and knowledge about literacy and can read and write, including mathematical knowledge.

The above information reveals that these organisations have attempted to bring about educational awareness; however, the quality is questionable. Therefore, the effectiveness should be assessed by both quality of service and the economy. Ghewa Tamang (name changed), one of the women's group leaders from Dalsingpakha in Markhu said *"I participated in 6 months course for two times and just know how to write my name but I cannot read and write so far I need"* (interviewed on 8 July, 1999).

More importantly, the literacy classes could not reach the ultra poor such as Kamaiya. Gram Chaudhar[26]—a Kamaiya

TABLE 5.10: Response on the benefits taken from the ALC classes

Description	*Markhu (N = 104)*	*Hekuli (N= 104)*	*Total (N=208)*
Don't know (%)	17	19	18
Not benefited (%)	19	20	20
Slight benefited (%)	36	34	35
Fairly benefited (%)	25	25	25
Highly benefited (%)	3	2	3

Source: Field Survey.

Note: Figures are rounded up.
(*don't know* = not known about the classes, *Not benefited* = known about literacy classes but not participated, *slight benefit* = have participated and learned only to sign but cannot read or write, *fairly benefited* = can read and write simple sentences, *and highly benefited* = good ability of reading and writing including simple mathematics).

living near the BASE central office expressed his views as *"Neither me nor my wife have attended the BASE literacy class. As my sons and daughters have also to support for earning daily food, they also have not enrolled school yet"* (interviewed on 20.4.2000; also see Box 5A).

However, some others who have attended the BASE literacy classes believe that such programmes gave a boost to sending their children to the school. These classes were also taken as an opportunity to deliver the message of local development, protection of forests, maintaining health and hygiene, and creating employment opportunities, etc. In the mid-1990s, the number of school enrolment was something nearly 42% were enrolled in school (boys 54% and girls 33%), which then rose to 74% (PLAN:1998, PLAN:1999). Similarly, the number of Tharu children enrolled was just 20% of the total, which grew to 65% in 1999. Girl children were also found increased in school enrolment, due to a positive drive in the educational system in this village. School enrolment during the last five years in Markhu and Hekuli is given in Table 5.11.

TABLE 5.11: Status of School Enrolment in Markhu and Hekuli

Area/Year	1995 (%)		1999 (%)	
	Boys	Girls	Boys	Girls
Markhu	54	33	82	64
Hekuli*	35	15	75	40

Source: PLAN: 1998; 1999; Interview with Purna Chaudhari and Jyoti Chaudhari.

Note: *estimated

Though the whole credit for increased enrolment could not go to PLAN International and BASE, their contributions could, of course, be taken as a positive indication. It has been found that NGOs have positive roles in the part of awareness creation of the people and also increasing enrolment in school. But the question may arise, at what cost? When analysing the cost of per class[27] it shows that the operational cost of PLAN International and BASE were more than the governmental department (see Table 5.12).

TABLE 5.12: Comparative Operational Costs of Adult Literacy Classes

Organisation	Unit Cost (NPR)	Remarks
PLAN International	22,000	Female literacy class for 16 and above age group (1–3 months basic practical issues, 40–9 months Naya Goreto I and II part) and 10–12 months Navajagaran (developed by COSAN)
BASE	11,364	Basic class for 14 and above age group (Naya Goreto, (6 months) or *Pashchim ko ful* developed by BASE (9 month).
District Education Office/HMGN	10,900	Developed by Ministry of Education/ HMGN Naya Goreto Part I & II (6 months)

Source: Concerned Office Records.

The District Education Office also provides literacy classes in Markhu and Hekuli. Similarly, the Village Development Scheme—a programme of Dang District Development

Committee—also conducted literacy classes in Hekuli. Lack of co-ordination can be explicitly seen which led to the functional overlap and uneconomic use of scarce resources in a country like Nepal. In this case, it can be said that there is more need to conduct literacy classes and the effectiveness is still a challenge in the study area.

Delivery of health services: As discussed in Section 5.4, the diseases commonly found in Markhu and Hekuli are related to both curative and preventive nature. As the government-created health alone has not been able to provide the required volume of services, other agencies such as PLAN International in Markhu and BASE in Hekuli, have also contributed to the delivery of health services, particularly egarding reproductive health. The nature of activities by these organisations is given in Table 5.13.

TABLE 5.13: PLAN International & BASE Health-related activities in Study Area

	PLAN International (Markhu)	*BASE (Hekuli)*
Health-related activities*	Mobile clinic running Medicine support for local Health Post Special support to medical treatment in hospitals Distribution of contraceptives Toilet construction Support for drinking water projects	Running community health clinic Training for 9 Traditional Birth Attendants and 1 Community Health Volunteers Support for construction of 15 wells at Rawat Gaun and Chakhora Gaun Health related orientation

Source: PLAN International Makwanur Cluster-I Office, BASE Office, Chokhara.

Note: * PLAN International has taken toilet construction and drinking water as the function of Habitat; however, in this study these items are included in health services.

PLAN delivers its health-related services mostly in co-operation with local Health Post, while BASE has created a community health clinic in Rawat Gaun to deliver its services; however, in some cases BASE was also found helping the local

Health Post to deliver health services. BASE trained Auxiliary midwives (ANM) have been delivering health services from this clinic.

The health-related supports such as distribution of contraceptives, primary health care, and organising mobile camps including dissemination of immunisation information to the villagers, and are some of the positive steps of both PLAN International and BASE. In this context, the interviewed persons were asked about the health services from these organisations. People found that they have used the immunisation information, and services from the traditional birth attendants. Sometimes they also go to other health centres for better treatment. The most important was that both PLAN International and BASE tried to train local healers and provide Traditional Birth Attendants who helped to deliver health services and also become effective as the villagers have more trust in these agents. In the words of Dhamkali Chaudhari, a resident of Hekuli Chakhaura Ward 8, *"After getting health volunteer training from BASE, and completion of literacy classes run by BASE I am delivering health-related services particularly to the women more efficiently. I bring family planning contraceptives from local Health Post and distribute particularly to the women"* (interview taken on 19.04.2000).

However, the poor section such as Kamaiya in Hekuli and also the poor people in Markhu have limited access in such services. Despite the limited scope and coverage, these health services were nevertheless helping the government's 'basic health for all' objective. Two reasons could be important, as both organisations tried to utilise locally accepted manpower such as TBA and faith healers, and also maintained good relations in connection with distribution of contraceptives and utilising their services with the local Health Post.

One major problem in these places was poor sanitation, and lack of proper health knowledge in Hekuli and improvement of household sanitation is still one of the biggest problems in the village. Awareness among the people regarding sanitation was very poor—people do not think much about sanitation and hygiene. Most of the people, more specifically the poor and illiterates, don't have a safe disposal system (toilet) or safe drinking water facilities at their homes. BASE village-level health volunteers started constructing pit latrines near their homes, which can be taken as a good starting in keeping sanitation. However, such efforts have not reached the people at large.

On the other hand, PLAN has also been supporting for construction of household/school toilets, which is a good idea of maintaining sanitation. Such supports cover the cost of construction materials such as corrugated sheets, pipe, cement, pan, and skilled labour. During the field observation, it was found that most of the PLAN families have constructed latrines from such supports besides their homes, however, only one out of eight of these constructed toilets were being used. One of the important reasons of not using these latrines was that latrine construction did not come under their felt need. They prefer to get their corrugated roofed houses rather than a good toilet. In the word of Ghewa, "*My house is thatched roof which is leaking water during the raining time. PLAN supported us toilet construction but we need corrugated sheets to roof the house.*" *(Ghewa Syandan Ward No. 2 Interviewed on Feb. 14, 2000).*

Despite most of them not using PLAN-supported toilets, they felt it had been fun to receive freely distributed toilet construction supports. In Sarbang village, some nine villagers have constructed latrines by using local materials. When PLAN International started to provide free support for constructing the latrines they demolished their locally-made latrines and waited for PLAN International's toilet support. When analysing this situation, two problems were distinctly seen. First, awareness of using latrines was lacking because construction of latrine can only be realised if it were properly utilised. People should understand the importance of using toilets. If they could understand the value of a safe disposal system, they could make their toilets by using the local materials as per their own interest. Second, the choice of costly construction materials (such as ceramic pan, cement plastered wall, corrugated sheets, etc.) could give a message for making fancy (in local context) latrine and it would be costly for repairing and maintenance, which may discourage making of latrines using local materials. It could ultimately create a problem of sustainability of the sanitation concept.

Clean water is essential for good health. Water management is poor in Dang district, particularly in villages like Hekuli. There is a problem of potable water in Hekuli. A few years back people used to fetch the water from local streams directly. The VDC has provided some public wells to the villagers. BASE also provided cement, some iron and equipment (block) for making concrete rings for the construction of wells. Altogether some 15 wells were constructed in Hekuli, which could be taken as a positive step. However, the management of the wells—cleaning, covering, repairing—is equally important. The wells were found uncovered and untidy. Apart from this, higher fertility rate and bigger family size particularly among the poor and the Tharu community are very common. The average family size in this VDC was 7.5 members against 5.7 of the national parameters. Child marriage is very common among Tharu, which contributed to the large number of children.

On the other hand, one of PLAN International's best works was supporting drinking water projects. At least four villages with 200 households got this facility from PLAN International. For this, PLAN provides all material costs and technician cost. PLAN also provides plumber training to two persons for taking care of every project. The beneficiaries have to collect NPR 1000 per tap for the repair of the drinking water system. Apart from this, they also have to manage local materials such as sand, aggregate and putting the water pipe under the surface. About the drinking water support, beneficiaries were requested to show their reaction. They showed their satisfaction and many of them liked to involve PLAN activities because they could get drinking water supports. However, some people such as Tirtha Lama—VDC chairman of Fakhel (interviewed on 9 July, 1999) showed his dissatisfaction about the cost (e.g., technician=s charge as local people contribute most of the project work).

Income-Generation Programme

Income is needed for a better livelihood. Income is one of the important indicators to measure the level of change brought by any intervention. Realising this fact, PLAN International in Markhu and BASE in Hekuli designed various activities to generate income for the beneficiaries.

The objectives set for livelihood domain of PLAN are as follows:

- ensure access to credit, agricultural services and strengthen community management and enhance social and economic capacities;
- increase capacity of targeted families and communities within PLAN working areas—to enable investment in social and economic services, which improves the quality of life of children, their families, and communities;
- to enable underprivileged families to earn sustainable incomes from their agricultural products and create opportunities for supplementary family incomes; and
- to organise skills training sessions mainly on agriculture production, including field practices and exposure visit during the training period (PLAN: 1998, 239, and PLAN: 1999, 218).

Similarly, BASE has also developed income-generation objectives from the very beginning of its establishment. The income-generating objectives were specified as capital formation, developing agricultural production through introducing improved seeds and enhancing training, encouraging establishing local handicraft industries, and developing a village banking system (BASE 1991; 1996). To achieve such objectives, PLAN International and BASE have developed the following activities in the study areas (see Table 5.14).

Distribution of improved seeds: To bring a change in the income level of the people, both PLAN and BASE decided to advance the production level of the villagers. Almost 95% of villagers were farmers and any scheme towards this direction

TABLE 5.14: PLAN International and BASE Income-Generating Activities in Study Area

	PLAN International (Markhu)	*BASE (Hekuli)*
Income-generation activities	• Distribution of seeds/ seedlings • Organising Demonstration visits • Skill-oriented training • Saving/credit schemes	Distribution of seeds/ seedlings Organising Demonstration visits Skill-oriented training Saving/credit schemes Special package to Kamaiya

Source: PLAN International, 1999; BASE office records.

could play important role. So PLAN International distributed vegetable seeds, potato seeds, maize seeds, and some pear seedlings to the PLAN families. During the field survey, some four plants of pear, plum, etc. were found planted at the farmers' kitchen-garden and reported that people got some vegetable seeds, potato seeds, maize seed, etc. in the last year. These seeds and saplings were distributed at a subsidised price (80%). Women's Group[28] requested PLAN to buy seeds. PLAN makes full payment for the seeds, but the beneficiaries have to pay just 20% of the real costs. This 20% also goes to the concerned groups' account.

Similarly, BASE also distributed improved vegetables, rice, and wheat seeds to some of the beneficiaries in Hekuli. The objective of such seed distribution was for increasing their farm production and supporting the family income. These seeds were distributed at a subsidised price. Few of the farmers found introducing some vegetable farming had irrigated land and access to markets.

To find out the respondents' response regarding the benefits from the seed/seedlings distribution scheme a question was asked, "How do you realise benefits from seed distribution scheme of PLAN International in case of Markhu and BASE in case of Hekuli?" The responses given in Table 5.15 give a disappointing picture, as only 3% of the people were highly benefited and 17% got fairly benefited from the seed/seedlings distribution schemes. The size of the slightly benefited group was only 19%, while the largest number 36% didn't realise any benefit, and 26% didn't even know about the seed distribution from these organisations.

TABLE 5.15: Response Regarding Benefit of Seed Distribution (in %)

Description	*Markhu (N= 104)*	*Hekuli (N= 104)*	*Total (N=208)*
Don't know	25	27	26
Not benefited	36	35	36
Slightly benefited	19	18	19
Fairly benefited	17	17	17
Highly benefited	3	3	3

Source: Field Survey.

Note:Figures are rounded.

(*Don't know* = not known about the seed distribution, *Not benefited* = could not realise any benefit, *Slightly benefited* = have got seeds and little bit benefit and supplement for home consumption, *Fairly benefited* = have enough for home consumption can also sell little bit, and *Highly benefited* = have enough production both for home consumption and support for cash income too).

When asked about the reasons for the ineffectiveness of the seed distribution scheme, the respondents gave the following reasons:

First, due to the lack of irrigation improved, seeds alone could not give much production. If the weather were good production could be better. If everybody's production is better, market again becomes a problem. So other vital resources such as irrigation, production procedures, markets connection were lacking in the farming programmes. Thus this scheme could not become very helpful to the people.

Second, compared to the bigger landholding groups, small landholding groups were deprived from this service as the size of their landholding is small and they mostly possess dry land (less fertile) which also make them afraid to introduce new input on their field.

Third, sometimes seeds were provided during the off-season and may not have been useful for more production.

In Markhu and Hekuli, seeds are also distributed by the governmental institutions such as Agricultural Service Centre, Veterinary Service Centre, and Co-operatives. Apart from this, some Markhu people used to buy such seeds from nearest markets such as from Palung, Bajrabarahi, Kathmandu; or the Hetauda and Hekuli people purchase from Tulsipur and Ghorahi bazaars. The problem can be seen in co-ordination between NGOs and other governmental offices, which also have been working in similar areas of activities. However, people enjoyed getting free (or nearly free) handouts from these NGOs. The market value and availability of these seeds were not that high — thus remain in the limit of the buying capacity. Local leading farmers also could provide such improved seeds. Whether the NGOs have to distribute seeds or make the people aware about the availability of seeds, production process, marketing of the outputs which were missing in the programmes of these NGOs.

Skill development training: One of the important reasons for poverty is lack of knowledge and skill for proper utilisation of available resources. Keeping this reality in mind, both PLAN International and BASE introduced skill development training schemes to enhance the productivity and employment opportunity of the people in their respective areas. PLAN has made various training packages such as tailoring, bamboo work, plumbing, veterinary, bee keeping and bee hive making to provide technical skill to the families for better income opportunities (PLAN, 1999, 282). Apart from these, PLAN also organised demonstration visits to some of the villagers. Similarly, BASE also tried to provide some skill development training from which the beneficiaries could get better employment in the farming/off-farm activities. The objective of such training was to expand the space of the working opportunities both in the agricultural and non-agricultural activities. According to the BASE field office source, three persons got Auxiliary Mid-Wives (ANM) training (ten months long), one person for CMA (ten months long) two persons for medical orientation (a week) and seven persons got agriculture/animal husbandry for five week-long training from BASE. BASE provided scholarships for ANM and CMA training participants, while other trainings were conducted by BASE itself. Apart from these, two persons got a week-long bicycle repair training, and another two got carpenter and mason training for two weeks from BASE.

Indeed skill development training even on such a small scale could be a help to the people if it helps to create some employment. In this context a question was asked the interviewees about the effectiveness of training, "Was the training component useful to the participants for enlarging their employment/income?" In Markhu, none of the training component become helpful to the people, as they could not introduce a new business or get any new employment; however, 40 women got a 3-month-long tailoring training and 9 women got 3-month-long bamboo work training and other short-term training. The reasons according to the trainees (based on the interview taken with *Urmila KC, Kanchhi Gole, Ram Maya Balami, and Fulmaya Syangdan of Markhu on 15.2.2000)* are as follows:

- duration of the training was not sufficient;
- there was not much scope for generating income;
- the participants were from among the non-damai[29] (non-traditional tailoring occupational caste);
- quality of the trainer was not much good; etc.
- Due to various reasons, organising organisations could not make the right choices to promote off-farming opportunities. Scope of work, quality of training, acceptability in the local context, saleability of outputs and other supporting aspects such as entrepreneurship development, etc. are other important aspects which were missing in the PLAN International training programme and could not be useful to generate extra employment/income of the target population.

After the completion of training of ANM and CMA, the participants were able to find job and also introduce self-employment; however, the other training participants were not able to introduce only an extra income-earning scheme. The most important was that none of the poor people like Kamaiya were provided such a training opportunity. Despite the importance of human resource development enabling the poor people for earning for their livelihood, training programmes could not contribute to off-farm employment because BASE also did not make a proper assessment of the scope of work, quality of training, and selection of appropriate candidates. In response to a question regarding the generation of off-farm employment, the respondents could not agree with the generation of extra off-farm employment from such skill development training (based on the interview with Ram Krishna Chaudhari and Ram Bahadur Chaudhari of Hekuli, interviewed on 20.4.2000).

Saving-credit scheme and mobilisation of local resources: Financial capital is the stock of money to which every person/family should have access. The saving and credit and also the saleability of other assets comprise financial capital, which is important for generating means of living. The other function regarding livelihood development was providing credits for investing in the income generating activities. Both PLAN International and BASE have encouraged women to save monthly and also to apply for credit when they require it. According to the group's decision the monthly savings was made in an average of NPR 10. Up to April 2000 the outstanding balance of saving in both Markhu and Hekuli was NPR 1,145,923, and also the outstanding credit was only NPR 469,500 (see Table 5.16).

It is curious that the size of outstanding saving is nearly three times greater than that of credit both in Markhu and Hekuli. Naturally, the formation of the saving habit is a good start, which would facilitate mobilising local resources in the productive sector. But compared to the outstanding saving balance, the credit business was not found to be of the same pace. When some of the group members were asked about this situation three problems were pointed out. First, they could not decide on the profitable use of such credit. Second, they

TABLE 5.16: Outstanding Balance of Saving-Credit in Markhu and Hekuli (in NPR)

Description	*PLAN International (Markhu)**	*BASE (Hekuli)*	*Total*
Outstanding balance (saving)	1,009,923	136,000	1,145,923
Outstanding balance (credit)	419,500	50,000	469,500
Total member	399	117	416

Source: CSD and PLAN International Office Records and also BASE Hekuli Office records.

Note: * *The amount and the members of the groups of Centre for Self-help Development (CSD) are also included as CSD was the Saving/credit operational partner of PLAN International since 1996; however, the partnership was broken after 1998. After 1998 PLAN International started to create women's groups from among the members of CSD women groups. Therefore most of the members of the women's groups become the members of both CSD and PLAN International.*

were afraid of the marketing problem. Finally, the rate of interest was high. This situation clearly shows that both PLAN International and BASE have not been considering entrepreneurship development, including the establishment of the market linkages. Though the nearest bigger markets of Markhu are Kathmandu, Hetauda and Tulsipur and Ghorahi for Hekuli, due to the lack of proper market linkages the produced goods were not sold. Without selling, it would be difficult to realise the real benefit of any venture. So the poor people could not venture into risky environments. However, PLAN held a five-day management and leadership development training especially for the women group's members. Similarly, BASE also tried to provide skill development training to a few of its beneficiaries. These situations show that the marketing component was missing in the training programme organised by both organisations though it is also one of the important elements of the income-generation cycle.

Before reaching NGOs in Markhu, there were already three financial institutions providing banking services. The interest rate of the SFDP (government credit unit based in Markhu area) was 16% while these NGOs were charging 20%–24% for their credits. Similarly, compared to BASE's interest rate (24%), Rural Development Bank's rate was quite reasonable (16%). Therefore the poor people were hesitant to utilise this loan. Due to the inability of the people's demand capacity, particularly of the poor, these governmental banks could not flow much credit to the people, though Rural Development Bank apparently can fulfill the financial need of the people. There was an absence for sharing the co-ordination between such financial institutions, which also work for the similar cause for the poor.

The BASE Village Committee in case of Hekuli and PLAN International in case of Markhu manage the saving/credit function with good faith. There was no systematic record keeping of the transaction of saving/credits. In an interview, the *Mool Samity*[30] chairperson Dev Maya Balami said about the management of such savings, "*Every month we all group members collect our savings and give to PLAN Sirs for keeping. I don't know exactly how much is the total amount of saving, however, we are collecting our money.*"

In case of misuse of such saving money or wrong project investment would create problems of accountability and responsibility. So far, the BASE Village Committee does not have any independent legal status of operating such loan business, and the legal question could create a more critical situation. Some of the members looked quite dissatisfied with this loan operation system of BASE's Village Committee. The management and institutionalisation aspect for handling such a saving/credit scheme was lacking, which raises the question of sustainability.

Special programme for Kamaiya: In relation to the special package to the Kamaiya, BASE has provided a few Kamaiyas NPR 5,000 to purchase a pair of oxen. This amount does not need to be paid back to BASE. Certainly, it was good help for those who got such financial support. If the person has a pair of bullocks and working hands, the person has more possibility for getting 'adhiya'[31] (share cropping) or could earn more from the agricultural labour. In an interview (20.4.2000) Bram

Chaudhari (name changed)—a local Kamaiya said, *"I got NPR 5.000 from BASE to purchase a pair of oxen. It makes me happy because I don't need to return. I hope it will help to get share cropping land and also more agricultural labour. I am also expecting some other help to construct my house which is in bad condition".*

But the question arises: "Is it a sustainable to help the poor like this?" Instead of developing an alternative income generating capability, the easy delivery could create dependency among the recipients and also create dissatisfaction among others who could not get such free supports. BASE was not found thinking toward other appropriate alternatives for these Kamaiyas' livelihoods. As agriculture is mostly dependent on monsoon rain, poor Tharus prefer to adopt the Kamaiya system more comfortably.

BASE has also introduced the Kamaiya children rehabilitation programme. According to this programme, children who lost their parents could get enrolled at this centre for food, lodging, and schooling opportunities. As an effort, a hostel has been constructed in Chakhora of Hekuli where 15 children from different parts of BASE's programme areas were accommodated. BASE's hostel approach of rehabilitation of these Kamaiya children is naturally commendable and a reasonable response in solving the Kamaiya problem in the area. However, the other orphans from non-Kamaiyas from the same area may feel discriminated against on one hand, and on the other hand the running cost of the hostel was totally depending on external funding. The future of such a scheme mostly depends on the permanent nature of income source, which was lacking in BASE programme. It can create a doubt for sustainability of this programme as well.

END NOTE

1. *Bari* is a dry land totally dependant upon good weather. Maize, millets, mustard seeds, and some vegetables such as climbers, radish, etc. can be produced in *bari*. The productivity and the value of *bari* is much less than *khet* (see also fn 6).
2. This lake is called Indrasarobar, and was created artificially as a reservoir for Kulekhani Hydropower project.

3. The streams are called *kholas*. Locally, some of these *kholas* are also called *Gard*. Many of these *kholas* are big during monsoon and dry in the summer in these places.
4. *Maghi* is a special day within Tharu community. They celebrate the 1st of Magh (Approximately 15th of January) as a festival of New Year.
5. *Ropani* is a scale of land measurement used in hilly parts of Nepal. Approximately 20 Ropani make a hectare.
6. *Khet* is a land used for rice plantation and has more productivity capacity than *bari*. So *khet* is considered an asset with high value. *Khet* can be all season irrigated or monsoon irrigated.
7. *Katha* is a land measurement system adopted particularly in Terai of Nepal. Altogether 20 *katha* make a *bigha*. Approximately 30 *katha* make a hectare.
8. A Kamaiya is an agricultural labourer who is mostly from among the poor Tharu families. They are used to work at a Zamindar's farm in a limited wage at least in an annual basis. Such Kamaiya system has been a common phenomenon particularly in the five districts such as Dang, Banke, Bardia, Kailali, and Kanchanpur of South/Western Nepal. These poor people even in the olden days and also at present mostly rely on working at a rich Zamindar's farm or other form of agricultural or non-agricultural labour. Due to the severe exploitation system, the poor people, particularly the Kamaiyas, have to work for their whole lifetime at Zamindar's place for their minimum survival. The government issued a Decree on 17 July, 2000 that no one could be eligible to hire a person or family as Kamaiya (for details see HMG Gadget 2000, Shrawan). In Dang district there were 1805 HHs with 12,124 Kamaiyas who have taken 40,38,000/loan (*Nepal Samachar Patra* (National Daily) (28 July, 2000). Such Kamaiyas in other districts were 30,462 in Kailali, 25,846 in Bardia, 7,945 in Kanchanpur, and 6,846 in Banke. (Junar Basnet "Kamaiya Fukuwa: Jeewan Yatra Kata" in *Yubamanch* Vol. 13, No. 03 (Shrawan) (18 Aug-17 Sep., 2000).
9. For some reason the real name of Kamaiya given in Box 5A is changed to Gram Chaudhari who is living in Hekuli near BASE Central Office. The annual salary of the Kamaiya family is calculated in Muri—a traditional measurement scale. The weight of a Muri (unmilled rice) is approximately 55 kg.
10. Zamindars are those persons who possess bigger size of land. In Terai, the Zamindari system was introduced nearly three

hundred years back. Some of the Zamindars had titles as Chaudharis who were also the moneylenders. Such Chaudharis were the local tax collectors and often worked as a local agent of the government. In Zamindari System was introduced for two reasons: first, the government used to give a big plot of land as a special 'gift' to those who could please the rulers or the local administrative agents, and second, those who could buy bigger size of land. As the Zamindars had plenty of lands, they used to hire local poor people as workers who are called Kamaiyas (see Hossain and Dhakal 1999; Backer 1998: 57-59; Odegaard, 1997).

11. The grass-roots organisations such as Gaun Panchayat at the village level, Nagar Panchayat at the town and Jilla Panchayat at the District level were created in 1963 according to the *Constitution of the Kingdom of Nepal 1962*. The names of these institutions have been changed to Village Development Committee and Municipality working at village and town respectively and District Development Committee at district level according to the *Constitution of the Kingdom of Nepal 1990* (for details see HMG/N, MoLJ, 1962; 1990).
12. The Local Election Act 1996 made a provision for a woman member from each Village and Municipality level Ward Committee and also the nomination of at least a woman and minimum of one from the minorities in Village Development Council, Municipality Council and District Development Council (see HMG/N, MoLD, 1998;1998).
13. Each person completing 75 years, widows over 60 years old, and the disabled are provided NPR 150/month as a social security support. This social security supports are distributed through VDC. Every VDC has to identify such persons and manage for distribution of social security.
14. The names of these schools are Shree Shakteswor Mahadev Primary School, Sarbang - 1; Shree Mahalaxmi Primary School, Nayagaun - 3; Shree Chandra Primary School, Sarbang - 4; Shree Khadpukhel Primary School, Khadpukhel - 5; Shree Rupadevi Primary School, Taumat - 6; Shree Balkumari Primary School, Bhirkharka - 6; and Shree Sharshoti Balbodhani Secondary School in Markhu - 8. Similarly the schools in Hekuli are: Birendra Secondary School, Hekuli – 8, Ratri Primary School, Baibang – 1, Sarsoti Primary School Padampur – 2, Laxmi Narayan Primary School, Salaura – 5, Sarsoti Primary School, Hekuli– 7, and Mirauli Enghish Boarding School, Mirauli - 4.

15. Open Schools are those which are not officially registered but where classes are runing like registered schools. They are run as branch schools of the nearest official school such as the schools of Khadpukhel, Bhirkharka are the branch of Saraswati Balbodhini Secondary School.
16. As PLAN International in Markhu and BASE in Hekuli were the major working non-governmental organisations, this dissertation made a study on the role of these two NGOs. For details also see Section 1.5 of Chapter One, and Section 5.4 of this Chapter.
17. Such help can be such as *makai* (maize) one to five *pathi* (approximately 4 to 20 kilograms), *chamal* (rice) 2 to 8 *mana* (approximately two mana of rice could be one kilogram), and money–10 Rupees from each house of his/her relatives. Still village people use Mana and Pathi as the local scale for measurement where Mana is one-eighth of part of a Pathi.
18. Forest Users' Groups (FUG) are formed from among the local villager and work on a voluntary basis. Traditionally, people living in village(s) control the local forest for the utilisation and conservation. The government abolished this practice during late 1950s and early 1960s, and all forests was nationalised and controlled by its administrative set-up. The consequence of this step led to more deforestation due to the inefficiency of governmental management system and corruption. Therefore, management of forest by the community has again restored since the early 1980s. According to the new provision the FUGs are free to protect, conserve, and utilise the forest products, however, community should be recognised by concerned governmental department—District Forest Office for building a system. Therefore, the FUGs are taken as community-based organisations in this study.
19. The family of a Foster Child is called Foster Child family or initially FC family or simply PLAN family. Normally PLAN collects funding resources from Foster Parents in the name of sponsorship to a Foster Child. It reaches the children with various programmes/activities through families and communities. Most of the PLAN programmes cover FC families only, while some activities include both PLAN families and non-PLAN families.
20. Cluster I consists 5 VDCs such as Markhu, Fakhel, Kulekhani, Sisneri and Tistung.
21. The Area Offices of BASE were 7 in Dang, one in Banke, two in

Bardia, two in Kailali, two in Kanchanpur, and two in Salyan.

22. Bal Kaksha (children class) were offered to those boys and/or girls who could not join school as regular classes. After completion of the one-year course they can join in grade four or five in the regular classes.
23. Altogether four schools such as Sakteswar Mahadev school, Khadpukhel Primary School, Balkumari Primary School, and Chandra Primary school in Markhu gots monthly salary of one teacher each from PLAN International.
24. The dialect of Tamangs differs from one place to another. Reading materials developed in Tamang language were not understandable to the Tamangs of this study area.
25. Total respondents were 208 of which 104 were from Markhu and 104 from Hekuli (also see Chapter I).
26. The name is changed for some reason and interview was taken on 20 April, 2000.
27. The average number of a literacy class is 20–25 participants.
28. In Markhu, PLAN International has created 20 women's groups comprising 399 members. From among these groups a co-operative named *Srijana Multipurpose Co-operative Association, Ltd* was registered in August 1999; however, the existing 20 groups were also found working as usual.
29. The traditional occupation of Damai caste is tailoring in Nepal. The Damais are also called Dalits, i.e., lower caste. The other caste may not have much occupational interest in tailoring.
30. PLAN International has created 20 women's groups in Markhu. From among these 20 groups a 13-member committee was created. This committee was called *Mool Samity.*
31. Adhiya is a system of equal sharing of the output of the cultivation, which is a common practice in Nepalese rural society.

6

Conclusions

The research problem was: "Are NGOs better institutional option for livelihood improvement of the people?" The purpose was to come up with the findings about the role of NGOs with regard to livelihood improvement of the people. The main emphasis was on analysing the NGOs' functions at the grass-roots and also reviewing the existing policy related to the functioning of NGOs in Nepal. The present research has reviewed poverty issues and explored how the findings can best be applied in the amelioration of livelihood both at the conceptual and practical levels. It reviews the efforts made to address poverty issues in the Nepalese context. It also presents the roles of NGOs in the planning process of the country and links their role and function to poverty eradication, legal status, management system and the problems they have been facing. In this context, this chapter summarises the main findings of the study. Livelihood issue should be seen in comprehensively and only a single sector may not able to achieve this goal.

The major parts of this section cover the NGOs as better option in the context of changing organisational landscape, bottlenecks for working through NGOs, contribution to the study and the implication of the study to different stockholders.

NGOS IN THE CHANGING ORGANISATIONAL LANDSCAPE

The volume and complexity of social problems particularly the livelihood condition of the people in developing countries such as in Nepal calls for new and effective roles of different organisations such as public, non-profit and for-profit organisations. Due to the shortfall of development efforts and bureaucratic nature of public organisations their roles in the public affairs management particularly for reaching out to the grass-roots for improving their livelihood have been criticised since the last quarter of the 20th century. The profit organisations, on the other hand, are comparatively efficient in management, however, are less sensitive to the problems of poorer section of the society because of the self-centred nature of the organisational culture. Therefore, such a situation demands an effective institutional arrangement, which should be voluntary in nature and efficient in the delivery particularly to the unreached and vulnerable section of the society. It appears that new inventions and solution of socio-economic problems result partially from institutional changes. Emergence of various social institutions has been impacted for the functioning styles and capacity of such organisation, which affected both social and individual behaviour and living condition of the people. Therefore, there is a gradual shift in the nature, scope, focus, methods and parameters and role of such organisations.

As modern NGOs are considered one of the major collective actors in the socio-economic process, their roles as development partners particularly in the Southern countries are increasingly considered as an effective vehicle for bringing social transformation, economic advancement and for furthering democratic governance. Thus, the significant emergence of the NGOs during recent years in development activities and on public agenda in developing counties can be identified as a significant political, social and economic trend. Their roles can be different according to the nature of problem to be addressed as said by Korten: *doer, mobiliser, catalyst* and *activist/educator.*

NGOs are also considered as potential alternative institutional framework for playing a catalytic role for micro-level social transformation and efficient mobiliser of local resources and effective delivery agents; however, some people consider NGOs as the agents of international corporate capital. Whatever the assumptions on the role of NGOs, the number of NGOs has expanded enormously during the last few decades.

The dramatic growth of NGOs in Nepal particularly in the last decade of the 20th century is due to the various reasons. *Firstly,* the changed international political arena and global environment and the development co-operation funding strategy of international donor agencies such as World Bank, OECD, ADB, etc., helped for opportunity to play the increased role in the socio-economic activities. *Secondly,* the democratisation of political system and economic liberalisation also contributed for proliferation of NGOs in Nepal. The liberalised legal provision related to registration, renewal and transfer of resources from the donor agencies also help for creating more and more NGOs in the country. *Thirdly,* the government has changed national development strategy and considered NGOs as development partners, which also encourages people for their participation in the national development activities through NGOs. All this provided a congenial environment for increasing both the international and national NGOs in Nepal particularly during the 1990s, however, existing literature on NGOs is still very little to know and understand. The most recent estimate indicates the number of INGOs and NGOs created in the country is as high as 100 and 25,000 respectively as against 50 INGOs and 220 national NGOs in 1990. In the study area too, not a single NGO existed before 1990. But up to the mid-1990s six NGOs in Markhu and five in Hekuli existed with diverse activities.

NGOs can play an active role in the creation of and mobilisation of assets, launch appropriate activities and create an environment to promote access to livelihood items. Due to their grass-roots attachment, direct approach, flexible and easy delivery to the needy groups/areas, they provide better services to their target group. However, there is a debate on their role in Nepal. NGOs as development partners of the government have vaguely specified in the policy documents and the lacuna of the policies regarding NGO function can be seen explicitly. It is natural that in the absence of a clear policy direction for selecting certain type of functions, target group or the area often subjected to the whim, caprices and/or simply interest of the intervening organisations such as NGOs and often direct/indirect direction of the donor organisations. Some of the important policy shortcomings for bringing NGOs to address livelihood issues in Nepal are as follows:

There is a lack of clear direction for the functions in terms of nature of works, types of target groups, geographical coverage, etc. that should be carried out through NGOs in Nepal.

Incorporation of NGOs activities in income-generation programmes in the governmental plans and programmes is also missing. The plans and programmes of the NGOs often found not on the basis of need of the people deprived from the basic needs but on the basis of available funding and interest of the concerned NGOs.

Most of the NGOs are guided by a project approach rather than a long-term approach with enhanced institutional capacity because the livelihood problem is tackled adopting both short-term and long-term approach. Hence, it is naturally difficult to solve the livelihood problem through a short-term approach.

Co-ordination is one of the missing parts of the NGO landscape. It is difficult to find out the type of NGOs based on the nature of work, capacity, know-how and geographical coverage. Though the Social Welfare Council—a governmental co-ordinating body—is responsible for co-ordinating both NGOs and INGOs, due to the lack of institutional capacity co-ordination function has become inefficient.

There is a severe lack of monitoring and evaluation of NGO activities in Nepal. Which organisation is responsible to take care of this function, i.e., which organisation—government, NGOs, donor agencies or the target beneficiaries is responsible to monitor and/or evaluate the NGO functions? Though SWC and the District Administration Office (CDO Office) are responsible for monitoring and evaluating NGO functions the monitoring and evaluation function has become weak due to lack of institutional capability.

On top of these problems, 70 per cent of the total NGOs are still concentrated in the urban places though the severity of problems is more in the rural places compared to urban areas. It indicates that the increased number of NGOs does not contribute much to improving the livelihood of the people living in poverty and other forms of vulnerability. Such situation also affects NGO dynamism in Nepal.

NGOS AND APPROPRIATENESS OF THEIR ACTIVITIES

The role of the sample NGOs particularly for meeting livelihoods of the poor people in the study area gives a mixed picture. These NGOs have been adopting a target group approach. This approach makes a clearer vision to address the problems of a certain section of society. PLAN international made a detail survey in its project areas and rank on the basis of *well-being ranking*[1]. The ranking was made on the basis of income level; household condition; landholding size; school enrolment of the children; and other assets portfolios, the poorer section of the society were selected as their target group. However, there must be at least a child for being the eligibility of a target household in the PLAN International programme area. In case of BASE target group, selection of target group was made on ethnic basis, i.e., Tharus are considered their target beneficiaries.

The selection of target beneficiary was also not without shortcomings. People felt often discriminated against in the case of not having any children even though they are also from among the low level of socio-economic backgrounds in case of the PLAN International programmes in Markhu. On the other hand, the selection criteria of target group in the BASE programmes could not include poor non-Tharus in Hekuli, which also discriminated against the other poor section of the society.

The matrix of poverty problems in Nepal particularly in the rural areas such as in Markhu and Hekuli is due to the various social and economic factors. As stated by Ellis (2000) and Chamber & Conway (1992) assets (natural, physical, human, financial and social capital), the activities, and access are important for improving livelihood of the people. Therefore, there should be a coinciding between the selection of NGO activities and need of the target beneficiaries. It depends on the availability and use of local resources, adaptability to the local environment, and for easy access for all particularly the poor and vulnerable.

Therefore, the intervening organisations with their appropriate and effective activities try to reach their target communities. The NGOs under question were found with multiple activities to address the community problems. Activities such as literacy class, skill-oriented training programmes, distribution of seeds, drinking water facilities, formation of groups, scheme of individual savings/credit are the common activities of both PLAN and BASE. Apart from these, PLAN launches special programmes to early childhood development programme to under six children while BASE has special programmes for the Kamaiyas.

Apart from these NGOs the governmental organisations in the study area and at district level have also similar type of activities, which are duplicated in the study area.

It is normal that people under livelihood problem expect some sort of help and co-operation from all kind of public, profit and non-profit organisations. As an intervening organisation PLAN in Markhu and BASE in Hekuli were also able somehow to give an impression to the people to voice and address their needs for building educational awareness, health services and other forms of social awareness. However, appropriateness of the different activities to address the poverty and accessibility of the project benefits to the most vulnerable sections was not given much care in the study areas. The skill development training such as tailoring and bamboo work in Markhu and livestock and agricultural training in Hekuli were not found much productive and beneficial to the target beneficiaries. Similarly, the construction of modern latrines using imported materials (such as ceramic pan, corrugated sheets, concrete structures) in the PLAN activities and distribution of chemical fertilisers in BASE activities were also not supporting for mobilising the locally available resources.

This situation also came as the donor agencies have a tendency to support such activities and the NGOs themselves are complacent in creativity in formulating newer programmes. NGOs often diversify activities to reach their resource collection strategy from foreign donor/agencies. The multiplicity of various activities of these NGOs represents national NGO characteristics in Nepal. It shows that NGOs are selective of activities and the target groups on the basis of their missions rather than the need of the society. In this context, it can be fairly said that NGOs should be more selective of those activities, which are feasible both for implementation and meeting the livelihood need of the community. Though the catch-all approach taken by NGOs helped them to generate more funding, it does not help to carry out all such activities in an effective way. However, these NGOs were able somehow to give an impression to the people particularly to Tharus in Hekuli and also FC families in Markhu to voice and address their needs for building educational awareness, health services and other forms of social awareness. However, appropriateness of the different activities to address the poverty and accessibility of the project benefits to the most vulnerable sections was not given much care. Hence, they lack in focus in potential area of success and more needy area of action.

IMPLICATIONS OF NGO ROLES

People naturally have great enthusiasm about the roles and function of NGOs and their relation with people to improve the livelihood status. The NGOs under study have direct contact with people and are involved in different functions through different users' groups, women's groups and other local indigenous groups for the delivery of their services. In the process of livelihood improvement of the people, the material affluence alone is not enough, they need association to work with and to use for a common good. The implication of NGO roles provides useful input to better design NGO policies and effective implementation mechanism. It also helps to assess the efficiency and effectiveness of social organisation and correct the shortcomings in the NGO functions.

Mobilisation of Resources

As NGOs have more grass-roots attachment they can better articulate local problems and motivate people for their participation. Participation can be in cash, kind and also in the form of labour. Therefore, the intervening organisation uses the participation as a strategy to involve the target beneficiaries in the project activities. Through this strategy, the intervening organisation focuses on resource mobilisation to implement their activities and meet their intended goals.

In Nepal, resource mobilisation through the NGO sector has dramatically increased during the 1990s. The total volume of resources channelled through this sector was NPR 7 million in 1990 which was increased by NPR 1,325 million in 2000. Of this total amount at least 85 per cent was channelled through foreign funding and only 15 per cent from the governmental organisations. However, there was still unaccounted volume of local resource mobilised through the NGO sector.

Apart from the external funding both PLAN and BASE have given their concern to mobilise local resources. Since local resource mobilisation helps to meet project inputs and also helps to make self-reliant, which ultimately contributes to long-term sustainability of the project. Sustainability is an important aspect of any organisational performance, which often depends on effective management, reliable source of financial resources, a good amount of public supports and a viable organisational process. People from both the study areas were found participative in the case of construction of wells in Hekuli and drinking water projects in Markhu. The value of local contribution from the supply of locally available raw materials and labour was up to 40 per cent in these projects. However, local contribution was absent in the activities such as Early Childhood Development in Markhu as such activity does not fall under the felt need of the local people.

In the case of financial resource mobilisation, both NGOs were found launching saving and credit schemes to improve the livelihood condition of the people. Most of the target groups particularly from among the women were found their involvement for saving function. During 1996–2000 total volume of net saving in Markhu was around four million rupees and NPR 160 thousand in Hekuli. Both of the NGO projects were found giving more concern to saving rather than credit. In fact, motivation plays a vital role in the saving function; however, there are more other important activities such as skills, technology, market networks and entrepreneurial capability which are critical for getting success of the credit function. Due to the absence in the effectiveness in the credit functions the stock of money collected as a saving was found unutilised both in Markhu and Hekuli which was much higher than the volume of credit.

The VDCs both in Markhu and Hekuli are also launching some of the developmental activities such as drinking water project. The cost of such projects mostly covered by mobilising local resources and also using the grants given from the central government. Similarly Rural Development Bank in Hekuli and Small Farmer Development Programme in Markhu have also been working for micro credit functions. Due to the grass-roots attachment NGOs' roles were more effective to motivate their beneficiaries for mobilising local resources but not necessarily success for implementing the resource utilisation functions. Therefore, NGOs roles can be more effective in awareness creation, which can facilitate mobilising the local resources. However, the tendency of NGOs in Nepal is found to be more active for channelling foreign resources than the mobilisation of local resources.

Gender Roles Enhanced

The study reveals that the NGOs act as change agent at the organisational landscape at the grass-roots level by organising the people, particularly women. People even among women's groups and also among different communities were organised to address their voice. In organising the unorganised people in constructive organisations NGOs in question acted as the impetus to change the organisational landscape at grassroots level. Altogether 400 women from 20 women groups in Markhu and 143 women from 11 groups in Hekuli were formed to work with the local people at the grass-roots. These groups mobilise local people particularly the women and children and the local resources. Such effort was found effective for community participation both for individual and social benefits. This effort expands spaces for more opportunities to bring the poor communities in the socio-economic functions. It also helps the people to exchange their co-operations for the gainful activities. Naturally, such group approach recognises the key role of women at the household and in society, facilitating their access to resources and thereby contributing to livelihood. This has a good effect on community participation and to voice and address women's needs. From the gender perspective, NGOs contribute to raising the general status of women; help in realising economic rights; and enhancement of new role to some extent.

Combine Effect

One of the issues often raised in different literatures and forums is about the Government–NGO relation in various aspects of socio-economic activities. The government of Nepal also realises this problem and considers NGOs as development partners for playing both complementary and supplementary roles. In both study areas, various organisations—public, private and also the non-profit organisations—have existed to carry out their programmes. As stated earlier, PLAN International and BASE have been implementing various forms of activities. Both organisations—BASE in Hekuli and PLAN in Markhu—experience show that the health delivery activities and also educational awareness activities are better co-ordinated with the existing local public health centres and also with local schools. In providing basic social services, these NGOs were found co-operating for strengthening schools, health services and other public institutions. The health-related activities and education/awareness activities run under these NGOs support for the national plan for providing basic health and education services to the concerned beneficiaries. These activities produced better performance compared with other activities such as distribution of seeds, imparting skill development training, running of saving/credit activities, which led to the duplication of resources.

As a result of increased awareness, school enrolments of children—both male and female—have gone up, participation in social and organisational activities have increased and household sanitation and health conditions have improved. This gives a notion of the better the co-ordination between Government and NGO better the performance of the NGO. It calls for a collective action among the different intervening institutions for the socio-economic transformation of local setting.

Demand-led Development Initiative

Both PLAN International and BASE programmes have been funded by foreign funding, i.e., almost all costs of PLAN International and 99.7 per cent of annual budget was covered by various international organisations including INGO and donor agencies. These NGOs have been found distributing some sort of handouts to the beneficiaries rather than prioritising on local resources mobilisation. There would be a great threat to these organisations for future programmes in the case of unavailability of foreign resources. They lack in focus in potential area of success and more needy area of action. Activities such as running of literacy class, distribution of seeds, formation of groups, scheme of individual savings/credit are duplicated by NGOs and other governmental organisations as well in the study area. This situation came about because the donor agencies have a tendency to support such activities and the NGOs themselves are complacent in creativity in formulating newer programmes. NGOs often diversify activities as their resource collection strategy. This leads to a dependency syndrome looking for only the grants and aid in the name of poor and helpless and raising question for their long-term sustainability.

As many of the target beneficiaries are deprived and unable to voice their demands, NGOs often have to define their needs, which represent their own value, interests and priorities. This situation constrained NGOs in question in creating demand-led development initiative. Therefore, there was a common tendency among poor people for seeking mercy, thus creating dependency and complaisance instead of creativity and independence both in Markhu and Hekuli.

Institutional Enhancement

The notion of 'comparative advantage' behind the NGOs' role can be expected in the case of the enhancement of their institutional capacity for translating the organisational policies and programmes into real action. This leads NGOs to become a better option for the socio-economic transformation particularly improving the livelihood of the people. Institutional capacity depends on an enhanced organisational structural, well trained and motivated human resources, a good management system which can develop effective programmes and implement them efficiently.

Both BASE and PLAN International try to address the local level problems by creating village-level committees, women groups, volunteer groups and also users' groups. BASE has a four-tier organisational structure of which the Village Committee works at the grass-roots level which also co-ordinates other volunteer groups and women groups. But PLAN International implements its activities through different working partners such as NGOs, local health posts, women groups, users' groups, etc. Theoretically, these village-level committees and groups have to plan and implement with technical/financial support of higher level committees in case of BASE and Cluster the level and also District-level PLAN International offices in the case of PLAN programmes. But in practice, the central-level Project Management Committee in case of BASE and PLAN District/Cluster office in case of PLAN International dictate the selection and implementation of their programmes.

From the present level of institutional process of the NGOs, one positive aspect has been started. Both organisations were found creating women's groups from among the local beneficiaries and involving them in local-level NGO activities. For activating them such groups have also been given a week-long phase-wise orientation training on leadership and management, which can help to sustain the local development initiatives. However, they require a few more years to institutionalise. The temporariness and short-term approach of these NGOs may not able to enhance capacity of local institution.

Stimulation of Local Initiative

Instead of articulating their behaviour in the right manner for using the available resources more aggressively for improving the livelihood in a village setting like Markhu and Hekuli the NGO programmes rather made them dependent and complaisance. However, the investment in social development in the area has created some positive attitude towards the organisation and created new expectations. The poverty problem could not be broken only with a small mercy of handouts.

The income-generating activities, on the other hand, produce fewer results for lack of holistic approach. These activities put more emphasis on distribution rather than developing human resource, entrepreneurial know-how and market. One positive indication was that people have been adopting saving habits after the introduction of NGO programmes. However, a large part of such saving remains unutilised. This indicates that NGOs have not been successful to stimulate local initiatives.

CONTRIBUTION OF THE STUDY

This study is an outcome of the research work conducted during 1998/2000 in some of the selected village communities after NGOs (such as PLAN International and BASE) have become active to implement their activities. The investment in social development in the study area has created some positive attitude towards the organisation and created new expectations. People found that NGOs like PLAN International in the case of Markhu and BASE in the case of Hekuli as new institutions to voice and address their needs. In providing basic social services in the area of literacy class, creating preventive health measures, and institutionalising social groups were some of the contributory activities of these NGOs. However, income-generating schemes of these NGOs for developing the livelihood of the people have had very limited impact. Various factors contribute to the livelihood of the people. As any single sector is hardly able to meet the expected level of livelihood of the people, it requires collaborative efforts, which not only fulfil the shortcomings of one sector but also help the effective use of different organisations working for the same cause. Hence this study provides a notion of more active and effective role and also the limitations of third sector organisations in the area of livelihood improvement of the people.

NGOs as development partners of the government have not been reflected in policy commitment. One of the reasons was that the government has not introduced specific policies to undertake development initiative through NGOs. Lack of clear direction for the functions that should be carried out through NGOs; absence of incorporation of NGOs' income-generation activities in the governmental plans and programmes; and lack of co-ordination and monitoring and evaluation of NGO activities are some of the policy shortcomings. Such situation also affects NGO dynamism in Nepal.

SUGGESTIONS FOR FURTHER STUDIES

NGOs can work to expand the welfare of the people. However, there are plenty of drawbacks. The challenge before the functioning of NGOs is how to establish its role in the broad array of organisational landscape. Should NGOs involve in all or have they special sector, and how NGOs can be institutionalised are some of the basic issues for discussion. Despite their important roles for the socio-economic upliftment of the people, NGOs have often been given some sort of impression such as "everywhere" and also "nowhere" dilemma. In the Nepalese context, the government has taken NGOs as development partners. Keeping in mind the increasing role of NGO sector further research is needed to explore effective modalities of partnership in terms of the areas, process and the volume and intensity of the functions.

In view of NGOs' growing dependency on foreign funding, a question has been raised from different quarters: "Can NGOs work without foreign funding"? On one hand, NGOs may lose their voluntarism and on the other hand, exploration of local resources may not be considered important. In this context, the other area of research could be NGOs and the scope of local resource mobilisation.

Similarly, various traditional organisations have been in operation in Nepal. Many of them have been in a critical position for their survival while the others have been running efficiently. They could have an important role in mobilising local resources such as human capital and other forms of resources. For this, further exploration is needed to find out the sustainability, dynamism and the capability of such traditional organisations which have more social value and have been working in the Nepalese local context.

CONCLUDING NOTE

NGOs have evolved in the natural course of time and space to meet the needs of the livelihood of society and country. People found these NGOs as new institutions to voice and address their needs. Therefore, government has come to accept NGOs as their helping support, to many of their developmental projects. NGOs' presence is felt to be inevitable and licensed to function according to their selective merits and self-credibility. Being non-profiteering voluntary NGOs their undoubted credibility depends on their stable self-supporting ability to maintain themselves to the required span of time till they achieve their targets. NGOs' presence is volatile as they indefinitely depend on uncertain donors.

A stable self-supporting NGO could be a part of a widely reputed large private enterprise with an interest to launch NGOs to promote selfless voluntary services. Thus, if NGOs could accomplish their formidable self-support for their own credibility, NGOs would be a perennial contribution to the well being of the people, society and nation as a whole and never be a substitution.

In the Nepalese context, NGOs can have better institutional option for the improvement of livelihood only in certain conditions. They must select only those activities, which are feasible to intervene at the grass-roots level, and can be managed easily. Such activities could be creation of awareness and development of human resources rather than distribution-oriented activities. Similarly, it also requires smooth collaboration and co-ordination among intervening organisations that are working for the same purpose to create synergy of efforts for implementing different activities successfully. NGOs should also develop their own capability for utilising local resources and implementing their programmes more effectively.

END NOTE

1. PLAN International made a detailed household survey in its project areas to decide the target group. On the basis of income, property, education and other assets, PLAN categorised into different groups and the terminology used as well-being ranking. Based on this ranking PLAN decided FC family and/ or non FC family.

Appendices

Appendix I: Questions for Beneficiaries (grass-roots level)

Re: Request letter for beneficiaries

Dear respondents,

I am Lecturer of the Central Department of Public Administration of Tribhuvan University and doing Ph.D. research. The topic of my research is *The Role of Non-governmental Organisation in the Improvement of Livelihood in Nepal.* As I understand, many of the governmental organisations, NGOs and private organisations are working in your localities. I have prepared this questionnaire to know the role of different organisations particularly NGOs in meeting livelihood of the people. In this context, I request you to participate for filling out this form as your experiences would be a valuable input to analyse and come to the conclusion. For your kind information any information given by you will be used only in the research purpose and maintained confidential.

Your cooperation in this regard will be highly appreciated.

With regards,

Tek Nath Dhakal,

Ph.D. Researcher, Central Department of Public Administration, Tribhuvan University, Kathmandu

****

Form No.................

Description about respondents

Type of house (roof)

a. thatched, b. tile/tin c. concrete

Size of land ownership

a. irrigated land ....(ha.)

b. dry land ....(ha.)

Major income source

a. own production b. animal /fish rearing

c. agriculture labour d. off farm labourer

e. weaving f. business

g. construction work h. transportation

i. employment j. if any other

Individual name (start from household chief)	Year	Relation with household chief	Sex 1. male 2. female	Education (No. of year in schooling)	Occupation 1. yes 2. no 3. not necessary	Income source, If yes, annual? 1. yes 2. no 3. not necessary	Involvement in social work. If yes, which organisation, what programme, when (year), what roles, and if any other)-
							Organisation programme year role if any
							Organisation programme year role if any
							Organisation programme year role if any
							Organisation programme year role if any

	Organisation programme year role if any
	Organisation programme year role if any
	Organisation programme year role if any
	Organisation programme year role if any

Circle the best answer from among the multiple choices

1. Does your family is benefited from the services of the following organisations?

(o) not known (1) no (2) little bit (3) fairly (4) benefited

A. Government Organisations

Primary school	-	-	0	1	2	3	4	-
Secondary school			0	1	2	3	4	
Healthpost				0	1	2	3	4
Village health worker		0	1	2	3	4		
Family planning volunteer		0	1	2	3	4		
Post office				0	1	2	3	4

B. Private organisations

Bank	-	-	-	-	0	1	2	3	4
Shops					0	1	2	3	4
Private dispensary/service		0	1	2	3	4			
Money lenders			0	1	2	3	4		
Sudeni				0	1	2	3	4	
Faith healers				0	1	2	3	4	
Traditional birth attendance	0	1	2	3	4				
Forest Users' group			0	1	2	3	4		

C. VDC

Road/foot trail construction/repair	0	1	2	3	4	-	-
Drinking water			0	1	2	3	4
Social security grant		0	1	2	3	4	
Recommendation			0	1	2	3	4
if any other...........			0	1	2	3	4

D. NGOs

Open school	-	-	-	0	1	2	3	4	-
Credit					0	1	2	3	4
Support through women group	0	1	2	3	4				
Health services			0	1	2	3	4		
Agriculture extension service	0	1	2	3	4				
ALC					0	1	2	3	4
Famine ration			0	1	2	3	4		
Drinking water			0	1	2	3	4		
Running of kindergarten school	0	1	2	3	4				
If any other				0	1	2	3	4	

i. List your needs for livelihood (up to five items)
   a. b. c. d. e.

ii. Apart from your own efforts, who else, institutions or individuals help to support your livelihood?
   a. b. c. d. e.

iii. If NGOs provide support for your livelihood, what are they doing to improve ?
   a. Enhance the intensity of traditional practices
   b. Provide new inputs in improved seeds/technology
   c. Provide skills-oriented training
   d. Market development for products
   e. Educational awareness
   f. Infrastructures
   g. Any other...

iv. How much income do you think has increased since NGOs started operating in your village? Please specify:

NPR.................monthly/annually and/or kind.................. monthly/annually

v. Are the NGO supports easily accessible to everybody in the village?

a. Elite b. Middle class c. Deprived class

vi. Do you think NGOs are bringing in negative effect(s) in society? yes/no

If yes, please specify them.

Appendix II: List of Persons interviewed

Government Officials

Aryal, Raj K., VDC Secretary and President, Indrasarobar Club, Markhu, interviewed on 15.4.2000 by Tek Nath Dhakal.

Chaudhari, Bhesh Bahadur, Rural Development Bank, Potali, Hekuli Inerviewed in Potali, on April 14, 2000 by Tek Nath Dhakal.

K.C., Krishna, Program Manager, DDC, Dang, Inerviewed in Ghorahi, on 10.4.2000 by Tek Nath Dhakal.

Sapkota Ms. Pashupati, Veterinary Service Center, Hekuli Inerviewed in Hekuli, on 13.4.2000 by Tek Nath Dhakal.

Nepal, Khemaraj, Jt. Secretary, Ministry of Local Development, inteviewed in Lalitpur on April 14, 2000 by Tek Nath.

Pokharel, Tika Prasad, Member Secretary, Social Welfare Council (SWC), Nepal. Interviewed in Kathmandu on 10.5.2000 by Tek Nath Dhakal.

Poudyal, Chandra Kanta Sharma, District Planning Adviser, Dang DDC. Ghorahi. Interviewed in Ghorahi on 8.4.2000 by Tek Nath Dhakal.

Sapkota, Saraswati, Agriculture Junior Technical Assistant, Dang, Inerviewed in Hekuli, on 114.4.2000 by Tek Nath Dhakal.

Shrestha, Ms. Urmila Secretary, MWCSW in Kathmandu on 15.05.2000 by Tek Nath.

Sriwastav, Rakesh, District Education Officer, Dang, Inerviewed in Ghorahi, on 10.4.2000 by Tek Nath Dhakal.

NGO Executives (Activists and employees)

Chaudhari, Dilli Bahadur, Founder President, BASE interviewed in Tulsipur, Dang on 10.17.1999 & 13.4.2000 by Tek Nath Dhakal.

Chaudhari, Churna Bahadur, Programme Director, Backward Education Society, Dang. Interviewed in Tulsipur, Dang on

19.5.1999 and [9.7.1999] by Tek Nath Dhakal and [Farhad Hossain].

Chaudhari, Purna Bahadur, Dang District President, Backward Education Society, Dang. Interviewed in Hekuli on 9.7.1999 by Tek Nath Dhakal and Farhad Hossain and again on 12.4.2000 in Hekuli by Tek Nath Dhakal.

Chaudhari, Jyoti, Founder President, SUPER interviewed in Hekuli, Dang on 4.11.2000 by Tek Nath Dhakal.

Chaudhari, Hallu Prasad, Education Programme Co-ordinator, Backward Education Society, Dang. Interviewed in Tulsipur, Dang on 19.5.1999 and 11.7.1999 by Tek Nath Dhakal and [Farhad Hossain].

Chaudhari, Gorakh Bahadur BASE employee, Chakhora, Hekuli Interviewed in Hekuli, on 13.4.2000 by Tek Nath Dhakal.

Gupta, Ram Narayan, District Manager, Makwanpur Inyerviewed in Hetauda, on 13.2.2000 by Marko, Ulvila and Tek Nath Dhakal.

Basnet, Bachchu Ram, Program Manager, Plan International Interviewed in Markhu, on 13.4.2000 by Marko Ulvila and Tek Nath Dhakal.

Neupane, Deepak, Livelihood Development Facilitator, Plan Makwanpu, Markhu interviewed on 13.4.2000 by Tek Nath Dhakal.

Acharya, Rajan, Plan Communication Facilitator interviewed in Markhu on 20.7.1999 by Tek Nath Dhakal and Farhad Hossain.

Basnet, Umesh, Plan Communication Facilitator in Markhu 20.7.1999 by Tek Nath Dhakal and Farhad Hossain.

Kattel, Dhanendra, Sub-branch Manager, CSD, Markhu, interviewed on 12.2.2000.

Local beneficiaries

Chaudhari, Ganga Ram (Kamaiya), Chakhaura, Hekuli Interviewed in Hekuli, on 13.4.2000 by Tek Nath Dhakal.

Chaudhari, Ram Bahadur, Field Motivator/SUPER, interviewed in Hekuli, Dang on 13.4.2000 by Tek Nath Dhakal.

Chaudhari, Ramkrishna, Local Boarding School Teacher, interviewed in Hekuli, Dang on 12.4.2000 by Tek Nath Dhakal.

Hamal, Mohan Kumari Farmr, Raut Gaun Inerviewed in Hekuli, on 13.4.2000 by Tek Nath Dhakal.

Adhikari, Salik Ram Farmer, Raut Gaun Interviewed in Hekuli, on 13.4.2000 by Tek Nath Dhakal.

Shah, A, Mirauli, Hekuli Inerviewed in Hekuli, on 14.4.2000 by Tek Nath Dhakal,

Acharya, Nimakanta Teacher, Birendra Secondary School, Hekuli interviewed in Hekuli, on 14.4.2000 by Tek Nath Dhakal,

Rana, Bhup Bahadur, Birendra Secondary School, Hekuli interviewed in Hekuli, on 14.4.2000 by Tek Nath Dhakal.

Chaudhari, Budhi Ram, Landless tenant, Chakhora, Hekuli Interviewed in Ghorahi, on 12.4.2000 by Tek Nath Dhakal.

Gole, Kanchhi, Sarbang, Markhu interviewed in Sarbang, on 24.02.2000 by Tek Nath.

Balami, Ram Maya, Taumat, Markhu Interviewed in Taumat on 24.02.2000 by Tek Nath.

Bista, Urmila, Bajrabanth, Markhu interviewed in Markhu, on 24.02.2000 by Tek Nath.

Thapa Ganga, Bajrabanth, interviewed in Markhu on 24.02.2000 by Tek Nath Dhakal.

Tamang, Fulmaya, Dalsingpakha, Markhu interviewed in Dalsingpakha, on 25.02.2000 by Tek Nath Dhakal.

Balami, Dilmaya, interviewed in Sanomakhu, on 25.02.2000 by Tek Nath Dhakal.

Waiba, Raj Man, Markhu, interviewed in Markhu on 25.02.2000 by Tek Nath Dhakal.

Appendix III : Plan-wise objectives and the resource allocation patterns

(NPR in Million)

Plan Period	*Plan Objectives*	*Expenditure*	*% in Social sector**
First (1956–1961)	To raise production and provide employment, to raise the standard of living and general well-being of all the people without any discrimination, to create simplified rules and regulations and necessary public co-operation for the success of the plan, to create economic base for the future plans and collect necessary statistics	214	13.3
Second (1962–1965)	To increase production to meet the needs of ever-increasing population and to provide the basis for future plan,	597	17.1

	to achieve economic stability, to provide additional employment opportunities, and to ensure social justice in the distribution of production		
Third (1965–1970	to improve agriculture sector, to develop basic infrastructures, to develop industrial sector, to diversify foreign trade, and to eradicate social injustice	1779	13.4
Fourth (1970–1975)	to maximise outputs, to establish the base for sustained and long-term economic growth, to expand and diversify international trade, to secure accelerated pace of development with maximum economic stability controlling price level, to make effective use of manpower resources and control population growth, and to create conditions conducive to the emergence of a society free from exploitation	3316	14.5
Fifth (1975–1980)	to make an increment in public utility services and production pattern, to make maximum utilisation of human resources, and to achieve regional balance and integration	88701	27.7
Sixth (1980–1985)	to increase production at faster rate, to increase productive employment opportunities, to meet minimum basic needs of the people such as food, firewood, drinking water, basic health services and sanitation, primary, vocational, and adult education, and minimum transport facilities	15583	25.6
Seventh (1985–1990)	to increase production at a higher rate, to increase opportunities for productive employment, and to fulfil the minimum basic needs of the people	29000	30.2

Eighth (1992–1997)	to generate faster and sustainable economic growth, to reduce regional imbalance, and to alleviate poverty	129.564,5r	33.28#
Ninth (1999–2002)	to alleviate poverty	189.580 e	33.3

Source: NPC, 1997; 1992; Sijapati,1997; Small Farmer Development Programme,1996; Paudyal, 1986).

Note: r = revised, e= estimated,
* covers only the expenses for education and health sectors
# 1996-7 price¤ 1996/7 price

Appendix IV: Long-term Projection of major Macroeconomic Indicators

SN	Indicators/ Plan period	F.Y. 1996/7	9th Plan (1997–2002)	10th Plan (2002–2007)	11th Plan (2007–2012)	12th Plan (2012–2017)
A	GDP Growth Rate (%)		6	7	7.5	8.3
	Agriculture		4	5	5	5
	Non-Agriculture		7.3	8.2	8.8	9.7
B	Contribution to DGP					
	Agriculture sector		38	34	30	25
	Non-agriculture sector		62	66	70	75
C	Investment (as a %age of DDP)		25	27	31	34
D	National saving (as a %age of GDP)		17	20	25	30
	Growth rate (per year)		8.8	10	12	12
E	Poverty and unemployment					
	People below poverty line (%age)	42	32	23	15	10
	Unemployment population (%age)	4.9	4	3.6	3.3	3
	Underemployed population (%age)	47	32	23	15	10

Source : NPC: 1998, 64 (HMG/N, Ninth Plan).

Note : FY = Fiscal Year

Post	No.	Representing	Remarks
Chairperson	1	Minister for Women, Children and Social Welfare	Ex-officio
Vice Chairman	1	Social Worker	Government Nominee
Member-Secretary	1	Social Worker	Government Nominee
Treasurer	1	Social Worker	Government Nominee
Member	1	Member, NPC (social Sector)	Representative Member
Member	1	Parliamentarian, Social Committee	Representative Member
Member	3	NGO Representative	Government Nominee
Member	4	Social worker (at least 1 female)	Government Nominee
Member	6	MoWCSW, MoH, MoLD, MoF, MoH, MoE	HMG/Ministry Representatives

Appendix V: Country-wise INGO Co-operation

S.N.	No.of INGO	Field of Cooperation	Total Amount (in US $)	%
1	20	United States of America	70,76,528	57.47
2	10	Japan	4,72,419	3.84
3	8	Canada	8,82,060	7.16
4.	8	Germany	2,98,000	2.42
5	8	United Kingdom	7,97,000	6.47
6	5	France	1,80,000	1.46
7	3	Australia	3,90,000	3.17
8	3	South Korea	9,70,000	7.88
9	3	Denmark	3,00,000	2.44
10	3	The Netherlands	1,48,000	1.20
11	3	Norway	71,000	0.58
12	3	Switzerland	3,90,000	3.17
13	2	Belgium	46,000	0.37
14	2	Italy	1,36,000	1.11
15	1	Finland	30,000	0.24
16	1	Sweden	26,000	0.21
17	1	Austria	1,00,000	0.81
Total	84		1,23,13,007	100.

Source: Calculated on the basis of SWC Office Records.

Appendix VI: Social Welfare Council Body

Source: Social Welfare Council Act 1992.

Appendix VII: Activities-wise Cooperation from the INGOs (Annual)

S.No.	*No.of INGO*	*Field of Cooperation*	*Total Amount (in US $)*	%
1	17	Community Development	19,20,060	16.10
2	11	Eye Care Service	6,34,334	5.10
3	14	Child Welfare/Orphanage	57,88,000	47.10
4	1	Women & Community Development	2,47,528	2.10
5	20	Health & Community Development	18,67,500	15.10
6	4	Disable	6,01,000	5.10
7	3	Water & Sanitation	3,86,000	3.10
8	2	Agriculture	1,90,500	2.10
9	10	Education	4,55,419	4.10
10	1	Housing	50,000	0.07
11	1	Dental Service	16,000	0.03
		Total	1,23,13,007	100

Source: SWC Office Records.

Appendix VIII: DONOR/INGOs FUNDING STATUS FOR BASE

S.N.	Name of the Donor	Funding total Grant	Duration	Exg. Rate US$1	Annual Grants	Annual Funding%	Programme	Working Area	Remarks
1	DANIDA	130,475,000	1996–2000	NPR 52,19	26,095,000	59.86%	Education Kamaiya, IGP	Kailali, Kanchanpur Salyan	from 1991
2	MS/Nepal	20,876,094,	Feb1998– Feb 2000		5,219,023	11.97%	Institutional Development	kailali, Kanchanpur Salyan	Beginning from Feb. 1997
3	TAF	1,654,440,	Jul 1997– Jul 1998		1,654,440	3.97%	Health (Family planning/clinic	Dang	Beginning from 1992
4	SCF/US	3,892,513,75	Sep 1997– Sep 1997		3,892,513,75	8.92%	IEC, Health, Ed. Agri. Eco. Opp.	Dang, Kailali	Tech. Support began 1992
5	UNDP	11,529,000,	Nov. 1997- Dec-99	NPR 63,00	5,533,920	12.69%	Socio-Eco.& Environ/Sustai	Kailali	Beginning Ju. 1997
6	PLAN International	1,195,636	May-1997 - Nov.'97		1,195,636	2.74%	Kamaiya/ Edu.	Bankey, Bardiya, Salyan	For only 6 months
	Grand Total	169,622,683,75			43,590,533,26	99.97%			

Source: BASE Office Records.

Appendix IX: BASE-Programme in Hekuli VDC (F.Y. 1999/2000)

Kamaiya and Advocacy Programme

Activities	*No. of beneficiary*	*Budget (NRP)*
Edu. support to Kamaiya children	42 Children	29,400
Stationary support		
Technical support enrolling in school		
Dress distribution		
Kamaiya Rehabilitation programme		10,000 Rs. to each Kamaiya
Kamaiya upliftment group	3 groups	no budget

Women Development and Income-generation Programme
Health-Programme
4 out reach mobile clinics
1 community health clinic
9 Traditional birth attendance
Community health volunteers
Education and awareness Programme

Activities	*No.of beneficiary (person)*	*Budget NPR*	*Remark*
Advance (3 class)	90	26,538	
Basic Class	2	22,728	
Girls education support	10	12,000	
Campus support	5	42,000	
School scholarship	3	5,400	
Support for ANM course	3	85,000	
Support for CMA course	1	35,000	
Medical orientation	2	5,000	
Workshop/Seminar	2	3,000	
Agriculture training	7 farmers	40,000	estimated data
Supervision/monitoring training to committee member	2 members	2,200	

Institutional Devt: Programme
20 Village committees (13 members in one committee)
1 area committee
Training to Village and area committee (first and second phase)

References

Acharya, Meena (1997): Non-Governmental Organisation (NGO)-Led Development Strategy in Nepal. In: Bhatachan, Krishna B. and Chaitanya Mishra (eds): *Developmental Practices in Nepal.* Kathmandu: Central Department of Sociology and Anthropology. pp. 69–99.

Acharya, Meena (2005): Nepal ko arthik vikas tatha baddo garivi. In: *Vikas* Quarterly Vol 13. Year 7. Kathmandu: Atmanirbhar Vikas Manch (SLF), Chaitra. pp. 64–73.

Acharya, Meena and Lynn Bennett (1981): *The Rural Women of Nepal: an Aggregate Analysis and Summary of 8 Village Studies.* Kathmandu: CEDA, Tribhuvan University.

Adhikari, Govinda (1999): Sankatma Pareko NGO Abhiyan. In: *Gorkhapatra* (Jan 23).

Adhikari, Shyam Prasad (1982): *Rural Development in Nepal, Problems and Prospects.* Lalitpur: Sajha Prakashan,

ADB (1999): *Background Paper for the Country Portfolio Review Mission,* (Unpublished). Kathmandu: Asian Development Bank.

ADB (1999): *Building Effective Institutions. Country Operational Strategy* Kathmandu: Asian Development Bank.

Agricultural Projects Services Centre (1995): *Nepal Agriculture Perspective Plan* (final Report). Kathmandu: National Planning Commission Secretariat. June.

Ahmad, Mokbul Morshed (2000): *Donors, NGOs, the State and Their Clients in Bangladesh.* Dhaka: Maniruddin Ahmed and Lutfun Nahar.

Al-Salem, Faisal S.A. (1977): The Ecological Dimensions of Development Administration. New Delhi: Associated Publishing House.

Alan, During (1992): *How Much Is Enough: The Consumer Society and the Future of the Earth*. New York: W.W. Norton.

Aminuzzaman, Salahuddin (1998): NGOs and the Grassroot Base Local Covernment in Bangladesh: A Study of Their Institutional Interaction. In: Farhad Hossain & Susanna, Mylllylä (eds.) (1998): *NGOs Under Challenge Dynamics and Drawbacks in Development*. Helsinki: Ministry of Foreign Affairs, Finland, 84–104.

Anheier, Helmut K., (1990): Private Voluntary Organisations and the Third World. The Case of Africa. In: Anheier, Helmut K. & Seibel, Wolfgang (eds. 1990): *The Third Sector. ComparativeStudies of Non-profit Organisations*. Berlin & New York: de Gruyter.

Anheier, Helmut K. & Wolfgang Seibel (1990): Introduction. In: Helmut K. Anheier and Wolfgang Seibel (eds.) (1990): *The Third Sector: Comparative Studies of Nonprofit Organisations*. Berlin/ New York: Walter de Gruyter.

Anheier, Helmut K. & Lester M Salamon (eds.) (1998): *The Non-profit Sector in the Developing World*. Manchester: Manchester University Press.

Arora, Ramesh Kumar (1972): *Comparative Public Administration: An Ecological Perspective*.New Delhi: Associated Publishing House. Department of Economic and Social Affairs, Development Administration: Current Approaches and Trends in Public Administration for National Development. New York: United Nations.

Barbara, Adams (1998): Neglect of Bhattarai's demands sparked "people's war". In: *http://www.info-nepal.com/p-eview/1998/05/080598/barbara.html* (5.6.2000). Quoted In: Ulvila, Marko (2000): Globalisation and the Role of Development NGOs in Political Participation in Bangladesh and Nepal (a paper presented at 3rd ISTR conference). Dublin: International Society for Third Sector Research. July 5–8.

Braibanti, Ralph (ed) (1969): Political and Administrative Development. Durham: Duke University Press Baral Jagadish R., and Koirala Kiran (1989): *Integrated Rural Development NEPAL*. New Delhi: Sterling Publishers Private Limited.

BASE-Nepal (2055 B.S.): *Backward Society Eduction Annual Report*. Dang: BASE.

BASE-Nepal (2054 B.S.): *Backward Society Eduction Annual Report*. Dang: BASE.

BASE-Nepal (2053 B.S) (1996): *Institutional Development Programme: Programme Directives 2053 B.S.* Tulsipur: BASE-Nepal.

Basnet, Tanuja (1998): *Health Program, BASE HEALTH PROGRAM –*

Annual Report (A Summary of Activities & Achievement, July 16, 1997 – July 15,1998). Dang: BASE.

Backer, Susanne (June 1998): *The Dichotomies of NGO Accountability: A Case Study of Backward Society Education (BASE) in Nepal.* Denmark: Copenhagen Business School, Department of Intercultural Communication and Management.

Bandhu, Agyat (1998): NGO haruko Antarnihit Swartha kasto Chha? (How is the implied interests of the NGOs?). In: *Jwala Weekly.* Feb 1998 (Magh 27, 2054) and Feb 1998 (Falgun 4, 2054). Kathmandu.

Bebbington, et.al, (1993): *Non-governmental Organisations and the State in Latin America.* London and New York: Routledge.

Bista, Dor Bahadur. (1990): *Fatalism and Development: Nepal's Struggle for Modernisation.* Calcutta: Orient Longman.

Bhattachan, Krishna B. (2000): "Voluntary Actions and Ethnicity in Nepal: Challenges and Limitations". In: Juha Vartola et.al. (eds.): *Development NGOs Facing the 21st Century Perspectives from South Asia.* Kathmandu: Institute for Human Development. pp. 74–80).

Bhattachan, Krishna B. (1999): "NGOs and INGOs In Nepal: Reality and Myth". In: Farhad Hossain, Marko Ulvila and Ware Newaz (eds.): *Learning NGOs and the Dynamics of Development Partnership.* Dhaka: Dhaka Ahsania Mission, pp. 269–280.

Bhattachan Krishna Bahadur (1999) Nepalma Karyarat Antarrastriya NGO ka Samasyaharu ek Charcha (in Nepali). In. *Khulla Bazzar* (fortnightly).Year 2, Vol. 4 Kathmandu, Saun 2056, pp. 21–22.

Bhattachan Krishna Bahadur (1998): "NGO & INGO in Nepal: Reality and Bhram"(in Nepali). *Vikas* (Quarterly) Vol. 7, No. 11. Kathmandu: Atmanirvar Bikas Manch.

Bista, Dor Bahadur (1994) *Fatalism and Development. Nepal's Struggle forModernization.* Calcutta: Orient Longman.

Begum, Afroza (2000): *Government-NGO Interface in Development Management Experiences of Selected Collaboration Models in Bangladesh.* Tampere: University of Tampere, Department of Administrative Science.

Booth, Charles (1903): *Life and Labour of the people in London.* London: Macmillan, Booth, David (ed.). *Rethinking Social Development. Theory, Research & Practice.* Essex: Longman. pp. 251–275.

Brabek, Anne Gordon. 1987. Development Alternatives: The Challenge for NGOs- An Overview of the Issues. *World Development* 15 (Supplement, Autumn): x–xiii)

Bratton Michael, (1989): The Politics of Government—N.G.O.

Relations in Africa. *World Development* 17 (4): 569–87).

Bratton, Michael (1988): The Politics of Government—N.G.O. Relations in Africa. *Word Development* 17 (4): 569–87.

Brett, E. (1993): Voluntary Organisations as Development Organisations: The Problem of Efficiency and Accountability. *Development and Change* 24 (2) 269–304.

Brown, I. David (1988): Organisational Barriers to NGO Strategic Action. In: *Proceedings of the ANGOC Regional Seminar on NGO Strategic Management in Asia.* Manila: ANGOC.

Brown, L. David and Korten, David C. (1991): Working More Effectively with Nongovernmental Organisations. In: Samuel Paul and Arturo Israel (eds.) (1991): *Nongovernmental Organisations and the World Bank Co-operation for Development.* Washington D.C.: World Bank. pp. 44-93.

Burkey, Stan (1993): *PEOPLE FIRST A Guide to self-reliant, Participatory Rural Development.* London: Zed Books Ltd.

Carter, Michael & R. Julian *(1997)*: *Poverty, Livelihood and Class in Rural South Africa.* Staff Paper Series No. 408. Madison: Agriculture and Applied Economics, University of Wisconsin, January. May.

CBS (1999): *Report on the Nepal Labour Force Survey 1998/99.* Kathmandu: Central Bureau of Statistics.

CBS (1997): *Nepal Living Standard Survey Vol. II.* Kathmandu: Central Bureau of Statistics.

CBS (1996): *Nepal Living Standards Survey Report 1996,* Vol. I. Kathmandu: Central Bureau of Statistics.

CBS (1993): *National Sample Census of Agriculture 1991/92.* Kathmandu: Central Bureau of Statistics.

CBS (1991): *Population Census.* Kathmandu: Central Bureau of Statistics.

CECI (1992): *The Potentials of Nepali NGOs. Vol. 1. & II.* Kathmandu: Canadian Centre for International Studies and Co-operation.

Central-level Program Implementation Committee (1999): *Bishweshwar with Poor Program Implementation Directives.* Lalitpur: Central-level Program Implementation committee.

Carney, D. (ed.). (1998): *Sustainable Rural Livelihoods: What Contribution Can We Make?* London: DFID.

Cernea, Michael (1988): *Nongovernmental Organisations and Local Development.* World Bank Discussion paper 40. Washington D.C.

Cernea, Micheel M. (1985): "Preface." In: Cernea, (ed*). Putting People First: Sociological Variables on Rural Development.* New York: Oxford University Press.

Chambers, Robert (1997): *Whose Reality Counts? Putting the First Last.* London: Intermediate Technology Publications.

Chambers, R. (1987): Sustainable Livelihood, Environment and Development: Putting Poor Rural People First. *IDS Discussion Paper.* No. 240. Brighton: IDS.

Chambers, Robert (1983): *Rural Development: Putting the Last First.* Harlow: Longman.

Chambers, R. and R. Conway (1992): Sustainable Rural Livelihoods: Practical Concepts for the 21st Century. *IDS Discussion Paper,* No. 296.

Chand, Diwakar (2000): Understanding Voluntary Action in Nepal. In: Juha Vartola *et.al.* (Eds.): *Development NGOs Facing the 21st Century Perspectives from South Asia.* Kathmandu: Institute for Human Development. pp. 65–73.

Chand, Diwakar (1999a): HMG Policy, INGOs Legal Status in Nepal, Role of SWC on INGOs and Utilisation of INGOs Aid. In: *Community Development Service Association: Social Development and INGOs Activities in Nepal 1999.* Kathmandu: Community Development Service Association.

Chand, Diwakar (1999b): *Views and Visions of Non-Governmental Organisation.* Kathmandu: ADAN.

Chand, Diwakar (1998): The Role of Civil Society in Democratisation NGO *perspective.* In: Shrestha, Anand (ed.), *The Role of Civil Society and Democratisation in Nepal.* Kathmandu: NEFAS.

Chand, Diwakar (1991): *Development through Non-Governmental Organisations in Nepal.* Kathmandu: Institute for National Development Research and Social Services (INDRASS).

Chaudhary, Churna Bahadur (1998): *BASE Nepal* (An unpublished monograph & office record). Tulsipur/Dang: Backward Society Education.

"Chintan", Gopal Siwakoti (2000): Foreign Intervention in Politics Through NGOs: A Case of the Left in Nepal. In: Juha Vartola et al. (eds.): *Development NGOs Facing the 21st Century Perspectives from South Asia.* Kathmandu: Institute for Human Development. pp. 134–143.

"Chintan", Gopal Siwakoti (1998): Gaisasa ra Yaska Bikalpahuru (NGOs and Its Alternatives). In: *Himal.* Kathmandu. Push-Magh, 2054, pp. 46–7.

Clark, John (1991): *Democratising Development: The Role of Voluntary Organisations.* Connecticut: Kumarian Press.

Clements, P. (1995): A Poverty-Oriented Cost-Benefit Approach to the Analysis of Development Projects, *World Development,* Vol.

23, No. 4, pp. 577–592.

Clements, P (1993): *An Approach to Poverty Alleviation for Large International Development Agencies*, World Development, Vol.21, No.10, pp.1633-1646

Community Development Service Association (1999): *Social Development and INGOs Activities in Nepal*. Kathmandu: Community Development Service Association.

COSAN (1997): *Final Report on Integrated community Development Program in Five VDCs of Makawanpur District (1995/96)*. Kathmandu: Community Support Association of Nepal.

CSD (1996): *Annual Progress Report 1996*. Kathmandu: Centre for Self-help Development.

Dahal, Dev Raj (1997): Role of Voluntary and Non-Profit Organisation in Local self-Governance. In: *The Journal of Development and Local Management* Vol. No. 1 May. Kathmandu: Local Development Training Academy.

Dahal, Dev Raj (1996): Emerging Development Thinking: Putting People at the Centre. In: Dahal Dev Raj and Kishor Kumar Guru-Gharana (eds) (1996): *Development Strategy For Nepal*. Kathmandu: NEFAS. pp. 1–12.

Dahal, Madan K. (1996): Outward-Oriented Economic Nationalism: A Model for Development in Nepal. In: Dahal Madan, K., Horst Mund (Eds.): *Social Economy and National Development Lessons from Nepalese Experience*. Kathmandu: Nepal Foundation for Advanced Studies (NEFAS), pp. 1–48.

Dahal, Peshal (1986): *Social Life in Nepal under the Malla*. Ph.D. Dissertation Submitted at Banaras Hindu University, India.

Dahal, Madan K & Dev Raj Dahal (Eds.) (1993): *ENVIRONMENT AND SUSTAINABLE DEVELOPMENT Issues in Nepalese Perspective*. Kathmandu: NEFAS.

Dahal, Dev Raj & Kishor Kumar Guru-gharana (eds.) (1996): *Developmnt Strategy for Nepal*. Kathmandu: NEFAS.

Dahal, Madan K. and Horst Mujnd (ed) (1996: *Social Economy and National Development Lessons from Nepalese Experience*. Kathmandu: NEFAS.

Dang, DDC (1995). *Dang District Profile. Dang: District Development Committee*. (in Nepali). Ghorahi, Dang District Development Committee.

Danida (Jan. 1995): Feasibility Study of Proposal for Danida Support. *A proposal submitted by BASE*. Kathmandu, Danida.

David I, Brown and David C. Korten 1989). *The Role of Voluntary Organisations in Development*: A concept paper prepared for the

World Bank. Boston, MA: Institute for Development Research, March 9.

Dhakal, Govind P. (2000): Foundation of an Autonomous Civil Society and the Environment of the Citizens in Nepal. In: Vartola, Juha et al. (eds.): Development NGOs Facing the 21st Century *Perspectives from South Asia*. Kathmandu: Institute for Human Development. pp. 109–120.

Dhakal, Tek Nath (2000d): Are Non-Governmental Organisations better Options for Development? Some Issues in the Nepasese Context. *A paper was presented at the annual conference Finnish Society for Administrative Studies* (Hallinnon Tutkimuksen Seura). Kuopio: University of Kuopio on 14–15 December.

Dhakal, Tek Nath (2000c): The Dynamics of Poverty Problem in Nepal. *A paper presented in an International Conference RICH and POOR Disparities, Perceptions, Consequences International and Intra-national Perspectives* (ISA-Working Group 6: Social Indicators and Social Reporting - Wissenschaftszentrum Berlin, Germany, October 13–14.

Dhakal, Tek Nath (2000b): Do NGOs Help for Livelihood Improvements? Observations from Markhu VDC in Nepal. *A paper presented in an International Seminar Making Sense of Development NGOs organised by 'NGO in Development Project. Tampere;* Department of Administrative Science, University of Tampere, August 28–29.

Dhakal, Tek Nath (2000a): Policy Perspective of NGO Operation in Nepal. In: Juha Vartola et al. (eds.): *Development NGOs Facing the 21st Century Perspectives from South Asia*. Kathmandu: Institute for Human Development, pp. 81–99.

Dhakal, Tek Nath (1999): Dynamics and Drawbacks of SWC's promotional Support to NGOs in Nepal. In: *PAAN Journal* (A Journal of Public Affairs Management), Volume: 8 & 9, Year 5. Kathmandu: Public Administration Association of Nepal, Jan/Feb, June/July, pp. 304-313, June/July.

Dhakal, Tek Nath (1997): *Government's Role for Rural Developent Enhancing Peple's Participation: A Case Study of Gongabu Village Development Committee of Kathmandu District* (A Study Report Submitted to University Grant Commission, Baneswar), Kathmandu: Tribhuvan University.

Dhakal, Tek Nath (August 1989): *Role of NGO, in Rural Development: A case of study of Save the Children Program in Takukot and Taku Majhlakuribot VDCs of Gorkha District.* A Dissertation submitted to the Department of Public Administration in partial fulfilment of Degree of Master in Public Administration, Kathmandu.

Dhakal, Tek Nath and Farhad Hossain (1999): The Fate of *Ghewa Tamang* and the Mercy of Non-governmental Organisations *The Impact & Relevance of Development Initiatives in Nepal.* Draft working document, NGOs in Development research Project, Tampere: University of Tampere.

Dhakal, Tek Nath & Marko, Ulvila (1999): *Institutional Analysis of Markhu VDC with Emphasis on Non-Governmental Organisation* (An unpublished Report on NGOs in Development Research Project Vorking Document 3), March.

Dhakal Tek Nath and Devkota Hridaya Raj (1996): *Socio-economic Impact of Rural Electrification Under PLAN International, Kathmandu Program Area.* Lalitpur: (An unpublished Report. Kathmandu: PLAN International.

District Education Office (1999): *Basic and Primary Education Programme: District Education Planning, Dang (2057-2061 B.S.).* (unofficially translated in English from Nepali). Dang: District Education Office.

Doglus, James (1987):Political Theories of Nonprofit Organisaton. In W.W. Powell (ed). *The Non-profit Sector: A Research Handbook. New Haven:* Yale University Press, p. 4354.

Drebek, Anne Gordon (1987): Development Alternatives: The Challenge for NGOs—An Overview of Issues. In: *World Development* 15, Supplement (August: ix–xv).

Drucker, P. (1990): *Managing the Non-Profit Organisation: Practices and Principles.* Harper Collins. New York: N.Y.

Drucker, P.F. (1986): *The Frontiers of Management: Where Tomorrow's Decisions are being Shaped Today.* Heinemann: London.

Edwards, M. &D. Hulme (1996): Too Close for Comfort? The Impact of Official Aid on Non-governmental Organisation. *World Development.* Vol.. 24 No. 6 pp. 961–973.

Edwards, Michael (1994): NGOs in the Age of Information *IDS Bulletin* Vol. 25, No. 2.

Ellis, Frank (2000): Rural Livelihood Diversity in Developing Countries. Oxford: Oxford University Press.

Ellis, Frank (1999): Rural Livelihood Diversity in Developing Countries: Evidence and Policy Implications. In: *ODI* (40). April.

Ellis, Frank (1998): Survey Article: Household strategies and Rural Livelihood Diversification. *The Journal of Development Studies.* Vol. 35, No. 1, pp. 1–38.

Emery, Fred E. et.al. (1978): *The Development of Organisations.* Conference Study paper prepared by the Societe International

Pour Le Development des Organisation (SIDO).

Esman, M. and N. Uphoff, (1984)(: Local Organisations: Intermediaries in rural development, Ithaca, NY: Cornell University Press.

Etzioni, A. (1973): "The Third Sector and Domestic Missions". In: PAR 33 (314–323).

Farrington, John et al. (1999). Sustainable Livelihoods in Practice: Early Applications of Concepts in Rural Areas. In: *ODI* (42), London: ODI, June, pp. 1–2.

Farrington, J. & Lewis, D.J. (eds) (1993): Introduction. In: Farrington, J. and Lewis, D.J. (eds.) (1993): *Non-Governmental Organisations and the State in Asia Rethinking Roles in Sustainable Agricultural Development*. London: Routledge.

Fisher, Julie (1993): *The Road from Rio: Sustainable Development and the Non-Government Movement in the Third World*. Westport, CT: Praeger Press.

Fowler, Alan (2000): *Striking a Balance A Guide to Enhancing the Effectiveness of Non-governmental Organisations in International Development*. London: Earthscan Publications Ltd.

Fukuyama, Francis (1995): *Trust: The Social Virtues and the Creation of Prosperity*. New York: The Free Press.

Gant, George F. (1979): *Development Administration: Concepts, Goals, Methods*. Madison, Wisconsin: The University of Wisconsin Press.

Gauder, Matt, Banjade, Janam Jay & Lowe, Lucky (1991): *Bold Action Social Eeducation*. (Report on the Problem Analysis and Planning workshop, Dang: BASE.

Ghimire, Jagadish (1999b): "NGO Development in Nepal" In: *Community Development Service Association: Social Development and INGOs Activities in Nepal*. Kathmandu: Community Development Service Association, pp. 7–8.

Ghimire, Jagadish (1999a): "Kunai Kunai Shaktishali Manchhe Ko NGO le karauday Rupaya Sharkarlai Suchana Nai Nadiee Nepal Lyairakhako Hunchha" (Interview). In *Khulla Bazzar* (fortnightly).Year 2, Vol. 4 Kathmandu, Saun 2056, pp. 35–36.

Ghimire, Jagadish (1998): Gai. Sa. Sa. Andolan: Chunauti Ra Paribartan. (in Nepali) *SMARIKA*. Kathmandu: NGO-Federation in Nepal.

Ghimire, Jagadish, Acharya, Narhari, et al: (nd.): *NGO Policy of Nepal: A Study*. Kathmandu: NGO Federation of Nepal: In: Rademacher, Anne & Tamang, Deepak (1995): *Democracy Development & NGOs:* Kathmandu: SEARCH: pp. 32–33.

Gidron, B., R. M. Kramer & L.M. Salamon (eds), (1992): *Government and the Third Sector. Emerging Relationships in Welfare States.* San Francisco: Jossey-Bass Publishers.

GTZ (1999): *Green Roads in Nepal, Best Practices Report.* Kathmandu: GTZ in Nepal, May.

Gurung, Harka (1998): *Nepal: Social Demography and Expressions.* Kathmandu: New ERA.

Gurung, Harka, 1989): *Nepal Dimensions of Development.* Kathmandu: Mrs. Saroj Gurung.

Gurung, Sant Bahadur (1998): *Rural Development Approaches in Nepal Some Experiences.* Kathmandu: DEVA Publication.

Guru-Gharana, Kishor Kumar (1992): Strategy Paper on: Poverty Alleviation and Human Development in Nepal: Macroeconomic and Sectoral Policies and Programmes. In: *Poverty Alleviation and Human Development in Nepal* (Proceedings of a National Seminar). Kathmandu: National Planning Commission, pp. 72–189.

Guru-Gharana, Kishor Kumar (1996a): Development Strategy for Nepal Perception from Below. In: Dahal, Dev Raj & Kishor Kumar Guru-Gharana (Eds.), *Development Strategy for Nepal.* Kathmandu: NEFAS.

Guru-gharana, Kishor Kumar (nd): Poverty Alleviation issues. In: *Social development in Nepal.* Kathmandu: UNAN.

Gyawali, Dipak (2000): Development Contradiction and Expectations From NGOs. In: Juha Vartola et al. (eds.): *Development NGOs Facing the 21st Century Perspectives from South Asia.* Kathmandu: Institute for Human Development. pp. 100–108.

Gyawali, Deepak (1998) Poverty Selling is Our Main Industry. In: *ViKas.* Vol 12. Year 7. Kathmandu: Atmanirbhar Vikas Manch (SLF), Poush, pp. 68–78.

Hannan, M.T. & J. Freeman (1977): *The Population Ecology of Organisations.American Journal of Sociology* 82, 929–964.

Hannan, M.T. & J. Freeman (1983): *Niche Width and the Dynamics of Organisational Populations. American Journal of Sociology* 88, 1116–1145.

Haq, Mahbub ul. (1997): *Human Development in South Asia 1997.* Dhaka: The University Press Limited.

Heady, Ferrel (1966): Public Administration: A Comparative Perspective. Englewood Cliffs: N.J: Prentice-Hall.

Heady, Ferrel & Sybil L. Stokes (eds.) 1962), Papers in Comparative Public Administration Ann Arbor: University of Michigan.

Heaphey, James P. (ed.) (1970): *Spatial Dimensions of Development*

Administration. Durham. Duke University Press.

HMG/N, MoF (2000): *Economic Survey* (Fiscal Year 1999–2000). Kathmandu: Ministry of Finance.

HMG/N, MoF (2000): *Budget Speech of the Fiscal Year 2000–2001*. Kathmandu: Ministry of Finance His Majesty's Government of Nepal.

HMG/N, MoF (1999): *Budget Speech of the Fiscal Year 1999–2000*. Kathmandu: Ministry of Finance.

HMG/N MoF (1995): *Budget Speech of the Fiscal Year 1995–96*. Kathmandu. Ministry of Finance.

HMG/N, MoLD (1999): *Introductory Book on Program/Projects under Ministry of Local Development*. Lalitpur: Ministry of Local Development.

HMG/N, MoLD (1999): *Local Self Governance Regulations 2056*. Kathmandu: Ministry of Local Development.

HMG/N, MoLD (1998): *Local Self Governance Act 2055*. Kathmandu: Ministry of Local Development.

HMG/N, MoLD (1998): Social Security Programme Implementation Directives (Updated). Kathmandu: Ministry of Local Development.

HMG/N MoLD (1992): *Village Development Act 1992*. Kathmandu. Ministry of Local Development.

HMG/N MoLD (1992): *Municipality Act 1992*. Kathmandu. Ministry of Local Development.

HMG/N MoLD (1992): *District Development Committee Act 1992*. Kathmandu. Ministry of Local Development.

HMG/N, MoLSW (1993): *Social Welfare Act 1992*. Kathmandu. Ministry of Labour and Social Welfare.

HMG/N, MoLJ (1977): *Social Service Act 1977*. Kathmandu: Ministry of Law & Justice.

HMG/N MoLJ (1993): *Natural Disaster and Relief Act 1993*. Kathmandu: Ministry of Law & Justice.

HMG/N MoLJ (1993): Handicapped Protection and Welfare Act 1993. Kathmandu: Ministry of Law & Justice.

HMG/N MoLJ (1992): *Children's Act 1992*. Kathmandu: Ministry of Law & Justice.

HMG/N, Law Books Management Board. (1991): *The Constitution of the Kingdom of Nepal, 2047 (1990)*. Kathmandu: Law Books Management Board.

HMG/N MoLJ (1962): *Nepal Adhirajya ko Sambibhan 2019*. The Constitution of the Kingdom of Nepal, 1962. Kathmandu: Ministry of Law & Justice.

HMG/N, MoLJ (1977): *Social Service Act 1977*. Kathmandu: Ministry of Law & Justice.

HMG/N, MoLJ (1963): Muluki Ain (Civil Code). Kathmandu: Ministry of Law & Justice.

HMG/N MoLJ (1962): *Nepal Adhirajya ko Sambibhan 2019* (The Constitution of the Kingdom of Nepal, 1962). Kathmandu: Ministry of Law & Justice.

HMG/N, NPC (1998): *The Ninth Plan (1997–2002)*. Kathmandu: National Planning Commission.

HMG/N, NPC: (1997): *Approach Paper of the Ninth Plan (1997–2002)*. Kathmandu: National Planning Commission,

HMG/N, NPC (1993): *The Eighth Plan (1992–1997)*. Kathmandu: National Planning Commission.

HMG/N, NPC, (1991): *Approach to the Eighth Year Plan (1992–1997)*. Kathmandu: National Planning Commission.

HMG/N, MWCSW (1999): Jagriti Women Income Generating Programme. Kathmandu: Ministry of Women, Children & Social Welfare.

Hossain, Farhad (1998): Development in Nepal: Possibilities through Non-Governmental Organisations. In: Farhad Hossain, Susanna Myllylä (eds.) *NGOs Under Challenge Dynamics and Drawbacks in Development*. Helsinki: Ministry of Foreign Affairs of Finland. Department for International Development Co-operation. pp. 105–125.

Hossain, Farhad (1998): *Administration of Development Projects by Nordic and Local Non-governmental Organisations: A Study of Their Sustainability in Sough Asian States of Bangladesh and Nepal*. A Licentiate Thesis in Administrative science submitted in University of Tampere, Department of Administrative Science.

Hossain, Farhad & Tek Nath Dhakal (1999) *Public, Private & Non-profits: Institutional Analysis of Hekuli VDC in Mid-Western Nepal*. NGOs in Development Project Working Document. Tampere, University of Tampere.

HRDC, (1995): *A review of NGOs involved in Democratisation Activities*. Kathmandu. pp. 27-33. http://www.elca.org/dcs/economiclife.html

IFAD (1999): *Nepal: Country Program Evaluation* (Unpublished), Vol. 1 & Vol. 2, Rome.

ILO (1976): Employment, Growth and Basic Needs: A One-World Problem. Geneva: ILO. *International Encyclopedia of the Social Sciences*, Social work, London, 1972.

Jain, S.C. (1981). Poverty to Prosperity in Nepal. Delhi: Development

Publishers.

James, E. (1987): "The Nonprofit Sector in Comparative Perspective. In W.W. Powell (ed.): The Nonprofit Sector: A Research Handbook. New Haven, Connecticut: Yale University Press.

Joshi, Angur Baba (1999): Social Service: A Most Potential Source of Fulfilment in Life. In: *Community Development Service Association: Social Development and INGOs Activities in Nepal.* Kathmandu: Community Development Service Association.

Karki, Arjun Kumar (1998): Relation between NGO, INGO and Foreign Donor Agency. (In Nepali). *Smarika.* Kathmandu: NGO-Federation in Nepal. Jan 5–6 1998, Kathmandu.

Kayastha, Pushpa Man (1986): *Integrated Rural Development programme.* Kathmandu: Ratna Pustak Bhandar.

K.C., Nirmala (1998): *A Study on Managerial and Performance Evaluation of Non-Governmental Organisations in Nepal* (Unpublished Thesis for Master's Degree in Public Administration). Kathmandu, Central Department of Public Administration, Tribhuvan University.

Khadka, Navin Singh (1997): "Mushrooms Called NGOs" In: *The Rising Nepal* (Nov 7, 1997). Kathmandu: *The Rising Nepal.*

Khadka, Shyam B. (1992): Overview of Poverty Alleviation Programmes. *Poverty Alleviation and Human Development in Nepal* (proceedings of a National Seminar 22–24 June 1992). Kathmandu: National Planning Commission.

Khan, M A (1997): *Poverty: concepts and Definitions.* Paper presented at the Asia Pacific Regional Launch and Workshop on the 1997 Human Development Report, 13–15 June.

Koirala, Govind, et al. (1992): Approaches to Poverty Alleviation in Nepal. In: *Poverty Alleviation and Human Development in Nepal* (Proceedings of a National Seminar 22–24 June, 1992). Kathmandu: National Planning Commission, pp. 1–52.

Korten, David C. (2000): Civil Society. (A draft presented at the International Society for Third Sector Research Dublin, Ireland –5 July, 2000.

Korten, David C. (1995): *When Corporations Rule the World.* London: Earthscan Publications Ltd.

Korten, David C. (1992) *Getting to the 2st Century.* New Delhi; Oxford and IBH Publishing Co. Pvt. Ltd.

Korten, David C. (1991): "The Role of Non-governmental Organisations in Development: Changing Patterns and Perspectives" In. Samuel Paul and Israel Arturo (eds.) (1991): *Nongovernmental Organisations and the World Bank Cooperation for Development*. Washington D.C.: World Bank pp. 20–43.

Korten David C. (1990): *Getting to the 21st Century: Voluntary Action and the Global Agenda*: Connetticut: Kumarian Press.

Korten, David C. (1987): Third Generation NGOs Strategies: A key to People-Centred Development. *World Development*.15, Autumn.

Korten, David C. (1988): "New Roles and Challenges for Asian NGOs." In: *Proceedings of the ANGOC Regional Seminar on NGO Strategic Management in Asia*. Manila: ANGOC.

Kothari, R. 1984. Party and State in Our Times: The Rise of Nonparty Political formation. *Alternatives* IX (Spring): 541–64).

Krashinsky, M. (1986) Transaction costs and a theory of the nonprofit organisation. In: S. Rose-Ackedrman (ed.): *The Economics of Nonprofit Institution*. New York: Oxford University Press.

Lama, Kanchan Verma (nd): Isues in Social Development: Social Integration Issues. In: Maskay, Bishwa Keshar (ed.) (1999): *Social Development in Nepal*. Kathmandu: Uunited Nations Association of Nepal, pp. 103–23.

Lama (ed) (1990): *NGOs in Nepal: Change and Challenge* (Proceedings of National Conference). Kathmandu: Search.

Lama, Mukta S. et al. (1992): Non-Governmental Organisations (NGOs) and Grassroots Development. In: *Administration & Management Review*. No. 6, NASC. January.

Lehmann, D. (1990): *Democracy and Development in Latin America. Economics, Politics and Religion in the Post-War Period*. Temple University Press.

Lipton, M.(1983): Poverty: Undernutrition and Hunger. *World Bank Staff Working Paper No. 597*. The World Bank.

Ludwid, Stiller F. (1989): *Integrated Rural Development Projects in Nepal: An Analysis Based on Project Evaluation Report*. Kathmandu: Canadian co-operation Office, February.

Lewis, D.J. (1993): NGO-Government Interaction in Bangladesh. In: Farrington, J. and Lewis, D.J. (eds.) *Non-Governmental Organisations and the State in Asia Rethinking Roles in Sustainable Agricultural Development*. London: Routledge.

Mahila Jagriti Program Implementation Committee (1999): *Mahila Jagriti Program Implementation Directives*. Kathmandu: Mahila Jagriti Program Implementation Committee.

Martinussen, John (1993): *Local Authorities in Nepal* (An Assessment of their Present Position and Proposals for Strengthening of Democracy at the Local Level). Kathmandu: Local Development Training Academy.

Mario Pardon (Autumn, 1987): "Non-Government Development Organisations: From Development Aid to Development Co-operation" *World Development*, Vol. 15.

Marsden, David and Peter Oakley (Eds.) (1990): *EVALUATING Social Development Projects*. (Development Guidelines No. 5). Banbury: Oxfam.

Maskay, Bishwa Keshar (1998): Non-Governmental Organisations in Development Search for a new Vision, Kathmandu: Centre for Development and Governance.

Mathur, Hari Mohan (1992): Administering People Centered Development. In: Arora, Ramesh K. (ed): *Politics and Administration in Changing Societies: Essays in Hohour of Professor Fred W. Riggs*. New Delhi: Associated Publishing House.

Maxwell, S. and M. Smith (1992): Household Food Security: A Conceptual Overview. Geneva: UNICEF.

McNulty, Stephanie (2000): The Role of NGOs in Latin America's Development: A Case Study of Peru. In: Hossain, Farhad, Marko Ulvila, Ware Newaz (eds.): *Learning NGOs and the Dynamics of Development partnership*. Dhaka: Dhaka Ahsania Mission, 247–268.

Meyer, C. (1992): A Step Back as Donors Shift Institution Building from The Public to The Private. *World Development*. Vol.. 20. No. 8. pp. 1115–1126.

Milton J. Esman and Norman Uphoff (1984): *Local Orgnaizations, Intermediaries in Rural Development* (Ithaca, New York: Rural Development committee, Cornell University.

Ministry of Foreign Affairs (1998): *Japan's Official Development Assistance*. Japan: Annual Report.

Mishra, Chaitanya (1998) "Why and How Nepalis are becoming poor?" In ViKas Quarterly Vol 12. Year 7. Kathmandu: Atmanirbhar Vikas Manch (SLF), Poush, pp. 27–37.

Montgomery, J.D. & W.L. Siffin (Eds.) (1966): *Approaches to Development: Politics, Administration and Change*. New York: McGraw-Hill.

Moris, David (1982): *Measuring the Condition of World Poor: The Physical Quality of life Index*. Delhi: Program Press.

Moshar, C.O. N. (1998) The Asset Vulnerability Framework: Reassessing Urban poverty Reduction Strategies. Worls Development, Vol. 26, No. 1, pp. 1–19.

National Planning Commission Secretariat & Ministry of Local Development (1998): Participatory Governance System in Nepal. *VIKAS (A Journal of People, Environment and Development)*.

Vol.18, National Planning Commission Secretariat, Nepal, June.

Nepal Samacharpatra, National Daily, 28 July, 2000

Nepal Samacharpatra, National Daily, 9 Aug, 2000

Nepal Samacharpatra (National Daily) (1999)

Nepal Samachar Patra (National Daily), Year 4, No. 39, 18 Feb., 1999

Nepal South Asia Centre (1998): *Nepal Human Development Report 1998*. Kathmandu: Nepal South Asia Centre.

Nepali, Gopal Singh (1965): The Newars, Bombay: United Asia Publications.

Nepali, Rohit Kumar (1999): "Role of NGOs: Follow Right Strategies" In: Nepali, Rohit Kumar (1996): *Role Model of Non-Governmental Development Organisations in Nepal*. Kathmandu: SAP-Nepal. pp. 40–6.

NGO Federation in Nepal (1991): *Proceedings of the National Level NGO Workshop*. (Kathmandu: (unpublished).

Nickson, Andrew (1992): The INGO Perception of Public Administration in Nepal. In: *Administration & Management Review*. No. 6, NASC. January.

Norman Uphoff and J. Cohen (1979?) *Feasibility and Application for Rural Development: Analysis of Asian Experience* Ithaca, New York: Rural Development committee, Cornell University.

North, Douglas (1990). *Institutes Institutional Change and Economic Performance*. New York: Cambridge University Press.

NPC HMG/N (1998): *The Ninth Plan (1997–2002)*. Kathmandu: National Planning Commission.

NPC, HMG/N (1997): *Approach Paper of the Ninth Plan (1997–2002)*. Kathmandu, National Planning Commission.

NPC, HMG/N (1992): *The Eighth Plan (1992–97)*. Kathmandu: National Planning Commission.

NPC, HMG/N (1991): *Approach Paper of the Eighth Plan (1992–1997)*. Kathmandu: National Planning Commission.

NPC, HMG/N (1986): *The Seventh Plan (1985–1990)*. Kathmandu, and National Planning Commission.

NPC, HMG/N 2044 B.S. (1987): *Aadharbhut Aabasyakta ko Paripurti ka Lagi Karyakram 2042-57 B.S* (Programme for Meeting Basic Needs 1986-2000). Kathmandu: National Planning Commission, His Majesty's Government of Nepal.

NPC, HMG/N (1977): Survey of Income, Employment and Consumption. Kathmandu, and National Planning Commission.

NRB (1988): Multipurpose Household Budget Survey. Kathmandu: Nepal Rastra Bank.

Oakley, P (1991): *Projects With People: The Practice of Participation in Rural Development.* Geneva: International Labour Office.

Oakley, Peter & Marsden, David (1990): *Approaches to Participation in Rural Development.* Geneva: International Labour Office.

Odegaard, Sigrun Eide (1998): "The BASE Movement land its Role in the Process of Democratisation and Development in Nepal". In: Farhad Hossain, Susanna Myllylä (eds.) NGOs Under Challenge *Dynamics and Drawbacks in Development.* Helsinki: Ministry of Foreign Affairs of Finland. pp. 164–76.

Odegaard, Sigrun Eide (1997): *From Caste to Ethnic Group? Modernisation and Forms of Social Identification among the Tharus of the Nepalese Tarai.* A thesis presented for Partial fulfilment of the Cand. Polit. Degree, at the Department and Museum of Anthropology, University of Oslo, July.

OECD (1989): *Sustainability in Development Programmes: A Compendium of Evaluation Experience.* Selected Issues in Aid Evaluation - 1. Paris: OECD.

OECD (1988): *Voluntary Aid for Development.* The Role of Non-Governmental Organisation, Paris: OECD.

OECD (1997): *Development Co-operation Report.* Development Assistance Committee. France: OECD.

OECD (1995). *Development Co-operation: Efforts and Policies of the Members of Development Assistance Committee. Chairman's Report.* Paris: OECD.

Oppenheimer, F.(1896): Die Siedlumgsgenossenschaft, Jena: Gustav Fisher. In: Seibel & Anheier HK(1990): Introduction. The Third Sector Comparative tudies of Nonprofit Organisations. Berlin, new York: Walter de Gruytor.

PACT (1987): *The Non-governmental Organisations Sector of Nepal.* A Study prepared by Team for USAID, Nepal, Private Agencies Collaborating Together (PACT).

Panday Devendra Raj (1999): Nepalma gaira sarkari shantghahaaru ko udaya, bikas ra halko avastha (Interview). In. *Khulla Bazzar* (fortnightly).Year 2, Vol. 4 Kathmandu, Saun 2056, pp. 10–11.

Panday, Devendra Raj 1999: *Nepal's Failed Development Reflections on the Mission and the Maladies.* Kathmandu:

Panday, Dr. Devendra Raj (1998): The more we got foreign assistance the more we become poor. In *ViKas Quarterly.* Vol 12. Year 7. Kathmandu: Atmanirbhar Vikas Manch, Poush, pp. 52–63.

Pandey, Nirmal Prasad (1999): NGO/INGO le kun rupma sahayog gariraheka chhanbhanekurako sahi Aakalan huna sakeko chhaina (Interview in Nepali). In. *Khulla Bazzar* (fortnightly).Year 2, Vol. 4 Kathmandu, Saun, pp. 8–9.

Pandey, Dr. Shushil Raj (2000b): Exploring Civil Society in Nepali Context: Are We Casually Donning Another Hat? In: *The Telegraph* (Weekly), Kathmandu, 01 November.

Pandey, D.R. and Shrestha, I (1985) *Non-Governmental Institutions and Process of Development in Nepal.* Kathmandu: Integrated Development Systems Pardon, M., (19987: Non Governmental Organisation: From Development Aid to Development Cooperation. *World Development,* 15, Supplement.

Paropakar (1997): *PAROPAKAR History of Service and Movement* (in Nepali). Kathmandu: Paropakar.

Paudel, Sharad (2055): Budol Garibi Bhelaka Garibharu. In: *Vikas Quarterly.* Vol 13. Year 7. Kathmandu: Atmanirbhar Vikas Manch, Chaitra. pp. 74–87)

Paul, Samuel (1991): Nongovernmental Organisations and the World Bank: An Overview. In: Paul: Samuel & Arturo Israel (Eds.) (1991): Nongovernmental Organisations and the World Bank *Co-operation for Development.* Washington D.C.: World Bank. pp. 1–19.

Paul, Samuel & Arturo Israel (Eds.) (1991): *Non-governmental Organisations and the World Bank Co-operation for Development.* Washington D. C.: The World Bank.

PLAN International (1999): *Annual Program Communication 1999.* Kathmandu: PLAN International.

PLAN International (1998): *Annual Program Communication 1998.* Kathmandu: PLAN International.

PLAN International (1996): *Worldwide Annual Report 1996.* Surrey: PLAN International.

PLAN International (1995): *PRA Based Village Profile of Markhu VDC.* Makwanpur: PLAN International.

Platteau, J.P. (1991): Traditional Systems of Social Security and Hunger Insurance: Past Achievements ad Modern Challenges. In: Ahmad et al., *Social Security in Developing Counties.* Oxford: Clarendon Press, pp. 112–170.

Pokharel, Tika Prasad (2000): NGOs and Their Functioning in Nepal. In: Juha Vartola *et.al.* (Eds.): *Development NGOs Facing the 21st Century Perspectives from South Asia.* Kathmandu: Institute for Human Development. pp. 55–64

Poudyal, Madhav P (1984): *Aspects of Public Administration in Nepal.* New Delhi: National Book Organisation.

Preuss, Hans Joachim (1998): The Challenges Facing NGOs. In: *The Rising Nepal* Feb 14, 1998. Kathmandu.

Pradhan, Bharat B.(1985): *Integrated Rural Development Projects in Nepal: A Review.* ICIMOD Occasional Paper No. 2. Kathmandu: ICIMOD, December.

PACT (1987): *The Non-governmental Organisations Sector of Nepal: A Study.* Kathmandu: Prepared by Private Agencies Collaborating Together Team for USAID.

Putnam, Robert D. (1993): The Prosperous Community: Social Capital and Public Affairs. *The American prospect 13 (Spring).* pp. 35–42.

Putnam, Robert (1993). *Making Democracy Work.* Princeton: Princeton University Press.

Pyakuryal, Bishwambhar & Dipendra Purush Dhakal (2000): *Foreign Aid: Challenges and Prospects* (Some Issues for Future Policy Consideration), A Report prepared for His Majesty's Government of Nepal, Ministry of Finance. Kathmandu.

Rademacher Anne (1995): Democracy Development & NGOs in Nepal. In. Rademacher, Anne Deepak Tamang. *Democracy Development & NGOs.* Kathmandu: SEARCH.

Ramana, D.V. (1977) *A Glossary of Some Terms used in Development and Planning.* Bangkok: UN Asian Development Institute.

Rastriyabhasa Niti Sujhav Ayog (RNSA) (1994): *Rastriyabhasa Niti Sujhav Ayog Prativedan.* (Report of the Advisory commission on Policy towards the National Languages). Kathmandu.

Salmen, Lawrence F. and A. Paige Eaves (1991): Interactions between Nongovernmental Organisations, Governments, and the World Bank: Evidence from Bank projects. In: Samuel Paul and Arturoo Israel (eds)) (1991): *Nongovernmental Organisations and the World Bank Co-operation for Development.* Washington D.C.: World Bank, pp. 94–133.

Regmi, Mahesh C., (1978), *Readings in Nepali Economic History.* Varanasi: Kishor Vidya Niketan.

Reardon, T. and S.A. Vosti (1995): Links Between Rural Poverty and the Environments in Developing Countries: Asset Categories and Investment Poverty, *World Development,* Vol. 23, No. 9, pp. 1495–1506.

Reichard C. (1988): Der Dritte Sektor. EnstchenFunktion und Problematik von 'Norprodit' - Organisation aus veraltungswissenschaftlicher Sicht'. Die Offentliche Verwaltung 41, 363–370.

Rein, M. /1971): "Problems in the Definition and Measurement of Poverty", In Townsend (1971): *The Concept of Poverty.* London: Heinemann.

Riddell, et al. (1995): Developing Country NGOs and Donor Governments. Reports to the Overseas Development Administration. London: Overseas Development Institute.

Riddell, R., and Robinson, M. (1995). *Non-governmental Organisations and Rural Poverty Alleviation*. Oxford: Clarendon Press.

Riggs, Fred W. (1964): Administration in Developing Countries: The theory of Prismatic Society. Boston: Houghton Mifflin.

Riggs, Fred W. (ed.) (1970): Frontiers of Development Administration, Durham: Duke University Press.

Riker, James V. 1991: Contending Perspectives for Interpreting Government NGO - Relations in South and South East Asia: Constrains, Challenges, and the Search for Common Ground in Rural Development. Background paper prepared for the APDC Regional Dialogue GO-NGO relations in Asia: Prospects and challenges for improving the Policy Environment for people centred Development: March 11–15, 1991. Chiengmai, Thailand, Malaysia: APDC.

Robinson, M. (1993): "Governance, Democracy and conditionality: NGOs and the New Policy Agenda." In: Clayton, A (ed.): *Governance Democracy and Conditionality: What Role for NGOs?* Oxford: INTRAC.

Robinson, M (1991). Evaluating The Impact of NGOs In Rural Poverty Alleviation. India Country Study. *Working Paper* 49. London: Overseas Development Institute.

Rose-Ackerman, Susan, (ed.) (1880): *The Economics of Non-profit Institutions: Studies in Structure and Policy*. Yale Studies on Nonprofit Organisation. New York: Oxford University Press.

Rowntree. S. (1901): *Poverty: A Study of Town Life*. London: Macmillan.

Salamon, Lester M. (1994). The Rise of the Non-profit Sector. In: Salamon, Lester M &, Helmut K. Anheier (1996): *The Emerging Non-profit Sector. An Overview. Manchester: Manchester University Press.*

Salamon, Lester M. and Helmut K. Anheier (1998): Social Origins of Civil Society: Explaining the Nonprofit Sector Cross-Nationally. In: *Voluntas: International Journal of Voluntary and Nonprofit Organisations*. 9 (3). New York and London: Plenum Press, September. pp. 213–248.

Salamon, Lester M &, Helmut K. Anheier (1996): In Search of the Non-profit Sector: The Question of Definition. *Voluntas*, 3, 2: 125–153.

Salamon. L.M. (1987): "Partners in Public Service: The Scope and Theory of government-non-profit relations." In: W. W. Powell (ed): *The Nonprofit Sector: A Research Handbook*, New Haven, Connecticut: Yale University Press, pp. 99–117.

Salmen, Lawrence F. and A. Paige Eaves (1991): Interactions between Nongovernmental Organisations, Governments, and the World Bank: Evidence from Bank projects. In: Paul, Samuel and Arturo Israeli (eds)) (1991): *Nongovernmental Organisations and the World Bank Co-operation for Development*. Washington D.C.: World Bank, pp. 94–133.

SAP-Nepal (1988): *Strengthening Nepalese Non-governmental Organisations: HRD Needs Assessment*. Kathmandu: SAP Nepal, July.

Scoones, I., (1998): *Sustainable Rural Livelihoods: A Framework for Analysis. IDS Working Paper*, No. 72.

Schumacher E.F. (19973): *Small is Beautiful*. New York: Harper and Row.

Seddon, David (1995): *Nepal—A State of Poverty*. New Delhi: Vikas Publishing House Pvt. Ltd.

Seddon, D. (1987): *Nepal—A State of Poverty*. New Delhi: Vikas Publishing House Pvt. Ltd.

Seibel, Wolfgang and Helmut K. Anheier (1990): Sociological and Political Science Approaches to the Third Sector. In: Anheier Helmut K., Wolfgang Seibel (Eds.): *The Third Sector Comparative studies of Non-profit Organisations*. Berlin, New York: Walter de Gruyter, pp. 7–20.

Sen, A (1981): *Poverty and Famines: An Essay on Entitlement and Deprivation*, New Delhi: Oxford: Oxford University Press.

Shah, Indra Bikram et al. (1986): *Social Service in Nepal: A Historical Perspective*. Kathmandu: Social Service National Co-ordination Council.

Shah, Vijaya (1999): *Role of INGOs for Resource Mobilisation in Nepal*. (A Thesis presented for Central Department of Public Administration, Faculty of Management, Tribhuvan University), Kathmandu.

Sharma, Sharad (1999): Nepalma Gairasarkari Sansthaharuko nalibeli. In: The *Gorkhapatra* (National Daily) (Ashoj, 7).

Siistiänen, Martti (2000): Social Capital, Power and the Third Sector. In: Martti, Kinnunen, Petri & Hietanen, Elina (eds.): The Third Sector in Finland *Review to Reassert of the Finnish Third Sector*. Helsinki: The Finnish Federation for Social Welfare and Health & University of Lapland. 2000.

Sijapati, Keshav Singh (1997): *Fundamentals of Nepalese Rural Economy*. Kathmandu: Ratna Pustak Bhandar.

Small Farmer Development Program (1996): *Small Farmer Development Program: Two Decades of Crusade Against Poverty*. Volume I. Kathmandu: Small Farmer Development Program.

Smillie, I. & H. Helmich (Des). (1993): *Non-Governmental Organisations and Governments: Stakeholders for Development*. Paris: OECD.

South Asia Partnership—Nepal (1996): *The Role of Non-Governmental Development Organisations in Sustainable Development* (Report of the National Workshop Jan. 31 to Feb. 2, 1996) Kathmandu, Nepal, December 1996.

Srinivasan, T.N. (1977): Poverty: Some Measurement Problems. In: *Conference Proceedings, 41st Seminar of the International Statistical Institute,* held at New Delhi.

Streeten, Paul (1979): *Constructive Features of a Basic Needs Approach to Development*. Mimeographed. Washington, DC: World Bank.

Streeten, P et al. (1981): *First things First: Meeting Basic Needs in Developing Countries,* Oxford University Press, Oxford.

Subedi, Chandra (1998): Sarkari Tatha Gairasarkari Sanstha Haruko Antarsambandha Ra Kanooni Prabadhan. (in Nepali). *SMARIKA*. Kathmndu: NGO-Federation in Nepal, January 5–6.

Subedi, Hem Raj: (1984): Special Feature of Guthi Samsthan Act 2041. (in Nepali) *Dharma Darsan*. Kathmandu.

Sukhatme, P.V. (1977): *Nutrition and Poverty*. New Delhi: Indian Agricultural Research Institute.

Sharma, S. K. (ed.)(1978): *Dynamics of Development: An International Perspective* (two Vols). Delhi: Concept Publishing House.

Swerdlow, Irving (1975): *The Public Administration of Economic Development*. New York: Praeger Publishers.

Swerdlow, Irving (ed.) 1963): *Development Administration: Concepts and Problems*. Syracus, N.Y.: Syracus University Press.

SWC (2000): *List of Non-Governmental Organisations Affiliated with Social Welfare Council. (Volume II)*. Kathmandu: Social Welfare Council.

SWC (1999): *List of Non-governmental Organisations Affiliated with Social Welfare Council*. (Volume - 1). Kathmandu: Social Welfare Council.

SWC (1998): *SWC News*. August-September 1998. Kathmandu: SWC.

SWC (1998): *Samajik Sewa Samachar*. Jestha-Ashar 2055: Kathmandu: SWC.

SWC (1998): *Samajik Sewa Samachar*. Kartik 2055: Kathmandu: SWC.

SWC (1997): *Samajik Sewa Samachar*. Shrawan-Aswin, 2054: Kathmandu: SWC.

Swift, J. (1998): *Factors Influencing the Dynamics of Livelihood Diversification and Rural Non-Farm Employment in Space and Time*, Rural Non-farm Employment Project, Chatham, UK: Natural Resources Institute, (Mimeo report).

Swift, J., (1989): Why Are Rural People Vulnerable to Famine?. *IDS Bulletin*, Vol. 20, No. 2, pp. 8–15.

Tamang, Deepak (1995): People's Government to People's Organisation. In: Rademacher, Anne Deepak Tamang. *Democracy Development & NGOs*. Kathmandu: SEARCH.

The Gorkhapatra. (National Daily), Dec 23, 1998. Kathmandu.

The Gorkhapatra. (National Daily), Jan 23, 1999. Kathmandu.

The Kantipur. (National Daily), Sept. 2000. Kathmandu.

The Kantipur. (National Daily), Sept. 1999. Kathmandu.

The Kantipur. (National Daily), Jan 08, 1998. Kathmandu.

The Kantipur (National Daily) (Poush 26, 2055).

The Kathmandu Post. (National Daily), August 1, 1998. Kathmandu.

The Kathmandu Post. (National Daily), Feb 12, 1999. Kathmandu.

The Kathmandu Post. (National Daily) February 25, 1999. Kathmandu.

The Rising Nepal. (National Daily) Feb. 14,1998. Kathmandu.

The Rising Nepal. (National Daily), 1999. Kathmandu.

The Rising Nepal. (National Daily) Dec. 23, 1997. Kathmandu: Nepal.

The Mahbub ul Haq Human Development Centre (1999): *Human Development inSouth Asia 1999*. Banglore: Ameena Saiyid, Oxford University Press.

Timilsina, P.P. (1999): Civil Society Organisations: their Dilemmas and Perspectives. In: *Community Development Service Association: Social Development and INGOs Activities in Nepal*. Kathmandu: Community Development Service Association.

Tiwari, Gopal Nidhi (nd): Pauranik Kalin Sewaparayan Jeevan Bitaune Mahan Byaktiharu. *Sewa*. Vol. 1 No. 4, pp. 7–8.

Townsend, Peter (1974): Poverty as Relative Deprivation: Resources and Styles of Living. In: Wedderburn D',(Ed). (1974):*Poverty, Inequality and Class Structure*. Cambridge: University Press.

Tuladhar, Jyoti (1991): *The Growth and Development of NGOs in the 1990s*. A seminar paper presented in "National NGO Conference" Kathmandu, Sept. 23–25.

Tvedt, Terje (1998a): Angels of Mercy or Development Diplomats? NGOs and Foreign Aid. Trenton: Africa World Press, Oxford: James Currey.

Tvedt, Terje (1998b): NGOs' Role at 'The End of History': Norwegian Policy and the New Paradigm. In: Hossain, Farhad & Susanna Myllyla, (eds. 1998): *NGOs Under Challenge: Dynamics and*

Drawbacks in Development. Helsinki: Ministry for Foreign Affairs of Finland, 63–83.

UNDP (1999): *Common Country Assessment*. Kathmandu: United Nations Development Program.

UNDP (1998): *Human Development Report 1998*. New York: UNDP, Oxford University Press.

UNDP (1997): *Human Development Report 1997*. New York: Oxford University Press.

UNDP (1994a): *Human Development Report 1994*. New York: Oxford University Press.

UNDP (1994b): *Sustainable Human Development*. New York: Oxford University Press.

UNDP (1994c): *Sustainable Human Development from Concept of Operation: A Guide for the Practitioners*. New York: Oxford University Press

UNDP (1993): *Human Development Report 1993*. New York: Oxford University Press.

UNDP (1991): *Human Development Report 1991*. New York: Oxford University Press.

United Nations (1995): *Report of the World Summit for Social Development:* Copenhagen, 6–12 March. New York: United Nations.

United Nations (1992): *Report of the UN Conference on Environment and Development Rio* de Janerio, 3–4 June 1992 Volume 1. New York: United Nations.

Van Dijk, M-P. (1994). *The effectiveness of NGOs: Insights from Danish, British and Dutch impact studies*. Schriften des Deutschen Ubersee-Institute Hamburg, No. 28, pp. 27–42, Hamburg.

Webster's New World Dictionary. (1980): Livelihood. 2d college Ed. New York: Simon and Schuster.

Weber, H. (1983): Geloste und Ungeloste probleme des Staatskirchenrechts. Neue Juristiche Wochenscharit 36, 2541-54 In: Seibel & Anheier H. K(1990): Introduction. *The Third Sector Comparative studies of Nonprofit Organisations*. Berlin, new York: Walter de Gruytor.

Weisbrod, Burton (1977): Towards a Theory of the Voluntary Nonprofit Sector in a Three-Sector Economy. In: Weisbrod B. (Ed), (1977): *The Voluntary Nonprofit Sector*. Lexington, MA: D.C. Heath, pp. 51–76.

Weisbrod, B.A., 1988, *The Nonprofit Economy*. Cambridge, MA: Harvard University Press.

Western Terai Poverty Alleviation Project (1997): *Western Terai Poverty*

Alleviation Project, Program Implementation Directives (2055). Kathmandu: Western Terai Poverty Alleviation Project.

William F. Fisher, (1997): *Doing Good? The Politics and Antipolitics of NGO Practices.* Annual Reviews Inc.

Williamson, O., (1985): *The Economic Institutions of Capitalism:* New York: Free Press.

Waldo, Dwight (ed.) (1970): *Temporal Dimensions of Development Administration.* Durham: Duke University Press.

Weidner, Edward (1964): *Technical Assistance in Public Administration Overseas: The Case for Developing Administration. Chicago.* Public Administration Service.

World Bank (1999): *Country Assistance Strategy 1999-2001.* Kathmandu: The World Bank.

World Bank (1995): *Working with NGOs: A Practical Guide to Opperational Collaboration between the World Bank and the Non-governmental Oranisations.* Washington, CDC: World Bank. *Country Assistance Strategy 1999-2001.* Kathmandu: The World Bank.

World Bank (1991): *Nepal: Relieving Poverty in Resources-Scarce Economy,* Vol. I, New York.

World Bank, 1990: *Nepal: Relieving Poverty n a Resource-Scarce Economy. A Joint World Bank/UNDP Study.* Report No. 8635-NEP. Country Department 1, Asia Region. Washington: World Bank.

World Bank (1989): *Involving NGOs in Bank Supported Activities, Operational Directives* No. 14.70. Washington D.C.

World Bank (1980): *Poverty and Human Development.* New York, Oxford.

World Bank (1979): *Nepal: Development Performance and Prospects.* Washington: D.C. World Bank.

Index